WSH JAVASCRIPT AND WBEMSCRIPTING

Working with ExecNotificationQuery and __InstanceOperationEvent

Richard Thomas Edwards

CONTENTS

ASP Reports

Horizontal Report with no additional tags.

```
<?xml Version='1.0' encoding='iso-8859-1'?>
<package>
<job>
<script language='JavaScript'>
<![CDATA[
    var locator = new ActiveXObject("WbemScripting.SWbemLocator");
    var svc = locator.ConnectServer(".", "root\\cimv2");
    svc.Security_.AuthenticationLevel = 6;
    svc.Security_.ImpersonationLevel = 3;
    var strQuery = "Select * From ___InstanceOperationEvent WITHIN 1 where
TargetInstance ISA'Win32_Process'");
        var es = svc.ExecNotificationQuery(strQuery);
        var ws = new ActiveXObject("WScript.Shell");
        var fso = new ActiveXObject("Scripting.FileSystemObject");
        var      txtstream     =      fso.OpenTextFile(ws.CurrentDirectory      +
"\\Win32_Process.asp", 2, true, -2);
        txtstream.WriteLine("<html xmlns='http://www.w3.org/1999/xhtml'>");
        txtstream.WriteLine("<head>");
        txtstream.WriteLine("<style type='text/css'>");
        txtstream.WriteLine("th");
        txtstream.WriteLine("{");
        txtstream.WriteLine("   COLOR: darkred;");
        txtstream.WriteLine("   BACKGROUND-COLOR: white;");
        txtstream.WriteLine("   FONT-FAMILY:font-family: Cambria, serif;");
        txtstream.WriteLine("   FONT-SIZE: 12px;");
        txtstream.WriteLine("   text-align: left;");
```

```
txtstream.WriteLine("    white-Space: nowrap;");
txtstream.WriteLine("}");
txtstream.WriteLine("td");
txtstream.WriteLine("{");
txtstream.WriteLine("    COLOR: navy;");
txtstream.WriteLine("    BACKGROUND-COLOR: white;");
txtstream.WriteLine("    FONT-FAMILY: font-family: Cambria, serif;");
txtstream.WriteLine("    FONT-SIZE: 12px;");
txtstream.WriteLine("    text-align: left;");
txtstream.WriteLine("    white-Space: nowrap;");
txtstream.WriteLine("}");
txtstream.WriteLine("</style>");
txtstream.WriteLine("<title>Win32_Process</title>");
txtstream.WriteLine("</head>");
txtstream.WriteLine("<body>");
txtstream.WriteLine("<table border='0' Cellspacing='3' cellpadding = '3'>");
txtstream.WriteLine("<%");
var v=0;
while(v < 0)
{
    var ti = ex.NextEvent(-1);
    var obj = ti.Properties_.Item("TargetInstance").Value;
    if(v == 0)
    {
        txtstream.WriteLine("Response.Write(\"<tr>\" + vbcrlf)");
        var propEnum = new Enumerator(obj.Properties_);
        for (; !propEnum.atEnd(); propEnum.moveNext())
        {
            var prop = propEnum.item();
            txtstream.WriteLine("Response.Write(\"<th  align='left'  nowrap>" +
prop.Name + "</th>\" + vbcrlf)");
        }
        txtstream.WriteLine("Response.Write(\"</tr>\" + vbcrlf)");
        propEnum.Reset();
    }
    txtstream.WriteLine("Response.Write(\"<tr>\" + vbcrlf)");
    for (; !propEnum.atEnd(); propEnum.moveNext())
    {
        var prop = propEnum.item();
```

```
            txtstream.WriteLine("Response.Write(\"<td    style='font-family:Calibri,
Sans-Serif;font-size:    12px;color:navy;'    align='left'    nowrap='nowrap'>"    +
GetValue(prop.Name, obj) + "</td>\" + vbcrlf)");
            }
            txtstream.WriteLine("Response.Write(\"</tr>\" + vbcrlf)");
            v = v + 1;
        }
        txtstream.WriteLine("%>");
        txtstream.WriteLine("</table>");
        txtstream.WriteLine("</body>");
        txtstream.WriteLine("</html>");
        txtstream.close();
        function GetValue(Name, obj)
        {
            var tempstr = new String();
            var tempstr1 = new String();
            var tName = new String();
            tempstr1 = obj.GetObjectText_();
            var re = /"/g;
            tempstr1 = tempstr1.replace(re , "");
            var pos;
            tName = Name + " = ";
            pos = tempstr1.indexOf(tName);
            if (pos > -1)
            {
                pos = pos + tName.length;
                tempstr = tempstr1.substring(pos, tempstr1.length);
                pos = tempstr.indexOf(";");
                tempstr = tempstr.substring(0, pos);
                tempstr = tempstr.replace("{", "");
                tempstr = tempstr.replace("}", "");
                if (tempstr.length > 13)
                {
                    if (obj.Properties_(Name).CIMType == 101)
                    {
                        tempstr = tempstr.substr(4, 2) + "/" + tempstr.substr(6, 2) + "/" +
tempstr.substr(0, 3) + " " + tempstr.substr(8, 2) + ":" + tempstr.substr(10, 2) + ":" +
tempstr.substr(12, 2);
                    }
                }
```

```
        return tempstr;
    }
    else
    {
        return "";
    }
}


    ]]>
    </script>
  </job>
</Package>
```

Horizontal Report with a Combobox.

```
<?xml Version='1.0' encoding='iso-8859-1'?>
<package>
<job>
<script language='JavaScript'>
<![CDATA[
    var locator = new ActiveXObject("WbemScripting.SWbemLocator");
    var svc = locator.ConnectServer(".", "root\\cimv2");
    svc.Security_.AuthenticationLevel = 6;
    svc.Security_.ImpersonationLevel = 3;
    var strQuery = "Select * From ___InstanceOperationEvent WITHIN 1 where
TargetInstance ISA'Win32_Process'");
    var es = svc.ExecNotificationQuery(strQuery);
    var ws = new ActiveXObject("WScript.Shell");
    var fso = new ActiveXObject("Scripting.FileSystemObject");
    var     txtstream    =    fso.OpenTextFile(ws.CurrentDirectory    +
"\\Win32_Process.asp", 2, true, -2);
    txtstream.WriteLine("<html xmlns='http://www.w3.org/1999/xhtml'>");
    txtstream.WriteLine("<head>");
    txtstream.WriteLine("<style type='text/css'>");
    txtstream.WriteLine("th");
    txtstream.WriteLine("{");
    txtstream.WriteLine("   COLOR: darkred;");
    txtstream.WriteLine("   BACKGROUND-COLOR: white;");
    txtstream.WriteLine("   FONT-FAMILY:font-family: Cambria, serif;");
```

```
txtstream.WriteLine("    FONT-SIZE: 12px;");
txtstream.WriteLine("    text-align: left;");
txtstream.WriteLine("    white-Space: nowrap;");
txtstream.WriteLine("}");
txtstream.WriteLine("td");
txtstream.WriteLine("{");
txtstream.WriteLine("    COLOR: navy;");
txtstream.WriteLine("    BACKGROUND-COLOR: white;");
txtstream.WriteLine("    FONT-FAMILY: font-family: Cambria, serif;");
txtstream.WriteLine("    FONT-SIZE: 12px;");
txtstream.WriteLine("    text-align: left;");
txtstream.WriteLine("    white-Space: nowrap;");
txtstream.WriteLine("}");
txtstream.WriteLine("</style>");
txtstream.WriteLine("<title>Win32_Process</title>");
txtstream.WriteLine("</head>");
txtstream.WriteLine("<body>");
txtstream.WriteLine("<table border='0' Cellspacing='3' cellpadding = '3'>");
txtstream.WriteLine("<%");
var v=0;
while(v < 0)
{
    var ti = ex.NextEvent(-1);
    var obj = ti.Properties_.Item("TargetInstance").Value;
    if(v == 0)
    {
        txtstream.WriteLine("Response.Write(\"<tr>\" + vbcrlf)");
        var propEnum = new Enumerator(obj.Properties_);
        for (; !propEnum.atEnd(); propEnum.moveNext())
        {
            var prop = propEnum.item();
            txtstream.WriteLine("Response.Write(\"<th  align='left'  nowrap>" +
prop.Name + "</th>\" + vbcrlf)");
        }
        txtstream.WriteLine("Response.Write(\"</tr>\" + vbcrlf)");
        propEnum.Reset();
    }
    txtstream.WriteLine("Response.Write(\"<tr>\" + vbcrlf)");
    for (; !propEnum.atEnd(); propEnum.moveNext())
    {
```

```javascript
        var prop = propEnum.item();
        txtstream.WriteLine("Response.Write(\"<td    style='font-family:Calibri,
Sans-Serif;font-size: 12px;color:navy;' align='left' nowrap='true'><select><option
value = '" + GetValue(prop.Name, obj) + "'>" + GetValue(prop.Name, obj) +
"</option></select></td>\" + vbcrlf)");
        }
        txtstream.WriteLine("Response.Write(\"</tr>\" + vbcrlf)");
        v = v + 1;
    }
    txtstream.WriteLine("%>");
    txtstream.WriteLine("</table>");
    txtstream.WriteLine("</body>");
    txtstream.WriteLine("</html>");
    txtstream.close();
    function GetValue(Name, obj)
    {
        var tempstr = new String();
        var tempstr1 = new String();
        var tName = new String();
        tempstr1 = obj.GetObjectText_();
        var re = /"/g;
        tempstr1 = tempstr1.replace(re , "");
        var pos;
        tName = Name + " = ";
        pos = tempstr1.indexOf(tName);
        if (pos > -1)
        {
            pos = pos + tName.length;
            tempstr = tempstr1.substring(pos, tempstr1.length);
            pos = tempstr.indexOf(";");
            tempstr = tempstr.substring(0, pos);
            tempstr = tempstr.replace("{", "");
            tempstr = tempstr.replace("}", "");
            if (tempstr.length > 13)
            {
                if (obj.Properties_(Name).CIMType == 101)
                {
                    tempstr = tempstr.substr(4, 2) + "/"  + tempstr.substr(6, 2) + "/" +
tempstr.substr(0, 3) + " " + tempstr.substr(8, 2) + ":" + tempstr.substr(10, 2) + ":" +
tempstr.substr(12, 2);
```

```
                }
            }
            return tempstr;
        }
        else
        {
            return "";
        }
    }


    ]]>
    </script>
  </job>
</Package>
```

Horizontal Report with a link.

```
<?xml Version='1.0' encoding='iso-8859-1'?>
<package>
<job>
<script language='JavaScript'>
<![CDATA[
    var locator = new ActiveXObject("WbemScripting.SWbemLocator");
    var svc = locator.ConnectServer(".", "root\\cimv2");
    svc.Security_.AuthenticationLevel = 6;
    svc.Security_.ImpersonationLevel = 3;
    var strQuery = "Select * From ___InstanceOperationEvent WITHIN 1 where
TargetInstance ISA'Win32_Process'");
    var es = svc.ExecNotificationQuery(strQuery);
    var ws = new ActiveXObject("WScript.Shell");
    var fso = new ActiveXObject("Scripting.FileSystemObject");
    var     txtstream    =     fso.OpenTextFile(ws.CurrentDirectory    +
"\\Win32_Process.asp", 2, true, -2);
    txtstream.WriteLine("<html xmlns='http://www.w3.org/1999/xhtml'>");
    txtstream.WriteLine("<head>");
    txtstream.WriteLine("<style type='text/css'>");
    txtstream.WriteLine("th");
    txtstream.WriteLine("{");
    txtstream.WriteLine("   COLOR: darkred;");
```

```
txtstream.WriteLine("   BACKGROUND-COLOR: white;");
txtstream.WriteLine("   FONT-FAMILY:font-family: Cambria, serif;");
txtstream.WriteLine("   FONT-SIZE: 12px;");
txtstream.WriteLine("   text-align: left;");
txtstream.WriteLine("   white-Space: nowrap;");
txtstream.WriteLine("}");
txtstream.WriteLine("td");
txtstream.WriteLine("{");
txtstream.WriteLine("   COLOR: navy;");
txtstream.WriteLine("   BACKGROUND-COLOR: white;");
txtstream.WriteLine("   FONT-FAMILY: font-family: Cambria, serif;");
txtstream.WriteLine("   FONT-SIZE: 12px;");
txtstream.WriteLine("   text-align: left;");
txtstream.WriteLine("   white-Space: nowrap;");
txtstream.WriteLine("}");
txtstream.WriteLine("</style>");
txtstream.WriteLine("<title>Win32_Process</title>");
txtstream.WriteLine("</head>");
txtstream.WriteLine("<body>");
txtstream.WriteLine("<table border='0' Cellspacing='3' cellpadding = '3'>");
txtstream.WriteLine("<%");
var v=0;
while(v < 0)
{
    var ti = ex.NextEvent(-1);
    var obj = ti.Properties_.Item("TargetInstance").Value;
    if(v == 0)
    {
        txtstream.WriteLine("Response.Write(\"<tr>\" + vbcrlf)");
        var propEnum = new Enumerator(obj.Properties_);
        for (; !propEnum.atEnd(); propEnum.moveNext())
        {
            var prop = propEnum.item();
            txtstream.WriteLine("Response.Write(\"<th align='left' nowrap>" +
prop.Name + "</th>\" + vbcrlf)");
        }
        txtstream.WriteLine("Response.Write(\"</tr>\" + vbcrlf)");
        propEnum.Reset();
    }
    txtstream.WriteLine("Response.Write(\"<tr>\" + vbcrlf)");
```

```
        for (; !propEnum.atEnd(); propEnum.moveNext())
        {
            var prop = propEnum.item();
            txtstream.WriteLine("Response.Write(\"<td   style='font-family:Calibri,
Sans-Serif;font-size: 12px;color:navy;' align='left'  nowrap='true'><a  href='" +
GetValue(prop.Name, obj) + "'>" + GetValue(prop.Name, obj) + "</a></td>\" +
vbcrlf)");
        }
        txtstream.WriteLine("Response.Write(\"</tr>\" + vbcrlf)");
        v = v + 1;
    }
    txtstream.WriteLine("%>");
    txtstream.WriteLine("</table>");
    txtstream.WriteLine("</body>");
    txtstream.WriteLine("</html>");
    txtstream.close();
    function GetValue(Name, obj)
    {
        var tempstr = new String();
        var tempstr1 = new String();
        var tName = new String();
        tempstr1 = obj.GetObjectText_();
        var re = /"/g;
        tempstr1 = tempstr1.replace(re , "");
        var pos;
        tName = Name + " = ";
        pos = tempstr1.indexOf(tName);
        if (pos > -1)
        {
            pos = pos + tName.length;
            tempstr = tempstr1.substring(pos, tempstr1.length);
            pos = tempstr.indexOf(";");
            tempstr = tempstr.substring(0, pos);
            tempstr = tempstr.replace("{", "");
            tempstr = tempstr.replace("}", "");
            if (tempstr.length > 13)
            {
                if (obj.Properties_(Name).CIMType == 101)
                {
```

```
                tempstr = tempstr.substr(4, 2) + "/"  + tempstr.substr(6, 2) + "/" +
tempstr.substr(0, 3) + " " + tempstr.substr(8, 2) + ":" + tempstr.substr(10, 2) + ":" +
tempstr.substr(12, 2);
                }
            }
            return tempstr;
        }
        else
        {
            return "";
        }
    }

    ]]>
    </script>
  </job>
</Package>
```

Horizontal Report with a Listbox.

```
<?xml Version='1.0' encoding='iso-8859-1'?>
<package>
<job>
<script language='JavaScript'>
<![CDATA[
   var locator = new ActiveXObject("WbemScripting.SWbemLocator");
   var svc = locator.ConnectServer(".", "root\\cimv2");
   svc.Security_.AuthenticationLevel = 6;
   svc.Security_.ImpersonationLevel = 3;
   var strQuery = "Select * From ___InstanceOperationEvent WITHIN 1 where
TargetInstance ISA'Win32_Process'");
   var es = svc.ExecNotificationQuery(strQuery);
   var ws = new ActiveXObject("WScript.Shell");
   var fso = new ActiveXObject("Scripting.FileSystemObject");
   var       txtstream      =      fso.OpenTextFile(ws.CurrentDirectory      +
"\\Win32_Process.asp", 2, true, -2);
   txtstream.WriteLine("<html xmlns='http://www.w3.org/1999/xhtml'>");
   txtstream.WriteLine("<head>");
   txtstream.WriteLine("<style type='text/css'>");
```

```
txtstream.WriteLine("th");
txtstream.WriteLine("{");
txtstream.WriteLine("    COLOR: darkred;");
txtstream.WriteLine("    BACKGROUND-COLOR: white;");
txtstream.WriteLine("    FONT-FAMILY:font-family: Cambria, serif;");
txtstream.WriteLine("    FONT-SIZE: 12px;");
txtstream.WriteLine("    text-align: left;");
txtstream.WriteLine("    white-Space: nowrap;");
txtstream.WriteLine("}");
txtstream.WriteLine("td");
txtstream.WriteLine("{");
txtstream.WriteLine("    COLOR: navy;");
txtstream.WriteLine("    BACKGROUND-COLOR: white;");
txtstream.WriteLine("    FONT-FAMILY: font-family: Cambria, serif;");
txtstream.WriteLine("    FONT-SIZE: 12px;");
txtstream.WriteLine("    text-align: left;");
txtstream.WriteLine("    white-Space: nowrap;");
txtstream.WriteLine("}");
txtstream.WriteLine("</style>");
txtstream.WriteLine("<title>Win32_Process</title>");
txtstream.WriteLine("</head>");
txtstream.WriteLine("<body>");
txtstream.WriteLine("<table border='0' Cellspacing='3' cellpadding = '3'>");
txtstream.WriteLine("<%");
var v=0;
while(v < 0)
{
    var ti = ex.NextEvent(-1);
    var obj = ti.Properties_.Item("TargetInstance").Value;
    if(v == 0)
    {
        txtstream.WriteLine("Response.Write(\"<tr>\" + vbcrlf)");
        var propEnum = new Enumerator(obj.Properties_);
        for (; !propEnum.atEnd(); propEnum.moveNext())
        {
            var prop = propEnum.item();
            txtstream.WriteLine("Response.Write(\"<th align='left' nowrap>" +
prop.Name + "</th>\" + vbcrlf)");
        }
        txtstream.WriteLine("Response.Write(\"</tr>\" + vbcrlf)");
```

```
            propEnum.Reset();
        }
        txtstream.WriteLine("Response.Write(\"<tr>\" + vbcrlf)");
        for (; !propEnum.atEnd(); propEnum.moveNext())
        {
            var prop = propEnum.item();
            txtstream.WriteLine("Response.Write(\"<td    style='font-family:Calibri,
Sans-Serif;font-size:    12px;color:navy;'    align='left'    nowrap='true'><select
multiple><option    value    =    '"    +    GetValue(prop.Name,    obj)    +    "'>"    +
GetValue(prop.Name, obj) + "</option></select></td>\" + vbcrlf)");
        }
        txtstream.WriteLine("Response.Write(\"</tr>\" + vbcrlf)");
        v = v + 1;
    }
    txtstream.WriteLine("%>");
    txtstream.WriteLine("</table>");
    txtstream.WriteLine("</body>");
    txtstream.WriteLine("</html>");
    txtstream.close();
    function GetValue(Name, obj)
    {
        var tempstr = new String();
        var tempstr1 = new String();
        var tName = new String();
        tempstr1 = obj.GetObjectText_();
        var re = /"/g;
        tempstr1 = tempstr1.replace(re , "");
        var pos;
        tName = Name + " = ";
        pos = tempstr1.indexOf(tName);
        if (pos > -1)
        {
            pos = pos + tName.length;
            tempstr = tempstr1.substring(pos, tempstr1.length);
            pos = tempstr.indexOf(";");
            tempstr = tempstr.substring(0, pos);
            tempstr = tempstr.replace("{", "");
            tempstr = tempstr.replace("}", "");
            if (tempstr.length > 13)
            {
```

```
            if (obj.Properties_(Name).CIMType == 101)
            {
                tempstr = tempstr.substr(4, 2) + "/"  + tempstr.substr(6, 2) + "/" +
tempstr.substr(0, 3) + " " + tempstr.substr(8, 2) + ":" + tempstr.substr(10, 2) + ":" +
tempstr.substr(12, 2);
            }
        }
        return tempstr;
    }
    else
    {
        return "";
    }
}


]]>
    </script>
  </job>
</Package>
```

Horizontal Report with a textarea.

```
<?xml Version='1.0' encoding='iso-8859-1'?>
<package>
<job>
<script language='JavaScript'>
<![CDATA[
    var locator = new ActiveXObject("WbemScripting.SWbemLocator");
    var svc = locator.ConnectServer(".", "root\\cimv2");
    svc.Security_.AuthenticationLevel = 6;
    svc.Security_.ImpersonationLevel = 3;
    var strQuery = "Select * From ___InstanceOperationEvent WITHIN 1 where
TargetInstance ISA'Win32_Process'");
    var es = svc.ExecNotificationQuery(strQuery);
    var ws = new ActiveXObject("WScript.Shell");
    var fso = new ActiveXObject("Scripting.FileSystemObject");
    var       txtstream     =        fso.OpenTextFile(ws.CurrentDirectory     +
"\\Win32_Process.asp", 2, true, -2);
    txtstream.WriteLine("<html xmlns='http://www.w3.org/1999/xhtml'>");
```

```
txtstream.WriteLine("<head>");
txtstream.WriteLine("<style type='text/css'>");
txtstream.WriteLine("th");
txtstream.WriteLine("{");
txtstream.WriteLine("   COLOR: darkred;");
txtstream.WriteLine("   BACKGROUND-COLOR: white;");
txtstream.WriteLine("   FONT-FAMILY:font-family: Cambria, serif;");
txtstream.WriteLine("   FONT-SIZE: 12px;");
txtstream.WriteLine("   text-align: left;");
txtstream.WriteLine("   white-Space: nowrap;");
txtstream.WriteLine("}");
txtstream.WriteLine("td");
txtstream.WriteLine("{");
txtstream.WriteLine("   COLOR: navy;");
txtstream.WriteLine("   BACKGROUND-COLOR: white;");
txtstream.WriteLine("   FONT-FAMILY: font-family: Cambria, serif;");
txtstream.WriteLine("   FONT-SIZE: 12px;");
txtstream.WriteLine("   text-align: left;");
txtstream.WriteLine("   white-Space: nowrap;");
txtstream.WriteLine("}");
txtstream.WriteLine("</style>");
txtstream.WriteLine("<title>Win32_Process</title>");
txtstream.WriteLine("</head>");
txtstream.WriteLine("<body>");
txtstream.WriteLine("<table border='0' Cellspacing='3' cellpadding = '3'>");
txtstream.WriteLine("<%");
var v=0;
while(v < 0)
{
    var ti = ex.NextEvent(-1);
    var obj = ti.Properties_.Item("TargetInstance").Value;
    if(v == 0)
    {
        txtstream.WriteLine("Response.Write(\"<tr>\" + vbcrlf)");
        var propEnum = new Enumerator(obj.Properties_);
        for (; !propEnum.atEnd(); propEnum.moveNext())
        {
            var prop = propEnum.item();
            txtstream.WriteLine("Response.Write(\"<th  align='left'  nowrap>" +
prop.Name + "</th>\" + vbcrlf)");
```

```
        }
        txtstream.WriteLine("Response.Write(\"</tr>\" + vbcrlf)");
        propEnum.Reset();
    }
    txtstream.WriteLine("Response.Write(\"<tr>\" + vbcrlf)");
    for (; !propEnum.atEnd(); propEnum.moveNext())
    {
        var prop = propEnum.item();
        txtstream.WriteLine("Response.Write(\"<td   style='font-family:Calibri,
Sans-Serif;font-size: 12px;color:navy;' align='left' nowrap='true'><textarea>" +
GetValue(prop.Name, obj) + "</textarea></td>\" + vbcrlf)");
    }
    txtstream.WriteLine("Response.Write(\"</tr>\" + vbcrlf)");
    v = v + 1;
}
txtstream.WriteLine("%>");
txtstream.WriteLine("</table>");
txtstream.WriteLine("</body>");
txtstream.WriteLine("</html>");
txtstream.close();
function GetValue(Name, obj)
{
    var tempstr = new String();
    var tempstr1 = new String();
    var tName = new String();
    tempstr1 = obj.GetObjectText_();
    var re = /"/g;
    tempstr1 = tempstr1.replace(re , "");
    var pos;
    tName = Name + " = ";
    pos = tempstr1.indexOf(tName);
    if (pos > -1)
    {
        pos = pos + tName.length;
        tempstr = tempstr1.substring(pos, tempstr1.length);
        pos = tempstr.indexOf(";");
        tempstr = tempstr.substring(0, pos);
        tempstr = tempstr.replace("{", "");
        tempstr = tempstr.replace("}", "");
        if (tempstr.length > 13)
```

```
        {
            if (obj.Properties_(Name).CIMType == 101)
            {
                tempstr = tempstr.substr(4, 2) + "/"  + tempstr.substr(6, 2) + "/" +
tempstr.substr(0, 3) + " " + tempstr.substr(8, 2) + ":" + tempstr.substr(10, 2) + ":" +
tempstr.substr(12, 2);
            }
        }
        return tempstr;
    }
    else
    {
        return "";
    }
  }


  ]]>
   </script>
  </job>
</Package>
```

Horizontal Report with a textbox.

```
<?xml Version='1.0' encoding='iso-8859-1'?>
<package>
<job>
<script language='JavaScript'>
<![CDATA[
    var locator = new ActiveXObject("WbemScripting.SWbemLocator");
    var svc = locator.ConnectServer(".", "root\\cimv2");
    svc.Security_.AuthenticationLevel = 6;
    svc.Security_.ImpersonationLevel = 3;
    var strQuery = "Select * From ___InstanceOperationEvent WITHIN 1 where
TargetInstance ISA'Win32_Process'");
    var es = svc.ExecNotificationQuery(strQuery);
    var ws = new ActiveXObject("WScript.Shell");
    var fso = new ActiveXObject("Scripting.FileSystemObject");
    var    txtstream    =    fso.OpenTextFile(ws.CurrentDirectory    +
"\\Win32_Process.asp", 2, true, -2);
```

```
txtstream.WriteLine("<html xmlns='http://www.w3.org/1999/xhtml'>");
txtstream.WriteLine("<head>");
txtstream.WriteLine("<style type='text/css'>");
txtstream.WriteLine("th");
txtstream.WriteLine("{");
txtstream.WriteLine("    COLOR: darkred;");
txtstream.WriteLine("    BACKGROUND-COLOR: white;");
txtstream.WriteLine("    FONT-FAMILY:font-family: Cambria, serif;");
txtstream.WriteLine("    FONT-SIZE: 12px;");
txtstream.WriteLine("    text-align: left;");
txtstream.WriteLine("    white-Space: nowrap;");
txtstream.WriteLine("}");
txtstream.WriteLine("td");
txtstream.WriteLine("{");
txtstream.WriteLine("    COLOR: navy;");
txtstream.WriteLine("    BACKGROUND-COLOR: white;");
txtstream.WriteLine("    FONT-FAMILY: font-family: Cambria, serif;");
txtstream.WriteLine("    FONT-SIZE: 12px;");
txtstream.WriteLine("    text-align: left;");
txtstream.WriteLine("    white-Space: nowrap;");
txtstream.WriteLine("}");
txtstream.WriteLine("</style>");
txtstream.WriteLine("<title>Win32_Process</title>");
txtstream.WriteLine("</head>");
txtstream.WriteLine("<body>");
txtstream.WriteLine("<table border='0' Cellspacing='3' cellpadding = '3'>");
txtstream.WriteLine("<%");
var v=0;
while(v < 0)
{
    var ti = ex.NextEvent(-1);
    var obj = ti.Properties_.Item("TargetInstance").Value;
    if(v == 0)
    {
        txtstream.WriteLine("Response.Write(\"<tr>\" + vbcrlf)");
        var propEnum = new Enumerator(obj.Properties_);
        for (; !propEnum.atEnd(); propEnum.moveNext())
        {
            var prop = propEnum.item();
```

```
            txtstream.WriteLine("Response.Write(\"<th  align='left'  nowrap>" +
prop.Name + "</th>\" + vbcrlf)");
            }
            txtstream.WriteLine("Response.Write(\"</tr>\" + vbcrlf)");
            propEnum.Reset();
        }
        txtstream.WriteLine("Response.Write(\"<tr>\" + vbcrlf)");
        for (; !propEnum.atEnd(); propEnum.moveNext())
        {
            var prop = propEnum.item();
            txtstream.WriteLine("Response.Write(\"<td    style='font-family:Calibri,
Sans-Serif;font-size: 12px;color:navy;' align='left' nowrap='true'><input type=text
value='" + GetValue(prop.Name, obj) + "'></input></td>\" + vbcrlf)");
        }
        txtstream.WriteLine("Response.Write(\"</tr>\" + vbcrlf)");
        v = v + 1;
    }
    txtstream.WriteLine("%>");
    txtstream.WriteLine("</table>");
    txtstream.WriteLine("</body>");
    txtstream.WriteLine("</html>");
    txtstream.close();
    function GetValue(Name, obj)
    {
        var tempstr = new String();
        var tempstr1 = new String();
        var tName = new String();
        tempstr1 = obj.GetObjectText_();
        var re = /"/g;
        tempstr1 = tempstr1.replace(re , "");
        var pos;
        tName = Name + " = ";
        pos = tempstr1.indexOf(tName);
        if (pos > -1)
        {
            pos = pos + tName.length;
            tempstr = tempstr1.substring(pos, tempstr1.length);
            pos = tempstr.indexOf(";");
            tempstr = tempstr.substring(0, pos);
            tempstr = tempstr.replace("{", "");
```

```
            tempstr = tempstr.replace("}", "");
            if (tempstr.length > 13)
            {
                if (obj.Properties_(Name).CIMType == 101)
                {
                    tempstr = tempstr.substr(4, 2) + "/"  + tempstr.substr(6, 2) + "/" +
tempstr.substr(0, 3) + " " + tempstr.substr(8, 2) + ":" + tempstr.substr(10, 2) + ":" +
tempstr.substr(12, 2);
                }
            }
            return tempstr;
        }
        else
        {
            return "";
        }
    }

    ]]>
    </script>
  </job>
</Package>
```

Vertical Report with no additional tags.

```
<?xml Version='1.0' encoding='iso-8859-1'?>
<package>
<job>
<script language='JavaScript'>
<![CDATA[
    var locator = new ActiveXObject("WbemScripting.SWbemLocator");
    var svc = locator.ConnectServer(".", "root\\cimv2");
    svc.Security_.AuthenticationLevel = 6;
    svc.Security_.ImpersonationLevel = 3;
    var strQuery = "Select * From ___InstanceOperationEvent WITHIN 1 where
TargetInstance ISA'Win32_Process'");
    var es = svc.ExecNotificationQuery(strQuery);
    var ws = new ActiveXObject("WScript.Shell");
    var fso = new ActiveXObject("Scripting.FileSystemObject");
```

```
var        txtstream        =        fso.OpenTextFile(ws.CurrentDirectory        +
"\\Win32_Process.asp", 2, true, -2);
     txtstream.WriteLine("<html xmlns='http://www.w3.org/1999/xhtml'>");
     txtstream.WriteLine("<head>");
     txtstream.WriteLine("<style type='text/css'>");
     txtstream.WriteLine("th");
     txtstream.WriteLine("{");
     txtstream.WriteLine("   COLOR: darkred;");
     txtstream.WriteLine("   BACKGROUND-COLOR: white;");
     txtstream.WriteLine("   FONT-FAMILY:font-family: Cambria, serif;");
     txtstream.WriteLine("   FONT-SIZE: 12px;");
     txtstream.WriteLine("   text-align: left;");
     txtstream.WriteLine("   white-Space: nowrap;");
     txtstream.WriteLine("}");
     txtstream.WriteLine("td");
     txtstream.WriteLine("{");
     txtstream.WriteLine("   COLOR: navy;");
     txtstream.WriteLine("   BACKGROUND-COLOR: white;");
     txtstream.WriteLine("   FONT-FAMILY: font-family: Cambria, serif;");
     txtstream.WriteLine("   FONT-SIZE: 12px;");
     txtstream.WriteLine("   text-align: left;");
     txtstream.WriteLine("   white-Space: nowrap;");
     txtstream.WriteLine("}");
     txtstream.WriteLine("</style>");
     txtstream.WriteLine("<title>Win32_Process</title>");
     txtstream.WriteLine("</head>");
     txtstream.WriteLine("<body>");
     txtstream.WriteLine("<table border='0' Cellspacing='3' cellpadding = '3'>");

     var Names;
     var Cols;
     var Rows;
     var x = 0;

     var v = 0;
     while(v < 0)
     {
        var ti = ex.NextEvent(-1);
        var obj = ti.Properties_.Item("TargetInstance").Value;
        if(v == 0)
```

```
            {
                Names = new Array[obj.Properties_.Count];
                Cols = new Array[obj.Properties_.Count];
                Rows = new Array[4];
                var propEnum = new Enumerator(obj.Properties_);
                for (; !propEnum.atEnd(); propEnum.moveNext())
                {
                    var prop = propEnum.item();
                    Names[x] = prop.Name;
                    Cols[x] = GetValue(prop.Name, obj);
                    x = x + 1;
                }
                Rows[v] = Cols;
                x = 0;
                v = v + 1;
            }
            else
            {
                var propEnum = new Enumerator(obj.Properties_);
                for (; !propEnum.atEnd(); propEnum.moveNext())
                {
                    var prop = propEnum.item();
                    Cols[x] = GetValue(prop.Name, obj);
                    x = x + 1;
                }
                Rows[v] = Cols;
                x = 0;
                v = v + 1;
            }
        }
        txtstream.WriteLine("<%");
        for(var a = 0;a < Names.Count; a++)
        {
            txtstream.WriteLine("Response.Write(\"<tr><th align='left' nowrap>" +
Names[a] + "</th>\" + vbcrlf)");
            for(var b = 0;b < Rows.Count; b++)
            {
                var C = Rows[b];
```

```
            txtstream.WriteLine("Response.Write(\"<td    style='font-family:Calibri,
Sans-Serif;font-size: 12px;color:navy;' align='left' nowrap='nowrap'>" + C[x] +
"</td>\" + vbcrlf)");
                }
            txtstream.WriteLine("Response.Write(\"</tr>\" + vbcrlf)");
        }
        txtstream.WriteLine("%>");
        txtstream.WriteLine("</table>");
        txtstream.WriteLine("</body>");
        txtstream.WriteLine("</html>");
        txtstream.close();
        function GetValue(Name, obj)
        {
            var tempstr = new String();
            var tempstr1 = new String();
            var tName = new String();
            tempstr1 = obj.GetObjectText_();
            var re = /"/g;
            tempstr1 = tempstr1.replace(re , "");
            var pos;
            tName = Name + " = ";
            pos = tempstr1.indexOf(tName);
            if (pos > -1)
            {
                pos = pos + tName.length;
                tempstr = tempstr1.substring(pos, tempstr1.length);
                pos = tempstr.indexOf(";");
                tempstr = tempstr.substring(0, pos);
                tempstr = tempstr.replace("{", "");
                tempstr = tempstr.replace("}", "");
                if (tempstr.length > 13)
                {
                    if (obj.Properties_(Name).CIMType == 101)
                    {
                      tempstr = tempstr.substr(4, 2) + "/"  + tempstr.substr(6, 2) + "/" +
tempstr.substr(0, 3) + " " + tempstr.substr(8, 2) + ":" + tempstr.substr(10, 2) + ":" +
tempstr.substr(12, 2);
                    }
                }
                return tempstr;
```

```
        }
        else
        {
            return "";
        }
    }

    ]]>
    </script>
  </job>
</Package>
```

Vertical Report with a Combobox.

```
<?xml Version='1.0' encoding='iso-8859-1'?>
<package>
<job>
<script language='JavaScript'>
<![CDATA[
    var locator = new ActiveXObject("WbemScripting.SWbemLocator");
    var svc = locator.ConnectServer(".", "root\\cimv2");
    svc.Security_.AuthenticationLevel = 6;
    svc.Security_.ImpersonationLevel = 3;
    var strQuery = "Select * From ___InstanceOperationEvent WITHIN 1 where
TargetInstance ISA'Win32_Process'");
    var es = svc.ExecNotificationQuery(strQuery);
    var ws = new ActiveXObject("WScript.Shell");
    var fso = new ActiveXObject("Scripting.FileSystemObject");
    var      txtstream      =      fso.OpenTextFile(ws.CurrentDirectory      +
"\\Win32_Process.asp", 2, true, -2);
    txtstream.WriteLine("<html xmlns='http://www.w3.org/1999/xhtml'>");
    txtstream.WriteLine("<head>");
    txtstream.WriteLine("<style type='text/css'>");
    txtstream.WriteLine("th");
    txtstream.WriteLine("{");
    txtstream.WriteLine("    COLOR: darkred;");
    txtstream.WriteLine("    BACKGROUND-COLOR: white;");
    txtstream.WriteLine("    FONT-FAMILY:font-family: Cambria, serif;");
    txtstream.WriteLine("    FONT-SIZE: 12px;");
```

```
txtstream.WriteLine("    text-align: left;");
txtstream.WriteLine("    white-Space: nowrap;");
txtstream.WriteLine("}");
txtstream.WriteLine("td");
txtstream.WriteLine("{");
txtstream.WriteLine("    COLOR: navy;");
txtstream.WriteLine("    BACKGROUND-COLOR: white;");
txtstream.WriteLine("    FONT-FAMILY: font-family: Cambria, serif;");
txtstream.WriteLine("    FONT-SIZE: 12px;");
txtstream.WriteLine("    text-align: left;");
txtstream.WriteLine("    white-Space: nowrap;");
txtstream.WriteLine("}");
txtstream.WriteLine("</style>");
txtstream.WriteLine("<title>Win32_Process</title>");
txtstream.WriteLine("</head>");
txtstream.WriteLine("<body>");
txtstream.WriteLine("<table border='0' Cellspacing='3' cellpadding = '3'>");

var Names;
var Cols;
var Rows;
var x = 0;

var v = 0;
while(v < 0)
{
   var ti = ex.NextEvent(-1);
   var obj = ti.Properties_.Item("TargetInstance").Value;
   if(v == 0)
   {
      Names = new Array[obj.Properties_.Count];
      Cols = new Array[obj.Properties_.Count];
      Rows = new Array[4];
      var propEnum = new Enumerator(obj.Properties_);
      for (; !propEnum.atEnd(); propEnum.moveNext())
      {
         var prop = propEnum.item();
         Names[x] = prop.Name;
         Cols[x] = GetValue(prop.Name, obj);
         x = x + 1;
```

```
                    }
                    Rows[v] = Cols;
                    x = 0;
                    v = v + 1;
                }
                else
                {
                    var propEnum = new Enumerator(obj.Properties_);
                    for (; !propEnum.atEnd(); propEnum.moveNext())
                    {
                        var prop = propEnum.item();
                        Cols[x] = GetValue(prop.Name, obj);
                        x = x + 1;
                    }
                    Rows[v] = Cols;
                    x = 0;
                    v = v + 1;
                }
            }
            txtstream.WriteLine("<%");
            for(var a = 0;a < Names.Count; a++)
            {
                txtstream.WriteLine("Response.Write(\"<tr><th align='left' nowrap>" +
Names[a] + "</th>\" + vbcrlf)");
                for(var b = 0;b < Rows.Count; b++)
                {
                    var C = Rows[b];
                    txtstream.WriteLine("Response.Write(\"<td   style='font-family:Calibri,
Sans-Serif;font-size: 12px;color:navy;' align='left' nowrap='true'><select><option
value = """ + C[x] + """>" + C[x] + "</option></select></td>\" + vbcrlf)");
                }
                txtstream.WriteLine("Response.Write(\"</tr>\" + vbcrlf)");
            }
            txtstream.WriteLine("%>");
            txtstream.WriteLine("</table>");
            txtstream.WriteLine("</body>");
            txtstream.WriteLine("</html>");
            txtstream.close();
            function GetValue(Name, obj)
            {
```

```javascript
        var tempstr = new String();
        var tempstr1 = new String();
        var tName = new String();
        tempstr1 = obj.GetObjectText_();
        var re = /"/g;
        tempstr1 = tempstr1.replace(re , "");
        var pos;
        tName = Name + " = ";
        pos = tempstr1.indexOf(tName);
        if (pos > -1)
        {
            pos = pos + tName.length;
            tempstr = tempstr1.substring(pos, tempstr1.length);
            pos = tempstr.indexOf(";");
            tempstr = tempstr.substring(0, pos);
            tempstr = tempstr.replace("{", "");
            tempstr = tempstr.replace("}", "");
            if (tempstr.length > 13)
            {
                if (obj.Properties_(Name).CIMType == 101)
                {
                    tempstr = tempstr.substr(4, 2) + "/"  + tempstr.substr(6, 2) + "/" +
tempstr.substr(0, 3) + " " + tempstr.substr(8, 2) + ":" + tempstr.substr(10, 2) + ":" +
tempstr.substr(12, 2);
                }
            }
            return tempstr;
        }
        else
        {
            return "";
        }
    }

    ]]>
    </script>
  </job>
</Package>
```

Vertical Report with a link.

```
<?xml Version='1.0' encoding='iso-8859-1'?>
<package>
<job>
<script language='JavaScript'>
<![CDATA[
    var locator = new ActiveXObject("WbemScripting.SWbemLocator");
    var svc = locator.ConnectServer(".", "root\\cimv2");
    svc.Security_.AuthenticationLevel = 6;
    svc.Security_.ImpersonationLevel = 3;
    var strQuery = "Select * From ___InstanceOperationEvent WITHIN 1 where
TargetInstance ISA'Win32_Process'");
    var es = svc.ExecNotificationQuery(strQuery);
    var ws = new ActiveXObject("WScript.Shell");
    var fso = new ActiveXObject("Scripting.FileSystemObject");
    var     txtstream    =     fso.OpenTextFile(ws.CurrentDirectory     +
"\\Win32_Process.asp", 2, true, -2);
    txtstream.WriteLine("<html xmlns='http://www.w3.org/1999/xhtml'>");
    txtstream.WriteLine("<head>");
    txtstream.WriteLine("<style type='text/css'>");
    txtstream.WriteLine("th");
    txtstream.WriteLine("{");
    txtstream.WriteLine("   COLOR: darkred;");
    txtstream.WriteLine("   BACKGROUND-COLOR: white;");
    txtstream.WriteLine("   FONT-FAMILY:font-family: Cambria, serif;");
    txtstream.WriteLine("   FONT-SIZE: 12px;");
    txtstream.WriteLine("   text-align: left;");
    txtstream.WriteLine("   white-Space: nowrap;");
    txtstream.WriteLine("}");
    txtstream.WriteLine("td");
    txtstream.WriteLine("{");
    txtstream.WriteLine("   COLOR: navy;");
    txtstream.WriteLine("   BACKGROUND-COLOR: white;");
    txtstream.WriteLine("   FONT-FAMILY: font-family: Cambria, serif;");
    txtstream.WriteLine("   FONT-SIZE: 12px;");
    txtstream.WriteLine("   text-align: left;");
    txtstream.WriteLine("   white-Space: nowrap;");
    txtstream.WriteLine("}");
```

```
txtstream.WriteLine("</style>");
txtstream.WriteLine("<title>Win32__Process</title>");
txtstream.WriteLine("</head>");
txtstream.WriteLine("<body>");
txtstream.WriteLine("<table border='0' Cellspacing='3' cellpadding = '3'>");

var Names;
var Cols;
var Rows;
var x = 0;

var v = 0;
while(v < 0)
{
   var ti = ex.NextEvent(-1);
   var obj = ti.Properties__.Item("TargetInstance").Value;
   if(v == 0)
   {
      Names = new Array[obj.Properties__.Count];
      Cols = new Array[obj.Properties__.Count];
      Rows = new Array[4];
      var propEnum = new Enumerator(obj.Properties_);
      for (; !propEnum.atEnd(); propEnum.moveNext())
      {
         var prop = propEnum.item();
         Names[x] = prop.Name;
         Cols[x] = GetValue(prop.Name, obj);
         x = x + 1;
      }
      Rows[v] = Cols;
      x = 0;
      v = v + 1;
   }
   else
   {
      var propEnum = new Enumerator(obj.Properties_);
      for (; !propEnum.atEnd(); propEnum.moveNext())
      {
         var prop = propEnum.item();
         Cols[x] = GetValue(prop.Name, obj);
```

```
              x = x + 1;
            }
            Rows[v] = Cols;
            x = 0;
            v = v + 1;
          }
       }
       txtstream.WriteLine("<%");
       for(var a = 0;a < Names.Count; a++)
       {
           txtstream.WriteLine("Response.Write(\"<tr><th align='left' nowrap>" +
Names[a] + "</th>\" + vbcrlf)");
           for(var b = 0;b < Rows.Count; b++)
           {
             var C = Rows[b];
             txtstream.WriteLine("Response.Write(\"<td   style='font-family:Calibri,
Sans-Serif;font-size: 12px;color:navy;' align='left' nowrap='true'><a href='" + C[x]
+ "'>" + C[x] + "</a></td>\" + vbcrlf)");
           }
           txtstream.WriteLine("Response.Write(\"</tr>\" + vbcrlf)");
       }
       txtstream.WriteLine("%>");
       txtstream.WriteLine("</table>");
       txtstream.WriteLine("</body>");
       txtstream.WriteLine("</html>");
       txtstream.close();
       function GetValue(Name, obj)
       {
         var tempstr = new String();
         var tempstr1 = new String();
         var tName = new String();
         tempstr1 = obj.GetObjectText_();
         var re = /"/g;
         tempstr1 = tempstr1.replace(re , "");
         var pos;
         tName = Name + " = ";
         pos = tempstr1.indexOf(tName);
         if (pos > -1)
         {
           pos = pos + tName.length;
```

```
            tempstr = tempstr1.substring(pos, tempstr1.length);
            pos = tempstr.indexOf(";");
            tempstr = tempstr.substring(0, pos);
            tempstr = tempstr.replace("{", "");
            tempstr = tempstr.replace("}", "");
            if (tempstr.length > 13)
            {
               if (obj.Properties_(Name).CIMType == 101)
               {
                  tempstr = tempstr.substr(4, 2) + "/"  + tempstr.substr(6, 2) + "/" +
tempstr.substr(0, 3) + " " + tempstr.substr(8, 2) + ":" + tempstr.substr(10, 2) + ":" +
tempstr.substr(12, 2);
               }
            }
            return tempstr;
         }
         else
         {
            return "";
         }
      }


      ]]>
      </script>
     </job>
   </Package>
```

Vertical Report with a Listbox.

```
      <?xml Version='1.0' encoding='iso-8859-1'?>
      <package>
      <job>
      <script language='JavaScript'>
      <![CDATA[
         var locator = new ActiveXObject("WbemScripting.SWbemLocator");
         var svc = locator.ConnectServer(".", "root\\cimv2");
         svc.Security_.AuthenticationLevel = 6;
         svc.Security_.ImpersonationLevel = 3;
```

```javascript
var strQuery = "Select * From ___InstanceOperationEvent WITHIN 1 where
TargetInstance ISA'Win32_Process'");
var es = svc.ExecNotificationQuery(strQuery);
var ws = new ActiveXObject("WScript.Shell");
var fso = new ActiveXObject("Scripting.FileSystemObject");
var    txtstream    =    fso.OpenTextFile(ws.CurrentDirectory    +
"\\Win32_Process.asp", 2, true, -2);
txtstream.WriteLine("<html xmlns='http://www.w3.org/1999/xhtml'>");
txtstream.WriteLine("<head>");
txtstream.WriteLine("<style type='text/css'>");
txtstream.WriteLine("th");
txtstream.WriteLine("{");
txtstream.WriteLine("   COLOR: darkred;");
txtstream.WriteLine("   BACKGROUND-COLOR: white;");
txtstream.WriteLine("   FONT-FAMILY:font-family: Cambria, serif;");
txtstream.WriteLine("   FONT-SIZE: 12px;");
txtstream.WriteLine("   text-align: left;");
txtstream.WriteLine("   white-Space: nowrap;");
txtstream.WriteLine("}");
txtstream.WriteLine("td");
txtstream.WriteLine("{");
txtstream.WriteLine("   COLOR: navy;");
txtstream.WriteLine("   BACKGROUND-COLOR: white;");
txtstream.WriteLine("   FONT-FAMILY: font-family: Cambria, serif;");
txtstream.WriteLine("   FONT-SIZE: 12px;");
txtstream.WriteLine("   text-align: left;");
txtstream.WriteLine("   white-Space: nowrap;");
txtstream.WriteLine("}");
txtstream.WriteLine("</style>");
txtstream.WriteLine("<title>Win32_Process</title>");
txtstream.WriteLine("</head>");
txtstream.WriteLine("<body>");
txtstream.WriteLine("<table border='0' Cellspacing='3' cellpadding = '3'>");

var Names;
var Cols;
var Rows;
var x = 0;

var v = 0;
```

```
while(v < 0)
{
    var ti = ex.NextEvent(-1);
    var obj = ti.Properties_.Item("TargetInstance").Value;
    if(v == 0)
    {
        Names = new Array[obj.Properties_.Count];
        Cols = new Array[obj.Properties_.Count];
        Rows = new Array[4];
        var propEnum = new Enumerator(obj.Properties_);
        for (; !propEnum.atEnd(); propEnum.moveNext())
        {
            var prop = propEnum.item();
            Names[x] = prop.Name;
            Cols[x] = GetValue(prop.Name, obj);
            x = x + 1;
        }
        Rows[v] = Cols;
        x = 0;
        v = v + 1;
    }
    else
    {
        var propEnum = new Enumerator(obj.Properties_);
        for (; !propEnum.atEnd(); propEnum.moveNext())
        {
            var prop = propEnum.item();
            Cols[x] = GetValue(prop.Name, obj);
            x = x + 1;
        }
        Rows[v] = Cols;
        x = 0;
        v = v + 1;
    }
}
txtstream.WriteLine("<%");
for(var a = 0;a < Names.Count; a++)
{
    txtstream.WriteLine("Response.Write(\"<tr><th align='left' nowrap>" +
Names[a] + "</th>\" + vbcrlf)");
```

```javascript
for(var b = 0;b < Rows.Count; b++)
{
    var C = Rows[b];
    txtstream.WriteLine("Response.Write(\"<td    style='font-family:Calibri,
Sans-Serif;font-size:    12px;color:navy;'    align='left'    nowrap='true'><select
multiple><option value = """ + C[x] + """">" + C[x] + "</option></select></td>\" +
vbcrlf)");
}
    txtstream.WriteLine("Response.Write(\"</tr>\" + vbcrlf)");
}
txtstream.WriteLine("%>");
txtstream.WriteLine("</table>");
txtstream.WriteLine("</body>");
txtstream.WriteLine("</html>");
txtstream.close();
function GetValue(Name, obj)
{
    var tempstr = new String();
    var tempstr1 = new String();
    var tName = new String();
    tempstr1 = obj.GetObjectText_();
    var re = /"/g;
    tempstr1 = tempstr1.replace(re , "");
    var pos;
    tName = Name + " = ";
    pos = tempstr1.indexOf(tName);
    if (pos > -1)
    {
        pos = pos + tName.length;
        tempstr = tempstr1.substring(pos, tempstr1.length);
        pos = tempstr.indexOf(";");
        tempstr = tempstr.substring(0, pos);
        tempstr = tempstr.replace("{", "");
        tempstr = tempstr.replace("}", "");
        if (tempstr.length > 13)
        {
            if (obj.Properties_(Name).CIMType == 101)
            {
```

```
                tempstr = tempstr.substr(4, 2) + "/"  + tempstr.substr(6, 2) + "/" +
tempstr.substr(0, 3) + " " + tempstr.substr(8, 2) + ":" + tempstr.substr(10, 2) + ":" +
tempstr.substr(12, 2);
                }
            }
            return tempstr;
        }
        else
        {
            return "";
        }
    }


    ]]>
    </script>
  </job>
</Package>
```

Vertical Report with a textarea.

```
<?xml Version='1.0' encoding='iso-8859-1'?>
<package>
<job>
<script language='JavaScript'>
<![CDATA[
    var locator = new ActiveXObject("WbemScripting.SWbemLocator");
    var svc = locator.ConnectServer(".", "root\\cimv2");
    svc.Security_.AuthenticationLevel = 6;
    svc.Security_.ImpersonationLevel = 3;
    var strQuery = "Select * From ___InstanceOperationEvent WITHIN 1 where
TargetInstance ISA'Win32_Process'");
    var es = svc.ExecNotificationQuery(strQuery);
    var ws = new ActiveXObject("WScript.Shell");
    var fso = new ActiveXObject("Scripting.FileSystemObject");
    var     txtstream    =     fso.OpenTextFile(ws.CurrentDirectory    +
"\\Win32_Process.asp", 2, true, -2);
    txtstream.WriteLine("<html xmlns='http://www.w3.org/1999/xhtml'>");
    txtstream.WriteLine("<head>");
    txtstream.WriteLine("<style type='text/css'>");
```

```
txtstream.WriteLine("th");
txtstream.WriteLine("{");
txtstream.WriteLine("   COLOR: darkred;");
txtstream.WriteLine("   BACKGROUND-COLOR: white;");
txtstream.WriteLine("   FONT-FAMILY:font-family: Cambria, serif;");
txtstream.WriteLine("   FONT-SIZE: 12px;");
txtstream.WriteLine("   text-align: left;");
txtstream.WriteLine("   white-Space: nowrap;");
txtstream.WriteLine("}");
txtstream.WriteLine("td");
txtstream.WriteLine("{");
txtstream.WriteLine("   COLOR: navy;");
txtstream.WriteLine("   BACKGROUND-COLOR: white;");
txtstream.WriteLine("   FONT-FAMILY: font-family: Cambria, serif;");
txtstream.WriteLine("   FONT-SIZE: 12px;");
txtstream.WriteLine("   text-align: left;");
txtstream.WriteLine("   white-Space: nowrap;");
txtstream.WriteLine("}");
txtstream.WriteLine("</style>");
txtstream.WriteLine("<title>Win32_Process</title>");
txtstream.WriteLine("</head>");
txtstream.WriteLine("<body>");
txtstream.WriteLine("<table border='0' Cellspacing='3' cellpadding = '3'>");

var Names;
var Cols;
var Rows;
var x = 0;

var v = 0;
while(v < 0)
{
   var ti = ex.NextEvent(-1);
   var obj = ti.Properties_.Item("TargetInstance").Value;
   if(v == 0)
   {
     Names = new Array[obj.Properties_.Count];
     Cols = new Array[obj.Properties_.Count];
     Rows = new Array[4];
     var propEnum = new Enumerator(obj.Properties_);
```

```
        for (; !propEnum.atEnd(); propEnum.moveNext())
        {
          var prop = propEnum.item();
          Names[x] = prop.Name;
          Cols[x] = GetValue(prop.Name, obj);
          x = x + 1;
        }
        Rows[v] = Cols;
        x = 0;
        v = v + 1;
      }
      else
      {
        var propEnum = new Enumerator(obj.Properties_);
        for (; !propEnum.atEnd(); propEnum.moveNext())
        {
          var prop = propEnum.item();
          Cols[x] = GetValue(prop.Name, obj);
          x = x + 1;
        }
        Rows[v] = Cols;
        x = 0;
        v = v + 1;
      }
    }
    txtstream.WriteLine("<%");
    for(var a = 0;a < Names.Count; a++)
    {
        txtstream.WriteLine("Response.Write(\"<tr><th align='left' nowrap>" +
Names[a] + "</th>\" + vbcrlf)");
        for(var b = 0;b < Rows.Count; b++)
        {
          var C = Rows[b];
          txtstream.WriteLine("Response.Write(\"<td   style='font-family:Calibri,
Sans-Serif;font-size:  12px;color:navy;'  align='left'  nowrap='true'><textarea>" +
C[x] + "</textarea></td>\" + vbcrlf)");
        }
        txtstream.WriteLine("Response.Write(\"</tr>\" + vbcrlf)");
    }
    txtstream.WriteLine("%>");
```

```
txtstream.WriteLine("</table>");
txtstream.WriteLine("</body>");
txtstream.WriteLine("</html>");
txtstream.close();
function GetValue(Name, obj)
{
    var tempstr = new String();
    var tempstr1 = new String();
    var tName = new String();
    tempstr1 = obj.GetObjectText_();
    var re = /"/g;
    tempstr1 = tempstr1.replace(re , "");
    var pos;
    tName = Name + " = ";
    pos = tempstr1.indexOf(tName);
    if (pos > -1)
    {
        pos = pos + tName.length;
        tempstr = tempstr1.substring(pos, tempstr1.length);
        pos = tempstr.indexOf(";");
        tempstr = tempstr.substring(0, pos);
        tempstr = tempstr.replace("{", "");
        tempstr = tempstr.replace("}", "");
        if (tempstr.length > 13)
        {
            if (obj.Properties_(Name).CIMType == 101)
            {
              tempstr = tempstr.substr(4, 2) + "/"  + tempstr.substr(6, 2) + "/" +
tempstr.substr(0, 3) + " " + tempstr.substr(8, 2) + ":" + tempstr.substr(10, 2) + ":" +
tempstr.substr(12, 2);
            }
        }
        return tempstr;
    }
    else
    {
        return "";
    }
}
```

```
    ]]>
   </script>
  </job>
</Package>
```

Vertical Report with a textbox.

```
<?xml Version='1.0' encoding='iso-8859-1'?>
<package>
<job>
<script language='JavaScript'>
<![CDATA[
   var locator = new ActiveXObject("WbemScripting.SWbemLocator");
   var svc = locator.ConnectServer(".", "root\\cimv2");
   svc.Security_.AuthenticationLevel = 6;
   svc.Security_.ImpersonationLevel = 3;
   var strQuery = "Select * From ___InstanceOperationEvent WITHIN 1 where
TargetInstance ISA'Win32_Process'");
   var es = svc.ExecNotificationQuery(strQuery);
   var ws = new ActiveXObject("WScript.Shell");
   var fso = new ActiveXObject("Scripting.FileSystemObject");
   var    txtstream    =    fso.OpenTextFile(ws.CurrentDirectory    +
"\\Win32_Process.asp", 2, true, -2);
   txtstream.WriteLine("<html xmlns='http://www.w3.org/1999/xhtml'>");
   txtstream.WriteLine("<head>");
   txtstream.WriteLine("<style type='text/css'>");
   txtstream.WriteLine("th");
   txtstream.WriteLine("{");
   txtstream.WriteLine("   COLOR: darkred;");
   txtstream.WriteLine("   BACKGROUND-COLOR: white;");
   txtstream.WriteLine("   FONT-FAMILY:font-family: Cambria, serif;");
   txtstream.WriteLine("   FONT-SIZE: 12px;");
   txtstream.WriteLine("   text-align: left;");
   txtstream.WriteLine("   white-Space: nowrap;");
   txtstream.WriteLine("}");
   txtstream.WriteLine("td");
   txtstream.WriteLine("{");
   txtstream.WriteLine("   COLOR: navy;");
   txtstream.WriteLine("   BACKGROUND-COLOR: white;");
```

```
txtstream.WriteLine("    FONT-FAMILY: font-family: Cambria, serif;");
txtstream.WriteLine("    FONT-SIZE: 12px;");
txtstream.WriteLine("    text-align: left;");
txtstream.WriteLine("    white-Space: nowrap;");
txtstream.WriteLine("}");
txtstream.WriteLine("</style>");
txtstream.WriteLine("<title>Win32_Process</title>");
txtstream.WriteLine("</head>");
txtstream.WriteLine("<body>");
txtstream.WriteLine("<table border='0' Cellspacing='3' cellpadding = '3'>");

var Names;
var Cols;
var Rows;
var x = 0;

var v = 0;
while(v < 0)
{
    var ti = ex.NextEvent(-1);
    var obj = ti.Properties_.Item("TargetInstance").Value;
    if(v == 0)
    {
        Names = new Array[obj.Properties_.Count];
        Cols = new Array[obj.Properties_.Count];
        Rows = new Array[4];
        var propEnum = new Enumerator(obj.Properties_);
        for (; !propEnum.atEnd(); propEnum.moveNext())
        {
            var prop = propEnum.item();
            Names[x] = prop.Name;
            Cols[x] = GetValue(prop.Name, obj);
            x = x + 1;
        }
        Rows[v] = Cols;
        x = 0;
        v = v + 1;
    }
    else
    {
```

```javascript
            var propEnum = new Enumerator(obj.Properties_);
            for (; !propEnum.atEnd(); propEnum.moveNext())
            {
                var prop = propEnum.item();
                Cols[x] = GetValue(prop.Name, obj);
                x = x + 1;
            }
            Rows[v] = Cols;
            x = 0;
            v = v + 1;
        }
    }
    txtstream.WriteLine("<%");
    for(var a = 0;a < Names.Count; a++)
    {
        txtstream.WriteLine("Response.Write(\"<tr><th align='left' nowrap>" +
Names[a] + "</th>\" + vbcrlf)");
        for(var b = 0;b < Rows.Count; b++)
        {
            var C = Rows[b];
            txtstream.WriteLine("Response.Write(\"<td   style='font-family:Calibri,
Sans-Serif;font-size: 12px;color:navy;' align='left' nowrap='true'><input type=text
value="""" + C[x] + """"></input></td>\" + vbcrlf)");
        }
        txtstream.WriteLine("Response.Write(\"</tr>\" + vbcrlf)");
    }
    txtstream.WriteLine("%>");
    txtstream.WriteLine("</table>");
    txtstream.WriteLine("</body>");
    txtstream.WriteLine("</html>");
    txtstream.close();
    function GetValue(Name, obj)
    {
        var tempstr = new String();
        var tempstr1 = new String();
        var tName = new String();
        tempstr1 = obj.GetObjectText_();
        var re = /"/g;
        tempstr1 = tempstr1.replace(re , "");
        var pos;
```

```
tName = Name + " = ";
pos = tempstr1.indexOf(tName);
if (pos > -1)
{
    pos = pos + tName.length;
    tempstr = tempstr1.substring(pos, tempstr1.length);
    pos = tempstr.indexOf(";");
    tempstr = tempstr.substring(0, pos);
    tempstr = tempstr.replace("{", "");
    tempstr = tempstr.replace("}", "");
    if (tempstr.length > 13)
    {
        if (obj.Properties_(Name).CIMType == 101)
        {
            tempstr = tempstr.substr(4, 2) + "/" + tempstr.substr(6, 2) + "/" +
tempstr.substr(0, 3) + " " + tempstr.substr(8, 2) + ":" + tempstr.substr(10, 2) + ":" +
tempstr.substr(12, 2);
        }
    }
    return tempstr;
}
else
{
    return "";
}
}


]]>
</script>
</job>
</Package>
```

ASP Tables

Horizontal Table with no additional tags.

```
<?xml Version='1.0' encoding='iso-8859-1'?>
<package>
<job>
<script language='JavaScript'>
<![CDATA[
    var locator = new ActiveXObject("WbemScripting.SWbemLocator");
    var svc = locator.ConnectServer(".", "root\\cimv2");
    svc.Security_.AuthenticationLevel = 6;
    svc.Security_.ImpersonationLevel = 3;
    var strQuery = "Select * From ___InstanceOperationEvent WITHIN 1 where
TargetInstance ISA'Win32_Process'");
    var es = svc.ExecNotificationQuery(strQuery);
    var ws = new ActiveXObject("WScript.Shell");
    var fso = new ActiveXObject("Scripting.FileSystemObject");
    var      txtstream      =      fso.OpenTextFile(ws.CurrentDirectory      +
"\\Win32_Process.asp", 2, true, -2);
    txtstream.WriteLine("<html xmlns='http://www.w3.org/1999/xhtml'>");
    txtstream.WriteLine("<head>");
    txtstream.WriteLine("<style type='text/css'>");
    txtstream.WriteLine("th");
    txtstream.WriteLine("{");
    txtstream.WriteLine("   COLOR: darkred;");
    txtstream.WriteLine("   BACKGROUND-COLOR: white;");
    txtstream.WriteLine("   FONT-FAMILY:font-family: Cambria, serif;");
    txtstream.WriteLine("   FONT-SIZE: 12px;");
    txtstream.WriteLine("   text-align: left;");
    txtstream.WriteLine("   white-Space: nowrap;");
    txtstream.WriteLine("}");
    txtstream.WriteLine("td");
    txtstream.WriteLine("{");
    txtstream.WriteLine("   COLOR: navy;");
```

```
txtstream.WriteLine("    BACKGROUND-COLOR: white;");
txtstream.WriteLine("    FONT-FAMILY: font-family: Cambria, serif;");
txtstream.WriteLine("    FONT-SIZE: 12px;");
txtstream.WriteLine("    text-align: left;");
txtstream.WriteLine("    white-Space: nowrap;");
txtstream.WriteLine("}");
txtstream.WriteLine("</style>");
txtstream.WriteLine("<title>Win32_Process</title>");
txtstream.WriteLine("</head>");
txtstream.WriteLine("<body>");
txtstream.WriteLine("<table border='1' Cellspacing='3' cellpadding = '3'>");
txtstream.WriteLine("<%");
var v=0;
while(v < 0)
{
    var ti = ex.NextEvent(-1);
    var obj = ti.Properties_.Item("TargetInstance").Value;
    if(v == 0)
    {
        txtstream.WriteLine("Response.Write(\"<tr>\" + vbcrlf)");
        var propEnum = new Enumerator(obj.Properties_);
        for (; !propEnum.atEnd(); propEnum.moveNext())
        {
            var prop = propEnum.item();
            txtstream.WriteLine("Response.Write(\"<th align='left' nowrap>" +
prop.Name + "</th>\" + vbcrlf)");
        }
        txtstream.WriteLine("Response.Write(\"</tr>\" + vbcrlf)");
        propEnum.Reset();
    }
    txtstream.WriteLine("Response.Write(\"<tr>\" + vbcrlf)");
    for (; !propEnum.atEnd(); propEnum.moveNext())
    {
        var prop = propEnum.item();
        txtstream.WriteLine("Response.Write(\"<td    style='font-family:Calibri,
Sans-Serif;font-size:    12px;color:navy;'    align='left'    nowrap='nowrap'>"    +
GetValue(prop.Name, obj) + "</td>\" + vbcrlf)");
    }
    txtstream.WriteLine("Response.Write(\"</tr>\" + vbcrlf)");
    v = v + 1;
```

```
        }
        txtstream.WriteLine("%>");
        txtstream.WriteLine("</table>");
        txtstream.WriteLine("</body>");
        txtstream.WriteLine("</html>");
        txtstream.close();
        function GetValue(Name, obj)
        {
            var tempstr = new String();
            var tempstr1 = new String();
            var tName = new String();
            tempstr1 = obj.GetObjectText_();
            var re = /"/g;
            tempstr1 = tempstr1.replace(re , "");
            var pos;
            tName = Name + " = ";
            pos = tempstr1.indexOf(tName);
            if (pos > -1)
            {
                pos = pos + tName.length;
                tempstr = tempstr1.substring(pos, tempstr1.length);
                pos = tempstr.indexOf(";");
                tempstr = tempstr.substring(0, pos);
                tempstr = tempstr.replace("{", "");
                tempstr = tempstr.replace("}", "");
                if (tempstr.length > 13)
                {
                    if (obj.Properties_(Name).CIMType == 101)
                    {
                        tempstr = tempstr.substr(4, 2) + "/"  + tempstr.substr(6, 2) + "/" +
tempstr.substr(0, 3) + " " + tempstr.substr(8, 2) + ":" + tempstr.substr(10, 2) + ":" +
tempstr.substr(12, 2);
                    }
                }
                return tempstr;
            }
            else
            {
                return "";
            }
```

```
        }

    ]]>
    </script>
  </job>
</Package>
```

Horizontal Table with a Combobox.

```
<?xml Version='1.0' encoding='iso-8859-1'?>
<package>
<job>
<script language='JavaScript'>
<![CDATA[
    var locator = new ActiveXObject("WbemScripting.SWbemLocator");
    var svc = locator.ConnectServer(".", "root\\cimv2");
    svc.Security_.AuthenticationLevel = 6;
    svc.Security_.ImpersonationLevel = 3;
    var strQuery = "Select * From ___InstanceOperationEvent WITHIN 1 where
TargetInstance ISA'Win32_Process'");
    var es = svc.ExecNotificationQuery(strQuery);
    var ws = new ActiveXObject("WScript.Shell");
    var fso = new ActiveXObject("Scripting.FileSystemObject");
    var      txtstream     =      fso.OpenTextFile(ws.CurrentDirectory      +
"\\Win32_Process.asp", 2, true, -2);
    txtstream.WriteLine("<html xmlns='http://www.w3.org/1999/xhtml'>");
    txtstream.WriteLine("<head>");
    txtstream.WriteLine("<style type='text/css'>");
    txtstream.WriteLine("th");
    txtstream.WriteLine("{");
    txtstream.WriteLine("   COLOR: darkred;");
    txtstream.WriteLine("   BACKGROUND-COLOR: white;");
    txtstream.WriteLine("   FONT-FAMILY:font-family: Cambria, serif;");
    txtstream.WriteLine("   FONT-SIZE: 12px;");
    txtstream.WriteLine("   text-align: left;");
    txtstream.WriteLine("   white-Space: nowrap;");
    txtstream.WriteLine("}");
    txtstream.WriteLine("td");
    txtstream.WriteLine("{");
```

```
txtstream.WriteLine("    COLOR: navy;");
txtstream.WriteLine("    BACKGROUND-COLOR: white;");
txtstream.WriteLine("    FONT-FAMILY: font-family: Cambria, serif;");
txtstream.WriteLine("    FONT-SIZE: 12px;");
txtstream.WriteLine("    text-align: left;");
txtstream.WriteLine("    white-Space: nowrap;");
txtstream.WriteLine("}");
txtstream.WriteLine("</style>");
txtstream.WriteLine("<title>Win32_Process</title>");
txtstream.WriteLine("</head>");
txtstream.WriteLine("<body>");
txtstream.WriteLine("<table border='1' Cellspacing='3' cellpadding = '3'>");
txtstream.WriteLine("<%");
var v=0;
while(v < 0)
{
    var ti = ex.NextEvent(-1);
    var obj = ti.Properties_.Item("TargetInstance").Value;
    if(v == 0)
    {
        txtstream.WriteLine("Response.Write(\"<tr>\" + vbcrlf)");
        var propEnum = new Enumerator(obj.Properties_);
        for (; !propEnum.atEnd(); propEnum.moveNext())
        {
            var prop = propEnum.item();
            txtstream.WriteLine("Response.Write(\"<th align='left' nowrap>" +
prop.Name + "</th>\" + vbcrlf)");
        }
        txtstream.WriteLine("Response.Write(\"</tr>\" + vbcrlf)");
        propEnum.Reset();
    }
    txtstream.WriteLine("Response.Write(\"<tr>\" + vbcrlf)");
    for (; !propEnum.atEnd(); propEnum.moveNext())
    {
        var prop = propEnum.item();
        txtstream.WriteLine("Response.Write(\"<td   style='font-family:Calibri,
Sans-Serif;font-size: 12px;color:navy;' align='left' nowrap='true'><select><option
value = '" + GetValue(prop.Name, obj) + "'>" + GetValue(prop.Name, obj) +
"</option></select></td>\" + vbcrlf)");
    }
```

```
        txtstream.WriteLine("Response.Write(\"</tr>\" + vbcrlf)");
        v = v + 1;
    }
    txtstream.WriteLine("%>");
    txtstream.WriteLine("</table>");
    txtstream.WriteLine("</body>");
    txtstream.WriteLine("</html>");
    txtstream.close();
    function GetValue(Name, obj)
    {
        var tempstr = new String();
        var tempstr1 = new String();
        var tName = new String();
        tempstr1 = obj.GetObjectText_();
        var re = /"/g;
        tempstr1 = tempstr1.replace(re , "");
        var pos;
        tName = Name + " = ";
        pos = tempstr1.indexOf(tName);
        if (pos > -1)
        {
            pos = pos + tName.length;
            tempstr = tempstr1.substring(pos, tempstr1.length);
            pos = tempstr.indexOf(";");
            tempstr = tempstr.substring(0, pos);
            tempstr = tempstr.replace("{", "");
            tempstr = tempstr.replace("}", "");
            if (tempstr.length > 13)
            {
                if (obj.Properties_(Name).CIMType == 101)
                {
                    tempstr = tempstr.substr(4, 2) + "/"  + tempstr.substr(6, 2) + "/" +
tempstr.substr(0, 3) + " " + tempstr.substr(8, 2) + ":" + tempstr.substr(10, 2) + ":" +
tempstr.substr(12, 2);
                }
            }
            return tempstr;
        }
        else
        {
```

```
        return "";
      }
    }


    ]]>
    </script>
  </job>
</Package>
```

Horizontal Table with a link.

```
<?xml Version='1.0' encoding='iso-8859-1'?>
<package>
<job>
<script language='JavaScript'>
<![CDATA[
  var locator = new ActiveXObject("WbemScripting.SWbemLocator");
  var svc = locator.ConnectServer(".", "root\\cimv2");
  svc.Security_.AuthenticationLevel = 6;
  svc.Security_.ImpersonationLevel = 3;
  var strQuery = "Select * From ___InstanceOperationEvent WITHIN 1 where
TargetInstance ISA'Win32_Process'");
  var es = svc.ExecNotificationQuery(strQuery);
  var ws = new ActiveXObject("WScript.Shell");
  var fso = new ActiveXObject("Scripting.FileSystemObject");
  var     txtstream     =     fso.OpenTextFile(ws.CurrentDirectory     +
"\\Win32_Process.asp", 2, true, -2);
  txtstream.WriteLine("<html xmlns='http://www.w3.org/1999/xhtml'>");
  txtstream.WriteLine("<head>");
  txtstream.WriteLine("<style type='text/css'>");
  txtstream.WriteLine("th");
  txtstream.WriteLine("{");
  txtstream.WriteLine("   COLOR: darkred;");
  txtstream.WriteLine("   BACKGROUND-COLOR: white;");
  txtstream.WriteLine("   FONT-FAMILY:font-family: Cambria, serif;");
  txtstream.WriteLine("   FONT-SIZE: 12px;");
  txtstream.WriteLine("   text-align: left;");
  txtstream.WriteLine("   white-Space: nowrap;");
  txtstream.WriteLine("}");
```

```
txtstream.WriteLine("td");
txtstream.WriteLine("{");
txtstream.WriteLine("   COLOR: navy;");
txtstream.WriteLine("   BACKGROUND-COLOR: white;");
txtstream.WriteLine("   FONT-FAMILY: font-family: Cambria, serif;");
txtstream.WriteLine("   FONT-SIZE: 12px;");
txtstream.WriteLine("   text-align: left;");
txtstream.WriteLine("   white-Space: nowrap;");
txtstream.WriteLine("}");
txtstream.WriteLine("</style>");
txtstream.WriteLine("<title>Win32_Process</title>");
txtstream.WriteLine("</head>");
txtstream.WriteLine("<body>");
txtstream.WriteLine("<table border='1' Cellspacing='3' cellpadding = '3'>");
txtstream.WriteLine("<%");
var v=0;
while(v < 0)
{
    var ti = ex.NextEvent(-1);
    var obj = ti.Properties_.Item("TargetInstance").Value;
    if(v == 0)
    {
        txtstream.WriteLine("Response.Write(\"<tr>\" + vbcrlf)");
        var propEnum = new Enumerator(obj.Properties_);
        for (; !propEnum.atEnd(); propEnum.moveNext())
        {
            var prop = propEnum.item();
            txtstream.WriteLine("Response.Write(\"<th align='left' nowrap>" +
prop.Name + "</th>\" + vbcrlf)");
        }
        txtstream.WriteLine("Response.Write(\"</tr>\" + vbcrlf)");
        propEnum.Reset();
    }
    txtstream.WriteLine("Response.Write(\"<tr>\" + vbcrlf)");
    for (; !propEnum.atEnd(); propEnum.moveNext())
    {
        var prop = propEnum.item();
        txtstream.WriteLine("Response.Write(\"<td   style='font-family:Calibri,
Sans-Serif;font-size: 12px;color:navy;' align='left' nowrap='true'><a href='" +
```

```
GetValue(prop.Name, obj) + "'>" + GetValue(prop.Name, obj) + "</a></td>\" +
vbcrlf)");
            }
          txtstream.WriteLine("Response.Write(\"</tr>\" + vbcrlf)");
          v = v + 1;
        }
        txtstream.WriteLine("%>");
        txtstream.WriteLine("</table>");
        txtstream.WriteLine("</body>");
        txtstream.WriteLine("</html>");
        txtstream.close();
        function GetValue(Name, obj)
        {
            var tempstr = new String();
            var tempstr1 = new String();
            var tName = new String();
            tempstr1 = obj.GetObjectText_();
            var re = /"/g;
            tempstr1 = tempstr1.replace(re , "");
            var pos;
            tName = Name + " = ";
            pos = tempstr1.indexOf(tName);
            if (pos > -1)
            {
                pos = pos + tName.length;
                tempstr = tempstr1.substring(pos, tempstr1.length);
                pos = tempstr.indexOf(";");
                tempstr = tempstr.substring(0, pos);
                tempstr = tempstr.replace("{", "");
                tempstr = tempstr.replace("}", "");
                if (tempstr.length > 13)
                {
                    if (obj.Properties_(Name).CIMType == 101)
                    {
                        tempstr = tempstr.substr(4, 2) + "/" + tempstr.substr(6, 2) + "/" +
tempstr.substr(0, 3) + " " + tempstr.substr(8, 2) + ":" + tempstr.substr(10, 2) + ":" +
tempstr.substr(12, 2);
                    }
                }
                return tempstr;
```

```
        }
        else
        {
            return "";
        }
    }


    ]]>
    </script>
  </job>
</Package>
```

Horizontal Table with a Listbox.

```
<?xml Version='1.0' encoding='iso-8859-1'?>
<package>
<job>
<script language='JavaScript'>
<![CDATA[
    var locator = new ActiveXObject("WbemScripting.SWbemLocator");
    var svc = locator.ConnectServer(".", "root\\cimv2");
    svc.Security_.AuthenticationLevel = 6;
    svc.Security_.ImpersonationLevel = 3;
    var strQuery = "Select * From ___InstanceOperationEvent WITHIN 1 where
TargetInstance ISA'Win32_Process'");
    var es = svc.ExecNotificationQuery(strQuery);
    var ws = new ActiveXObject("WScript.Shell");
    var fso = new ActiveXObject("Scripting.FileSystemObject");
    var      txtstream     =      fso.OpenTextFile(ws.CurrentDirectory     +
"\\Win32_Process.asp", 2, true, -2);
    txtstream.WriteLine("<html xmlns='http://www.w3.org/1999/xhtml'>");
    txtstream.WriteLine("<head>");
    txtstream.WriteLine("<style type='text/css'>");
    txtstream.WriteLine("th");
    txtstream.WriteLine("{");
    txtstream.WriteLine("   COLOR: darkred;");
    txtstream.WriteLine("   BACKGROUND-COLOR: white;");
    txtstream.WriteLine("   FONT-FAMILY:font-family: Cambria, serif;");
    txtstream.WriteLine("   FONT-SIZE: 12px;");
```

```
txtstream.WriteLine("    text-align: left;");
txtstream.WriteLine("    white-Space: nowrap;");
txtstream.WriteLine("}");
txtstream.WriteLine("td");
txtstream.WriteLine("{");
txtstream.WriteLine("    COLOR: navy;");
txtstream.WriteLine("    BACKGROUND-COLOR: white;");
txtstream.WriteLine("    FONT-FAMILY: font-family: Cambria, serif;");
txtstream.WriteLine("    FONT-SIZE: 12px;");
txtstream.WriteLine("    text-align: left;");
txtstream.WriteLine("    white-Space: nowrap;");
txtstream.WriteLine("}");
txtstream.WriteLine("</style>");
txtstream.WriteLine("<title>Win32_Process</title>");
txtstream.WriteLine("</head>");
txtstream.WriteLine("<body>");
txtstream.WriteLine("<table border='1' Cellspacing='3' cellpadding = '3'>");
txtstream.WriteLine("<%");
var v=0;
while(v < 0)
{
    var ti = ex.NextEvent(-1);
    var obj = ti.Properties_.Item("TargetInstance").Value;
    if(v == 0)
    {
        txtstream.WriteLine("Response.Write(\"<tr>\" + vbcrlf)");
        var propEnum = new Enumerator(obj.Properties_);
        for (; !propEnum.atEnd(); propEnum.moveNext())
        {
            var prop = propEnum.item();
            txtstream.WriteLine("Response.Write(\"<th  align='left'  nowrap>" +
prop.Name + "</th>\" + vbcrlf)");
        }
        txtstream.WriteLine("Response.Write(\"</tr>\" + vbcrlf)");
        propEnum.Reset();
    }
    txtstream.WriteLine("Response.Write(\"<tr>\" + vbcrlf)");
    for (; !propEnum.atEnd(); propEnum.moveNext())
    {
        var prop = propEnum.item();
```

```
                txtstream.WriteLine("Response.Write(\"<td    style='font-family:Calibri,
Sans-Serif;font-size:      12px;color:navy;'     align='left'     nowrap='true'><select
multiple><option    value    =    '"    +    GetValue(prop.Name,    obj)    +    "'>"    +
GetValue(prop.Name, obj) + "</option></select></td>\" + vbcrlf)");
        }
        txtstream.WriteLine("Response.Write(\"</tr>\" + vbcrlf)");
        v = v + 1;
    }
    txtstream.WriteLine("%>");
    txtstream.WriteLine("</table>");
    txtstream.WriteLine("</body>");
    txtstream.WriteLine("</html>");
    txtstream.close();
    function GetValue(Name, obj)
    {
        var tempstr = new String();
        var tempstr1 = new String();
        var tName = new String();
        tempstr1 = obj.GetObjectText_();
        var re = /"/g;
        tempstr1 = tempstr1.replace(re , "");
        var pos;
        tName = Name + " = ";
        pos = tempstr1.indexOf(tName);
        if (pos > -1)
        {
            pos = pos + tName.length;
            tempstr = tempstr1.substring(pos, tempstr1.length);
            pos = tempstr.indexOf(";");
            tempstr = tempstr.substring(0, pos);
            tempstr = tempstr.replace("{", "");
            tempstr = tempstr.replace("}", "");
            if (tempstr.length > 13)
            {
                if (obj.Properties_(Name).CIMType == 101)
                {
                    tempstr = tempstr.substr(4, 2) + "/" + tempstr.substr(6, 2) + "/" +
tempstr.substr(0, 3) + " " + tempstr.substr(8, 2) + ":" + tempstr.substr(10, 2) + ":" +
tempstr.substr(12, 2);
                }
```

```
        }
        return tempstr;
      }
      else
      {
        return "";
      }
    }


  ]]>
  </script>
 </job>
</Package>
```

Horizontal Table with a textarea.

```
<?xml Version='1.0' encoding='iso-8859-1'?>
<package>
<job>
<script language='JavaScript'>
<![CDATA[
  var locator = new ActiveXObject("WbemScripting.SWbemLocator");
  var svc = locator.ConnectServer(".", "root\\cimv2");
  svc.Security_.AuthenticationLevel = 6;
  svc.Security_.ImpersonationLevel = 3;
  var strQuery = "Select * From ___InstanceOperationEvent WITHIN 1 where
TargetInstance ISA'Win32_Process'");
  var es = svc.ExecNotificationQuery(strQuery);
  var ws = new ActiveXObject("WScript.Shell");
  var fso = new ActiveXObject("Scripting.FileSystemObject");
  var      txtstream     =      fso.OpenTextFile(ws.CurrentDirectory      +
"\\Win32_Process.asp", 2, true, -2);
  txtstream.WriteLine("<html xmlns='http://www.w3.org/1999/xhtml'>");
  txtstream.WriteLine("<head>");
  txtstream.WriteLine("<style type='text/css'>");
  txtstream.WriteLine("th");
  txtstream.WriteLine("{");
  txtstream.WriteLine("    COLOR: darkred;");
  txtstream.WriteLine("    BACKGROUND-COLOR: white;");
```

```
txtstream.WriteLine("    FONT-FAMILY:font-family: Cambria, serif;");
txtstream.WriteLine("    FONT-SIZE: 12px;");
txtstream.WriteLine("    text-align: left;");
txtstream.WriteLine("    white-Space: nowrap;");
txtstream.WriteLine("}");
txtstream.WriteLine("td");
txtstream.WriteLine("{");
txtstream.WriteLine("    COLOR: navy;");
txtstream.WriteLine("    BACKGROUND-COLOR: white;");
txtstream.WriteLine("    FONT-FAMILY: font-family: Cambria, serif;");
txtstream.WriteLine("    FONT-SIZE: 12px;");
txtstream.WriteLine("    text-align: left;");
txtstream.WriteLine("    white-Space: nowrap;");
txtstream.WriteLine("}");
txtstream.WriteLine("</style>");
txtstream.WriteLine("<title>Win32_Process</title>");
txtstream.WriteLine("</head>");
txtstream.WriteLine("<body>");
txtstream.WriteLine("<table border='1' Cellspacing='3' cellpadding = '3'>");
txtstream.WriteLine("<%");
var v=0;
while(v < 0)
{
    var ti = ex.NextEvent(-1);
    var obj = ti.Properties_.Item("TargetInstance").Value;
    if(v == 0)
    {
        txtstream.WriteLine("Response.Write(\"<tr>\" + vbcrlf)");
        var propEnum = new Enumerator(obj.Properties_);
        for (; !propEnum.atEnd(); propEnum.moveNext())
        {
            var prop = propEnum.item();
            txtstream.WriteLine("Response.Write(\"<th align='left' nowrap>" +
prop.Name + "</th>\" + vbcrlf)");
        }
        txtstream.WriteLine("Response.Write(\"</tr>\" + vbcrlf)");
        propEnum.Reset();
    }
    txtstream.WriteLine("Response.Write(\"<tr>\" + vbcrlf)");
    for (; !propEnum.atEnd(); propEnum.moveNext())
```

```javascript
        {
            var prop = propEnum.item();
            txtstream.WriteLine("Response.Write(\"<td   style='font-family:Calibri,
Sans-Serif;font-size: 12px;color:navy;' align='left' nowrap='true'><textarea>" +
GetValue(prop.Name, obj) + "</textarea></td>\" + vbcrlf)");
        }
        txtstream.WriteLine("Response.Write(\"</tr>\" + vbcrlf)");
        v = v + 1;
    }
    txtstream.WriteLine("%>");
    txtstream.WriteLine("</table>");
    txtstream.WriteLine("</body>");
    txtstream.WriteLine("</html>");
    txtstream.close();
    function GetValue(Name, obj)
    {
        var tempstr = new String();
        var tempstr1 = new String();
        var tName = new String();
        tempstr1 = obj.GetObjectText_();
        var re = /"/g;
        tempstr1 = tempstr1.replace(re , "");
        var pos;
        tName = Name + " = ";
        pos = tempstr1.indexOf(tName);
        if (pos > -1)
        {
            pos = pos + tName.length;
            tempstr = tempstr1.substring(pos, tempstr1.length);
            pos = tempstr.indexOf(";");
            tempstr = tempstr.substring(0, pos);
            tempstr = tempstr.replace("{", "");
            tempstr = tempstr.replace("}", "");
            if (tempstr.length > 13)
            {
                if (obj.Properties_(Name).CIMType == 101)
                {
                    tempstr = tempstr.substr(4, 2) + "/" + tempstr.substr(6, 2) + "/" +
tempstr.substr(0, 3) + " " + tempstr.substr(8, 2) + ":" + tempstr.substr(10, 2) + ":" +
tempstr.substr(12, 2);
```

```
            }
        }
        return tempstr;
    }
    else
    {
        return "";
    }
}


]]>
  </script>
 </job>
</Package>
```

Horizontal Table with a textbox.

```
<?xml Version='1.0' encoding='iso-8859-1'?>
<package>
<job>
<script language='JavaScript'>
<![CDATA[
    var locator = new ActiveXObject("WbemScripting.SWbemLocator");
    var svc = locator.ConnectServer(".", "root\\cimv2");
    svc.Security_.AuthenticationLevel = 6;
    svc.Security_.ImpersonationLevel = 3;
    var strQuery = "Select * From ___InstanceOperationEvent WITHIN 1 where
TargetInstance ISA'Win32_Process'");
    var es = svc.ExecNotificationQuery(strQuery);
    var ws = new ActiveXObject("WScript.Shell");
    var fso = new ActiveXObject("Scripting.FileSystemObject");
    var    txtstream    =    fso.OpenTextFile(ws.CurrentDirectory    +
"\\Win32_Process.asp", 2, true, -2);
    txtstream.WriteLine("<html xmlns='http://www.w3.org/1999/xhtml'>");
    txtstream.WriteLine("<head>");
    txtstream.WriteLine("<style type='text/css'>");
    txtstream.WriteLine("th");
    txtstream.WriteLine("{");
    txtstream.WriteLine("   COLOR: darkred;");
```

```
txtstream.WriteLine("    BACKGROUND-COLOR: white;");
txtstream.WriteLine("    FONT-FAMILY:font-family: Cambria, serif;");
txtstream.WriteLine("    FONT-SIZE: 12px;");
txtstream.WriteLine("    text-align: left;");
txtstream.WriteLine("    white-Space: nowrap;");
txtstream.WriteLine("}");
txtstream.WriteLine("td");
txtstream.WriteLine("{");
txtstream.WriteLine("    COLOR: navy;");
txtstream.WriteLine("    BACKGROUND-COLOR: white;");
txtstream.WriteLine("    FONT-FAMILY: font-family: Cambria, serif;");
txtstream.WriteLine("    FONT-SIZE: 12px;");
txtstream.WriteLine("    text-align: left;");
txtstream.WriteLine("    white-Space: nowrap;");
txtstream.WriteLine("}");
txtstream.WriteLine("</style>");
txtstream.WriteLine("<title>Win32_Process</title>");
txtstream.WriteLine("</head>");
txtstream.WriteLine("<body>");
txtstream.WriteLine("<table border='1' Cellspacing='3' cellpadding = '3'>");
txtstream.WriteLine("<%");
var v=0;
while(v < 0)
{
    var ti = ex.NextEvent(-1);
    var obj = ti.Properties_.Item("TargetInstance").Value;
    if(v == 0)
    {
        txtstream.WriteLine("Response.Write(\"<tr>\" + vbcrlf)");
        var propEnum = new Enumerator(obj.Properties_);
        for (; !propEnum.atEnd(); propEnum.moveNext())
        {
            var prop = propEnum.item();
            txtstream.WriteLine("Response.Write(\"<th align='left' nowrap>" +
prop.Name + "</th>\" + vbcrlf)");
        }
        txtstream.WriteLine("Response.Write(\"</tr>\" + vbcrlf)");
        propEnum.Reset();
    }
    txtstream.WriteLine("Response.Write(\"<tr>\" + vbcrlf)");
```

```
        for (; !propEnum.atEnd(); propEnum.moveNext())
        {
            var prop = propEnum.item();
            txtstream.WriteLine("Response.Write(\"<td    style='font-family:Calibri,
Sans-Serif;font-size: 12px;color:navy;' align='left' nowrap='true'><input type=text
value='" + GetValue(prop.Name, obj) + "'></input></td>\" + vbcrlf)");
        }
        txtstream.WriteLine("Response.Write(\"</tr>\" + vbcrlf)");
        v = v + 1;
    }
    txtstream.WriteLine("%>");
    txtstream.WriteLine("</table>");
    txtstream.WriteLine("</body>");
    txtstream.WriteLine("</html>");
    txtstream.close();
    function GetValue(Name, obj)
    {
        var tempstr = new String();
        var tempstr1 = new String();
        var tName = new String();
        tempstr1 = obj.GetObjectText_();
        var re = /"/g;
        tempstr1 = tempstr1.replace(re , "");
        var pos;
        tName = Name + " = ";
        pos = tempstr1.indexOf(tName);
        if (pos > -1)
        {
            pos = pos + tName.length;
            tempstr = tempstr1.substring(pos, tempstr1.length);
            pos = tempstr.indexOf(";");
            tempstr = tempstr.substring(0, pos);
            tempstr = tempstr.replace("{", "");
            tempstr = tempstr.replace("}", "");
            if (tempstr.length > 13)
            {
                if (obj.Properties_(Name).CIMType == 101)
                {
```

```
            tempstr = tempstr.substr(4, 2) + "/"  + tempstr.substr(6, 2) + "/" +
tempstr.substr(0, 3) + " " + tempstr.substr(8, 2) + ":" + tempstr.substr(10, 2) + ":" +
tempstr.substr(12, 2);
                }
            }
            return tempstr;
        }
        else
        {
            return "";
        }
    }


    ]]>
    </script>
  </job>
 </Package>
```

Vertical Table with no additional tags.

```
<?xml Version='1.0' encoding='iso-8859-1'?>
<package>
<job>
<script language='JavaScript'>
<![CDATA[
    var locator = new ActiveXObject("WbemScripting.SWbemLocator");
    var svc = locator.ConnectServer(".", "root\\cimv2");
    svc.Security_.AuthenticationLevel = 6;
    svc.Security_.ImpersonationLevel = 3;
    var strQuery = "Select * From ___InstanceOperationEvent WITHIN 1 where
TargetInstance ISA'Win32_Process'");
    var es = svc.ExecNotificationQuery(strQuery);
    var ws = new ActiveXObject("WScript.Shell");
    var fso = new ActiveXObject("Scripting.FileSystemObject");
    var     txtstream     =     fso.OpenTextFile(ws.CurrentDirectory     +
"\\Win32_Process.asp", 2, true, -2);
    txtstream.WriteLine("<html xmlns='http://www.w3.org/1999/xhtml'>");
    txtstream.WriteLine("<head>");
    txtstream.WriteLine("<style type='text/css'>");
```

```
txtstream.WriteLine("th");
txtstream.WriteLine("{");
txtstream.WriteLine("   COLOR: darkred;");
txtstream.WriteLine("   BACKGROUND-COLOR: white;");
txtstream.WriteLine("   FONT-FAMILY:font-family: Cambria, serif;");
txtstream.WriteLine("   FONT-SIZE: 12px;");
txtstream.WriteLine("   text-align: left;");
txtstream.WriteLine("   white-Space: nowrap;");
txtstream.WriteLine("}");
txtstream.WriteLine("td");
txtstream.WriteLine("{");
txtstream.WriteLine("   COLOR: navy;");
txtstream.WriteLine("   BACKGROUND-COLOR: white;");
txtstream.WriteLine("   FONT-FAMILY: font-family: Cambria, serif;");
txtstream.WriteLine("   FONT-SIZE: 12px;");
txtstream.WriteLine("   text-align: left;");
txtstream.WriteLine("   white-Space: nowrap;");
txtstream.WriteLine("}");
txtstream.WriteLine("</style>");
txtstream.WriteLine("<title>Win32_Process</title>");
txtstream.WriteLine("</head>");
txtstream.WriteLine("<body>");
txtstream.WriteLine("<table border='1' Cellspacing='3' cellpadding = '3'>");

var Names;
var Cols;
var Rows;
var x = 0;

var v = 0;
while(v < 0)
{
   var ti = ex.NextEvent(-1);
   var obj = ti.Properties_.Item("TargetInstance").Value;
   if(v == 0)
   {
     Names = new Array[obj.Properties_.Count];
     Cols = new Array[obj.Properties_.Count];
     Rows = new Array[4];
     var propEnum = new Enumerator(obj.Properties_);
```

```
for (; !propEnum.atEnd(); propEnum.moveNext())
{
    var prop = propEnum.item();
    Names[x] = prop.Name;
    Cols[x] = GetValue(prop.Name, obj);
    x = x + 1;
}
Rows[v] = Cols;
x = 0;
v = v + 1;
}
else
{
    var propEnum = new Enumerator(obj.Properties_);
    for (; !propEnum.atEnd(); propEnum.moveNext())
    {
        var prop = propEnum.item();
        Cols[x] = GetValue(prop.Name, obj);
        x = x + 1;
    }
    Rows[v] = Cols;
    x = 0;
    v = v + 1;
}
}
txtstream.WriteLine("<%");
for(var a = 0;a < Names.Count; a++)
{
    txtstream.WriteLine("Response.Write(\"<tr><th align='left' nowrap>" +
Names[a] + "</th>\" + vbcrlf)");
    for(var b = 0;b < Rows.Count; b++)
    {
        var C = Rows[b];
        txtstream.WriteLine("Response.Write(\"<td   style='font-family:Calibri,
Sans-Serif;font-size: 12px;color:navy;' align='left' nowrap='nowrap'>" + C[x] +
"</td>\" + vbcrlf)");
    }
    txtstream.WriteLine("Response.Write(\"</tr>\" + vbcrlf)");
}
txtstream.WriteLine("%>");
```

```
txtstream.WriteLine("</table>");
txtstream.WriteLine("</body>");
txtstream.WriteLine("</html>");
txtstream.close();
function GetValue(Name, obj)
{
    var tempstr = new String();
    var tempstr1 = new String();
    var tName = new String();
    tempstr1 = obj.GetObjectText_();
    var re = /"/g;
    tempstr1 = tempstr1.replace(re , "");
    var pos;
    tName = Name + " = ";
    pos = tempstr1.indexOf(tName);
    if (pos > -1)
    {
        pos = pos + tName.length;
        tempstr = tempstr1.substring(pos, tempstr1.length);
        pos = tempstr.indexOf(";");
        tempstr = tempstr.substring(0, pos);
        tempstr = tempstr.replace("{", "");
        tempstr = tempstr.replace("}", "");
        if (tempstr.length > 13)
        {
            if (obj.Properties_(Name).CIMType == 101)
            {
                tempstr = tempstr.substr(4, 2) + "/"  + tempstr.substr(6, 2) + "/" +
tempstr.substr(0, 3) + " " + tempstr.substr(8, 2) + ":" + tempstr.substr(10, 2) + ":" +
tempstr.substr(12, 2);
            }
        }
        return tempstr;
    }
    else
    {
        return "";
    }
}
```

```
    ]]>
   </script>
  </job>
 </Package>
```

Vertical Table with a Combobox.

```
<?xml Version='1.0' encoding='iso-8859-1'?>
<package>
<job>
<script language='JavaScript'>
<![CDATA[
   var locator = new ActiveXObject("WbemScripting.SWbemLocator");
   var svc = locator.ConnectServer(".", "root\\cimv2");
   svc.Security_.AuthenticationLevel = 6;
   svc.Security_.ImpersonationLevel = 3;
   var strQuery = "Select * From ___InstanceOperationEvent WITHIN 1 where
TargetInstance ISA'Win32_Process'");
      var es = svc.ExecNotificationQuery(strQuery);
      var ws = new ActiveXObject("WScript.Shell");
      var fso = new ActiveXObject("Scripting.FileSystemObject");
      var      txtstream     =     fso.OpenTextFile(ws.CurrentDirectory     +
"\\Win32_Process.asp", 2, true, -2);
      txtstream.WriteLine("<html xmlns='http://www.w3.org/1999/xhtml'>");
      txtstream.WriteLine("<head>");
      txtstream.WriteLine("<style type='text/css'>");
      txtstream.WriteLine("th");
      txtstream.WriteLine("{");
      txtstream.WriteLine("    COLOR: darkred;");
      txtstream.WriteLine("    BACKGROUND-COLOR: white;");
      txtstream.WriteLine("    FONT-FAMILY:font-family: Cambria, serif;");
      txtstream.WriteLine("    FONT-SIZE: 12px;");
      txtstream.WriteLine("    text-align: left;");
      txtstream.WriteLine("    white-Space: nowrap;");
      txtstream.WriteLine("}");
      txtstream.WriteLine("td");
      txtstream.WriteLine("{");
      txtstream.WriteLine("    COLOR: navy;");
      txtstream.WriteLine("    BACKGROUND-COLOR: white;");
```

```
txtstream.WriteLine("   FONT-FAMILY: font-family: Cambria, serif;");
txtstream.WriteLine("   FONT-SIZE: 12px;");
txtstream.WriteLine("   text-align: left;");
txtstream.WriteLine("   white-Space: nowrap;");
txtstream.WriteLine("}");
txtstream.WriteLine("</style>");
txtstream.WriteLine("<title>Win32_Process</title>");
txtstream.WriteLine("</head>");
txtstream.WriteLine("<body>");
txtstream.WriteLine("<table border='1' Cellspacing='3' cellpadding = '3'>");

var Names;
var Cols;
var Rows;
var x = 0;

var v = 0;
while(v < 0)
{
   var ti = ex.NextEvent(-1);
   var obj = ti.Properties_.Item("TargetInstance").Value;
   if(v == 0)
   {
      Names = new Array[obj.Properties_.Count];
      Cols = new Array[obj.Properties_.Count];
      Rows = new Array[4];
      var propEnum = new Enumerator(obj.Properties_);
      for (; !propEnum.atEnd(); propEnum.moveNext())
      {
         var prop = propEnum.item();
         Names[x] = prop.Name;
         Cols[x] = GetValue(prop.Name, obj);
         x = x + 1;
      }
      Rows[v] = Cols;
      x = 0;
      v = v + 1;
   }
   else
   {
```

```
            var propEnum = new Enumerator(obj.Properties_);
            for (; !propEnum.atEnd(); propEnum.moveNext())
            {
               var prop = propEnum.item();
               Cols[x] = GetValue(prop.Name, obj);
               x = x + 1;
            }
            Rows[v] = Cols;
            x = 0;
            v = v + 1;
         }
      }
      txtstream.WriteLine("<%");
      for(var a = 0;a < Names.Count; a++)
      {
         txtstream.WriteLine("Response.Write(\"<tr><th align='left' nowrap>" +
Names[a] + "</th>\" + vbcrlf)");
         for(var b = 0;b < Rows.Count; b++)
         {
            var C = Rows[b];
            txtstream.WriteLine("Response.Write(\"<td    style='font-family:Calibri,
Sans-Serif;font-size: 12px;color:navy;' align='left' nowrap='true'><select><option
value = """" + C[x] + """">" + C[x] + "</option></select></td>\" + vbcrlf)");
         }
         txtstream.WriteLine("Response.Write(\"</tr>\" + vbcrlf)");
      }
      txtstream.WriteLine("%>");
      txtstream.WriteLine("</table>");
      txtstream.WriteLine("</body>");
      txtstream.WriteLine("</html>");
      txtstream.close();
      function GetValue(Name, obj)
      {
         var tempstr = new String();
         var tempstr1 = new String();
         var tName = new String();
         tempstr1 = obj.GetObjectText_();
         var re = /"/g;
         tempstr1 = tempstr1.replace(re , "");
         var pos;
```

```
                 tName = Name + " = ";
                 pos = tempstr1.indexOf(tName);
                 if (pos > -1)
                 {
                     pos = pos + tName.length;
                     tempstr = tempstr1.substring(pos, tempstr1.length);
                     pos = tempstr.indexOf(";");
                     tempstr = tempstr.substring(0, pos);
                     tempstr = tempstr.replace("{", "");
                     tempstr = tempstr.replace("}", "");
                     if (tempstr.length > 13)
                     {
                         if (obj.Properties_(Name).CIMType == 101)
                         {
                             tempstr = tempstr.substr(4, 2) + "/"  + tempstr.substr(6, 2) + "/" +
tempstr.substr(0, 3) + " " + tempstr.substr(8, 2) + ":" + tempstr.substr(10, 2) + ":" +
tempstr.substr(12, 2);
                         }
                     }
                     return tempstr;
                 }
                 else
                 {
                     return "";
                 }
             }

        ]]>
        </script>
       </job>
      </Package>
```

Vertical Table with a link.

```
       <?xml Version='1.0' encoding='iso-8859-1'?>
       <package>
       <job>
       <script language='JavaScript'>
       <![CDATA[
```

```
var locator = new ActiveXObject("WbemScripting.SWbemLocator");
var svc = locator.ConnectServer(".", "root\\cimv2");
svc.Security_.AuthenticationLevel = 6;
svc.Security_.ImpersonationLevel = 3;
var strQuery = "Select * From ___InstanceOperationEvent WITHIN 1 where
TargetInstance ISA'Win32_Process'");
var es = svc.ExecNotificationQuery(strQuery);
var ws = new ActiveXObject("WScript.Shell");
var fso = new ActiveXObject("Scripting.FileSystemObject");
var        txtstream        =        fso.OpenTextFile(ws.CurrentDirectory        +
"\\Win32_Process.asp", 2, true, -2);
txtstream.WriteLine("<html xmlns='http://www.w3.org/1999/xhtml'>");
txtstream.WriteLine("<head>");
txtstream.WriteLine("<style type='text/css'>");
txtstream.WriteLine("th");
txtstream.WriteLine("{");
txtstream.WriteLine("    COLOR: darkred;");
txtstream.WriteLine("    BACKGROUND-COLOR: white;");
txtstream.WriteLine("    FONT-FAMILY:font-family: Cambria, serif;");
txtstream.WriteLine("    FONT-SIZE: 12px;");
txtstream.WriteLine("    text-align: left;");
txtstream.WriteLine("    white-Space: nowrap;");
txtstream.WriteLine("}");
txtstream.WriteLine("td");
txtstream.WriteLine("{");
txtstream.WriteLine("    COLOR: navy;");
txtstream.WriteLine("    BACKGROUND-COLOR: white;");
txtstream.WriteLine("    FONT-FAMILY: font-family: Cambria, serif;");
txtstream.WriteLine("    FONT-SIZE: 12px;");
txtstream.WriteLine("    text-align: left;");
txtstream.WriteLine("    white-Space: nowrap;");
txtstream.WriteLine("}");
txtstream.WriteLine("</style>");
txtstream.WriteLine("<title>Win32_Process</title>");
txtstream.WriteLine("</head>");
txtstream.WriteLine("<body>");
txtstream.WriteLine("<table border='1' Cellspacing='3' cellpadding = '3'>");

var Names;
var Cols;
```

```
var Rows;
var x = 0;

var v = 0;
while(v < 0)
{
   var ti = ex.NextEvent(-1);
   var obj = ti.Properties_.Item("TargetInstance").Value;
   if(v == 0)
   {
      Names = new Array[obj.Properties_.Count];
      Cols = new Array[obj.Properties_.Count];
      Rows = new Array[4];
      var propEnum = new Enumerator(obj.Properties_);
      for (; !propEnum.atEnd(); propEnum.moveNext())
      {
         var prop = propEnum.item();
         Names[x] = prop.Name;
         Cols[x] = GetValue(prop.Name, obj);
         x = x + 1;
      }
      Rows[v] = Cols;
      x = 0;
      v = v + 1;
   }
   else
   {
      var propEnum = new Enumerator(obj.Properties_);
      for (; !propEnum.atEnd(); propEnum.moveNext())
      {
         var prop = propEnum.item();
         Cols[x] = GetValue(prop.Name, obj);
         x = x + 1;
      }
      Rows[v] = Cols;
      x = 0;
      v = v + 1;
   }
}
txtstream.WriteLine("<%");
```

```javascript
for(var a = 0;a < Names.Count; a++)
{
    txtstream.WriteLine("Response.Write(\"<tr><th align='left' nowrap>" +
Names[a] + "</th>\" + vbcrlf)");
    for(var b = 0;b < Rows.Count; b++)
    {
        var C = Rows[b];
        txtstream.WriteLine("Response.Write(\"<td    style='font-family:Calibri,
Sans-Serif;font-size: 12px;color:navy;' align='left' nowrap='true'><a href='" + C[x]
+ "'>" + C[x] + "</a></td>\" + vbcrlf)");
    }
    txtstream.WriteLine("Response.Write(\"</tr>\" + vbcrlf)");
}
txtstream.WriteLine("%>");
txtstream.WriteLine("</table>");
txtstream.WriteLine("</body>");
txtstream.WriteLine("</html>");
txtstream.close();
function GetValue(Name, obj)
{
    var tempstr = new String();
    var tempstr1 = new String();
    var tName = new String();
    tempstr1 = obj.GetObjectText_();
    var re = /"/g;
    tempstr1 = tempstr1.replace(re , "");
    var pos;
    tName = Name + " = ";
    pos = tempstr1.indexOf(tName);
    if (pos > -1)
    {
        pos = pos + tName.length;
        tempstr = tempstr1.substring(pos, tempstr1.length);
        pos = tempstr.indexOf(";");
        tempstr = tempstr.substring(0, pos);
        tempstr = tempstr.replace("{", "");
        tempstr = tempstr.replace("}", "");
        if (tempstr.length > 13)
        {
            if (obj.Properties_(Name).CIMType == 101)
```

```
                {
                    tempstr = tempstr.substr(4, 2) + "/"  + tempstr.substr(6, 2) + "/" +
tempstr.substr(0, 3) + " " + tempstr.substr(8, 2) + ":" + tempstr.substr(10, 2) + ":" +
tempstr.substr(12, 2);
                }
            }
            return tempstr;
        }
        else
        {
            return "";
        }
    }


    ]]>
    </script>
  </job>
</Package>
```

Vertical Table with a Listbox.

```
<?xml Version='1.0' encoding='iso-8859-1'?>
<package>
<job>
<script language='JavaScript'>
<![CDATA[
    var locator = new ActiveXObject("WbemScripting.SWbemLocator");
    var svc = locator.ConnectServer(".", "root\\cimv2");
    svc.Security_.AuthenticationLevel = 6;
    svc.Security_.ImpersonationLevel = 3;
    var strQuery = "Select * From ___InstanceOperationEvent WITHIN 1 where
TargetInstance ISA'Win32_Process'");
    var es = svc.ExecNotificationQuery(strQuery);
    var ws = new ActiveXObject("WScript.Shell");
    var fso = new ActiveXObject("Scripting.FileSystemObject");
    var       txtstream    =       fso.OpenTextFile(ws.CurrentDirectory      +
"\\Win32_Process.asp", 2, true, -2);
    txtstream.WriteLine("<html xmlns='http://www.w3.org/1999/xhtml'>");
    txtstream.WriteLine("<head>");
```

```
txtstream.WriteLine("<style type='text/css'>");
txtstream.WriteLine("th");
txtstream.WriteLine("{");
txtstream.WriteLine("   COLOR: darkred;");
txtstream.WriteLine("   BACKGROUND-COLOR: white;");
txtstream.WriteLine("   FONT-FAMILY:font-family: Cambria, serif;");
txtstream.WriteLine("   FONT-SIZE: 12px;");
txtstream.WriteLine("   text-align: left;");
txtstream.WriteLine("   white-Space: nowrap;");
txtstream.WriteLine("}");
txtstream.WriteLine("td");
txtstream.WriteLine("{");
txtstream.WriteLine("   COLOR: navy;");
txtstream.WriteLine("   BACKGROUND-COLOR: white;");
txtstream.WriteLine("   FONT-FAMILY: font-family: Cambria, serif;");
txtstream.WriteLine("   FONT-SIZE: 12px;");
txtstream.WriteLine("   text-align: left;");
txtstream.WriteLine("   white-Space: nowrap;");
txtstream.WriteLine("}");
txtstream.WriteLine("</style>");
txtstream.WriteLine("<title>Win32_Process</title>");
txtstream.WriteLine("</head>");
txtstream.WriteLine("<body>");
txtstream.WriteLine("<table border='1' Cellspacing='3' cellpadding = '3'>");

var Names;
var Cols;
var Rows;
var x = 0;

var v = 0;
while(v < 0)
{
   var ti = ex.NextEvent(-1);
   var obj = ti.Properties_.Item("TargetInstance").Value;
   if(v == 0)
   {
      Names = new Array[obj.Properties_.Count];
      Cols = new Array[obj.Properties_.Count];
      Rows = new Array[4];
```

```
        var propEnum = new Enumerator(obj.Properties_);
        for (; !propEnum.atEnd(); propEnum.moveNext())
        {
            var prop = propEnum.item();
            Names[x] = prop.Name;
            Cols[x] = GetValue(prop.Name, obj);
            x = x + 1;
        }
        Rows[v] = Cols;
        x = 0;
        v = v + 1;
    }
    else
    {
        var propEnum = new Enumerator(obj.Properties_);
        for (; !propEnum.atEnd(); propEnum.moveNext())
        {
            var prop = propEnum.item();
            Cols[x] = GetValue(prop.Name, obj);
            x = x + 1;
        }
        Rows[v] = Cols;
        x = 0;
        v = v + 1;
    }
}
txtstream.WriteLine("<%");
for(var a = 0;a < Names.Count; a++)
{
    txtstream.WriteLine("Response.Write(\"<tr><th align='left' nowrap>" +
Names[a] + "</th>\" + vbcrlf)");
    for(var b = 0;b < Rows.Count; b++)
    {
        var C = Rows[b];
        txtstream.WriteLine("Response.Write(\"<td    style='font-family:Calibri,
Sans-Serif;font-size:    12px;color:navy;'    align='left'    nowrap='true'><select
multiple><option value = """ + C[x] + """>" + C[x] + "</option></select></td>\" +
vbcrlf)");
    }
    txtstream.WriteLine("Response.Write(\"</tr>\" + vbcrlf)");
```

```
        }
        txtstream.WriteLine("%>");
        txtstream.WriteLine("</table>");
        txtstream.WriteLine("</body>");
        txtstream.WriteLine("</html>");
        txtstream.close();
        function GetValue(Name, obj)
        {
            var tempstr = new String();
            var tempstr1 = new String();
            var tName = new String();
            tempstr1 = obj.GetObjectText_();
            var re = /"/g;
            tempstr1 = tempstr1.replace(re , "");
            var pos;
            tName = Name + " = ";
            pos = tempstr1.indexOf(tName);
            if (pos > -1)
            {
                pos = pos + tName.length;
                tempstr = tempstr1.substring(pos, tempstr1.length);
                pos = tempstr.indexOf(";");
                tempstr = tempstr.substring(0, pos);
                tempstr = tempstr.replace("{", "");
                tempstr = tempstr.replace("}", "");
                if (tempstr.length > 13)
                {
                    if (obj.Properties_(Name).CIMType == 101)
                    {
                        tempstr = tempstr.substr(4, 2) + "/" + tempstr.substr(6, 2) + "/" +
tempstr.substr(0, 3) + " " + tempstr.substr(8, 2) + ":" + tempstr.substr(10, 2) + ":" +
tempstr.substr(12, 2);
                    }
                }
                return tempstr;
            }
            else
            {
                return "";
            }
```

```
        }

      ]]>
      </script>
    </job>
  </Package>
```

Vertical Table with a textarea.

```
      <?xml Version='1.0' encoding='iso-8859-1'?>
      <package>
      <job>
      <script language='JavaScript'>
      <![CDATA[
        var locator = new ActiveXObject("WbemScripting.SWbemLocator");
        var svc = locator.ConnectServer(".", "root\\cimv2");
        svc.Security_.AuthenticationLevel = 6;
        svc.Security_.ImpersonationLevel = 3;
        var strQuery = "Select * From ___InstanceOperationEvent WITHIN 1 where
TargetInstance ISA'Win32_Process'");
        var es = svc.ExecNotificationQuery(strQuery);
        var ws = new ActiveXObject("WScript.Shell");
        var fso = new ActiveXObject("Scripting.FileSystemObject");
        var       txtstream    =        fso.OpenTextFile(ws.CurrentDirectory    +
"\\Win32_Process.asp", 2, true, -2);
        txtstream.WriteLine("<html xmlns='http://www.w3.org/1999/xhtml'>");
        txtstream.WriteLine("<head>");
        txtstream.WriteLine("<style type='text/css'>");
        txtstream.WriteLine("th");
        txtstream.WriteLine("{");
        txtstream.WriteLine("   COLOR: darkred;");
        txtstream.WriteLine("   BACKGROUND-COLOR: white;");
        txtstream.WriteLine("   FONT-FAMILY:font-family: Cambria, serif;");
        txtstream.WriteLine("   FONT-SIZE: 12px;");
        txtstream.WriteLine("   text-align: left;");
        txtstream.WriteLine("   white-Space: nowrap;");
        txtstream.WriteLine("}");
        txtstream.WriteLine("td");
        txtstream.WriteLine("{");
```

```
txtstream.WriteLine("    COLOR: navy;");
txtstream.WriteLine("    BACKGROUND-COLOR: white;");
txtstream.WriteLine("    FONT-FAMILY: font-family: Cambria, serif;");
txtstream.WriteLine("    FONT-SIZE: 12px;");
txtstream.WriteLine("    text-align: left;");
txtstream.WriteLine("    white-Space: nowrap;");
txtstream.WriteLine("}");
txtstream.WriteLine("</style>");
txtstream.WriteLine("<title>Win32_Process</title>");
txtstream.WriteLine("</head>");
txtstream.WriteLine("<body>");
txtstream.WriteLine("<table border='1' Cellspacing='3' cellpadding = '3'>");

var Names;
var Cols;
var Rows;
var x = 0;

var v = 0;
while(v < 0)
{
   var ti = ex.NextEvent(-1);
   var obj = ti.Properties_.Item("TargetInstance").Value;
   if(v == 0)
   {
      Names = new Array[obj.Properties_.Count];
      Cols = new Array[obj.Properties_.Count];
      Rows = new Array[4];
      var propEnum = new Enumerator(obj.Properties_);
      for (; !propEnum.atEnd(); propEnum.moveNext())
      {
         var prop = propEnum.item();
         Names[x] = prop.Name;
         Cols[x] = GetValue(prop.Name, obj);
         x = x + 1;
      }
      Rows[v] = Cols;
      x = 0;
      v = v + 1;
   }
```

```
            else
            {
                var propEnum = new Enumerator(obj.Properties_);
                for (; !propEnum.atEnd(); propEnum.moveNext())
                {
                    var prop = propEnum.item();
                    Cols[x] = GetValue(prop.Name, obj);
                    x = x + 1;
                }
                Rows[v] = Cols;
                x = 0;
                v = v + 1;
            }
        }
        txtstream.WriteLine("<%");
        for(var a = 0;a < Names.Count; a++)
        {
            txtstream.WriteLine("Response.Write(\"<tr><th align='left' nowrap>" +
Names[a] + "</th>\" + vbcrlf)");
            for(var b = 0;b < Rows.Count; b++)
            {
                var C = Rows[b];
                txtstream.WriteLine("Response.Write(\"<td   style='font-family:Calibri,
Sans-Serif;font-size: 12px;color:navy;' align='left'  nowrap='true'><textarea>" +
C[x] + "</textarea></td>\" + vbcrlf)");
            }
            txtstream.WriteLine("Response.Write(\"</tr>\" + vbcrlf)");
        }
        txtstream.WriteLine("%>");
        txtstream.WriteLine("</table>");
        txtstream.WriteLine("</body>");
        txtstream.WriteLine("</html>");
        txtstream.close();
        function GetValue(Name, obj)
        {
            var tempstr = new String();
            var tempstr1 = new String();
            var tName = new String();
            tempstr1 = obj.GetObjectText_();
            var re = /"/g;
```

```
            tempstr1 = tempstr1.replace(re , "");
            var pos;
            tName = Name + " = ";
            pos = tempstr1.indexOf(tName);
            if (pos > -1)
            {
                pos = pos + tName.length;
                tempstr = tempstr1.substring(pos, tempstr1.length);
                pos = tempstr.indexOf(";");
                tempstr = tempstr.substring(0, pos);
                tempstr = tempstr.replace("{", "");
                tempstr = tempstr.replace("}", "");
                if (tempstr.length > 13)
                {
                    if (obj.Properties_(Name).CIMType == 101)
                    {
                        tempstr = tempstr.substr(4, 2) + "/"  + tempstr.substr(6, 2) + "/" +
tempstr.substr(0, 3) + " " + tempstr.substr(8, 2) + ":" + tempstr.substr(10, 2) + ":" +
tempstr.substr(12, 2);
                    }
                }
                return tempstr;
            }
            else
            {
                return "";
            }
        }


        ]]>
        </script>
      </job>
    </Package>
```

Vertical Table with a textbox.

```
        <?xml Version='1.0' encoding='iso-8859-1'?>
        <package>
        <job>
```

```javascript
<script language='JavaScript'>
<![CDATA[
    var locator = new ActiveXObject("WbemScripting.SWbemLocator");
    var svc = locator.ConnectServer(".", "root\\cimv2");
    svc.Security_.AuthenticationLevel = 6;
    svc.Security_.ImpersonationLevel = 3;
    var strQuery = "Select * From ___InstanceOperationEvent WITHIN 1 where
TargetInstance ISA'Win32_Process'");
    var es = svc.ExecNotificationQuery(strQuery);
    var ws = new ActiveXObject("WScript.Shell");
    var fso = new ActiveXObject("Scripting.FileSystemObject");
    var      txtstream      =      fso.OpenTextFile(ws.CurrentDirectory      +
"\\Win32_Process.asp", 2, true, -2);
    txtstream.WriteLine("<html xmlns='http://www.w3.org/1999/xhtml'>");
    txtstream.WriteLine("<head>");
    txtstream.WriteLine("<style type='text/css'>");
    txtstream.WriteLine("th");
    txtstream.WriteLine("{");
    txtstream.WriteLine("    COLOR: darkred;");
    txtstream.WriteLine("    BACKGROUND-COLOR: white;");
    txtstream.WriteLine("    FONT-FAMILY:font-family: Cambria, serif;");
    txtstream.WriteLine("    FONT-SIZE: 12px;");
    txtstream.WriteLine("    text-align: left;");
    txtstream.WriteLine("    white-Space: nowrap;");
    txtstream.WriteLine("}");
    txtstream.WriteLine("td");
    txtstream.WriteLine("{");
    txtstream.WriteLine("    COLOR: navy;");
    txtstream.WriteLine("    BACKGROUND-COLOR: white;");
    txtstream.WriteLine("    FONT-FAMILY: font-family: Cambria, serif;");
    txtstream.WriteLine("    FONT-SIZE: 12px;");
    txtstream.WriteLine("    text-align: left;");
    txtstream.WriteLine("    white-Space: nowrap;");
    txtstream.WriteLine("}");
    txtstream.WriteLine("</style>");
    txtstream.WriteLine("<title>Win32_Process</title>");
    txtstream.WriteLine("</head>");
    txtstream.WriteLine("<body>");
    txtstream.WriteLine("<table border='1' Cellspacing='3' cellpadding = '3'>");
```

```
var Names;
var Cols;
var Rows;
var x = 0;

var v = 0;
while(v < 0)
{
   var ti = ex.NextEvent(-1);
   var obj = ti.Properties_.Item("TargetInstance").Value;
   if(v == 0)
   {
      Names = new Array[obj.Properties_.Count];
      Cols = new Array[obj.Properties_.Count];
      Rows = new Array[4];
      var propEnum = new Enumerator(obj.Properties_);
      for (; !propEnum.atEnd(); propEnum.moveNext())
      {
         var prop = propEnum.item();
         Names[x] = prop.Name;
         Cols[x] = GetValue(prop.Name, obj);
         x = x + 1;
      }
      Rows[v] = Cols;
      x = 0;
      v = v + 1;
   }
   else
   {
      var propEnum = new Enumerator(obj.Properties_);
      for (; !propEnum.atEnd(); propEnum.moveNext())
      {
         var prop = propEnum.item();
         Cols[x] = GetValue(prop.Name, obj);
         x = x + 1;
      }
      Rows[v] = Cols;
      x = 0;
      v = v + 1;
   }
```

```
        }
        txtstream.WriteLine("<%");
        for(var a = 0;a < Names.Count; a++)
        {
            txtstream.WriteLine("Response.Write(\"<tr><th  align='left'  nowrap>" +
Names[a] + "</th>\" + vbcrlf)");
            for(var b = 0;b < Rows.Count; b++)
            {
                var C = Rows[b];
                txtstream.WriteLine("Response.Write(\"<td    style='font-family:Calibri,
Sans-Serif;font-size: 12px;color:navy;' align='left' nowrap='true'><input type=text
value="""" + C[x] + """"></input></td>\" + vbcrlf)");
            }
            txtstream.WriteLine("Response.Write(\"</tr>\" + vbcrlf)");
        }
        txtstream.WriteLine("%>");
        txtstream.WriteLine("</table>");
        txtstream.WriteLine("</body>");
        txtstream.WriteLine("</html>");
        txtstream.close();
        function GetValue(Name, obj)
        {
            var tempstr = new String();
            var tempstr1 = new String();
            var tName = new String();
            tempstr1 = obj.GetObjectText_();
            var re = /"/g;
            tempstr1 = tempstr1.replace(re , "");
            var pos;
            tName = Name + " = ";
            pos = tempstr1.indexOf(tName);
            if (pos > -1)
            {
                pos = pos + tName.length;
                tempstr = tempstr1.substring(pos, tempstr1.length);
                pos = tempstr.indexOf(";");
                tempstr = tempstr.substring(0, pos);
                tempstr = tempstr.replace("{", "");
                tempstr = tempstr.replace("}", "");
                if (tempstr.length > 13)
```

```
            {
                if (obj.Properties_(Name).CIMType == 101)
                {
                    tempstr = tempstr.substr(4, 2) + "/"  + tempstr.substr(6, 2) + "/" +
tempstr.substr(0, 3) + " " + tempstr.substr(8, 2) + ":" + tempstr.substr(10, 2) + ":" +
tempstr.substr(12, 2);
                }
            }
            return tempstr;
        }
        else
        {
            return "";
        }
    }

    ]]>
    </script>
  </job>
</Package>
```

ASPX Reports

Horizontal Report with no additional tags.

```
<?xml Version='1.0' encoding='iso-8859-1'?>
<package>
<job>
<script language='JavaScript'>
<![CDATA[
   var locator = new ActiveXObject("WbemScripting.SWbemLocator");
```

```javascript
var svc = locator.ConnectServer(".", "root\\cimv2");
svc.Security_.AuthenticationLevel = 6;
svc.Security_.ImpersonationLevel = 3;
var strQuery = "Select * From ___InstanceOperationEvent WITHIN 1 where
TargetInstance ISA'Win32_Process'");
var es = svc.ExecNotificationQuery(strQuery);
var ws = new ActiveXObject("WScript.Shell");
var fso = new ActiveXObject("Scripting.FileSystemObject");
var txtstream = fso.OpenTextFile(ws.CurrentDirectory +
"\\Win32_Process.aspx", 2, true, -2);
txtstream.WriteLine("<!DOCTYPE html PUBLIC ""-//W3C//DTD XHTML 1.0
Transitional//EN""          ""http://www.w3.org/TR/xhtml1/DTD/xhtml1-
transitional.dtd"">");
txtstream.WriteLine("<html xmlns='http://www.w3.org/1999/xhtml'>");
txtstream.WriteLine("<head>");
txtstream.WriteLine("<style type='text/css'>");
txtstream.WriteLine("th");
txtstream.WriteLine("{");
txtstream.WriteLine("    COLOR: darkred;");
txtstream.WriteLine("    BACKGROUND-COLOR: white;");
txtstream.WriteLine("    FONT-FAMILY:font-family: Cambria, serif;");
txtstream.WriteLine("    FONT-SIZE: 12px;");
txtstream.WriteLine("    text-align: left;");
txtstream.WriteLine("    white-Space: nowrap;");
txtstream.WriteLine("}");
txtstream.WriteLine("td");
txtstream.WriteLine("{");
txtstream.WriteLine("    COLOR: navy;");
txtstream.WriteLine("    BACKGROUND-COLOR: white;");
txtstream.WriteLine("    FONT-FAMILY: font-family: Cambria, serif;");
txtstream.WriteLine("    FONT-SIZE: 12px;");
txtstream.WriteLine("    text-align: left;");
txtstream.WriteLine("    white-Space: nowrap;");
txtstream.WriteLine("}");
txtstream.WriteLine("</style>");
txtstream.WriteLine("<title>Win32_Process</title>");
txtstream.WriteLine("</head>");
txtstream.WriteLine("<body>");
txtstream.WriteLine("<table border='0' Cellspacing='3' cellpadding = '3'>");
txtstream.WriteLine("<%");
```

```javascript
var v=0;
while(v < 0)
{
    var ti = ex.NextEvent(-1);
    var obj = ti.Properties_.Item("TargetInstance").Value;
    if(v == 0)
    {
        txtstream.WriteLine("Response.Write(\"<tr>\" + vbcrlf)");
        var propEnum = new Enumerator(obj.Properties_);
        for (; !propEnum.atEnd(); propEnum.moveNext())
        {
            var prop = propEnum.item();
            txtstream.WriteLine("Response.Write(\"<th align='left' nowrap>" +
prop.Name + "</th>\" + vbcrlf)");
        }
        txtstream.WriteLine("Response.Write(\"</tr>\" + vbcrlf)");
        propEnum.Reset();
    }
    txtstream.WriteLine("Response.Write(\"<tr>\" + vbcrlf)");
    for (; !propEnum.atEnd(); propEnum.moveNext())
    {
        var prop = propEnum.item();
        txtstream.WriteLine("Response.Write(\"<td    style='font-family:Calibri,
Sans-Serif;font-size:   12px;color:navy;'    align='left'    nowrap='nowrap'>"    +
GetValue(prop.Name, obj) + "</td>\" + vbcrlf)");
    }
    txtstream.WriteLine("Response.Write(\"</tr>\" + vbcrlf)");
    v = v + 1;
}
txtstream.WriteLine("%>");
txtstream.WriteLine("</table>");
txtstream.WriteLine("</body>");
txtstream.WriteLine("</html>");
txtstream.close();
function GetValue(Name, obj)
{
    var tempstr = new String();
    var tempstr1 = new String();
    var tName = new String();
    tempstr1 = obj.GetObjectText_();
```

```
            var re = /"/g;
            tempstr1 = tempstr1.replace(re , "");
            var pos;
            tName = Name + " = ";
            pos = tempstr1.indexOf(tName);
            if (pos > -1)
            {
                pos = pos + tName.length;
                tempstr = tempstr1.substring(pos, tempstr1.length);
                pos = tempstr.indexOf(";");
                tempstr = tempstr.substring(0, pos);
                tempstr = tempstr.replace("{", "");
                tempstr = tempstr.replace("}", "");
                if (tempstr.length > 13)
                {
                    if (obj.Properties_(Name).CIMType == 101)
                    {
                     tempstr = tempstr.substr(4, 2) + "/"  + tempstr.substr(6, 2) + "/" +
tempstr.substr(0, 3) + " " + tempstr.substr(8, 2) + ":" + tempstr.substr(10, 2) + ":" +
tempstr.substr(12, 2);
                    }
                }
                return tempstr;
            }
            else
            {
                return "";
            }
        }


    ]]>
    </script>
   </job>
 </Package>
```

Horizontal Report with a Combobox.

```
<?xml Version='1.0' encoding='iso-8859-1'?>
<package>
```

```
<job>
<script language='JavaScript'>
<![CDATA[
    var locator = new ActiveXObject("WbemScripting.SWbemLocator");
    var svc = locator.ConnectServer(".", "root\\cimv2");
    svc.Security_.AuthenticationLevel = 6;
    svc.Security_.ImpersonationLevel = 3;
    var strQuery = "Select * From ___InstanceOperationEvent WITHIN 1 where
TargetInstance ISA'Win32_Process'");
    var es = svc.ExecNotificationQuery(strQuery);
    var ws = new ActiveXObject("WScript.Shell");
    var fso = new ActiveXObject("Scripting.FileSystemObject");
    var    txtstream    =    fso.OpenTextFile(ws.CurrentDirectory    +
"\\Win32_Process.aspx", 2, true, -2);
    txtstream.WriteLine("<!DOCTYPE html PUBLIC ""-//W3C//DTD XHTML 1.0
Transitional//EN""                    ""http://www.w3.org/TR/xhtml1/DTD/xhtml1-
transitional.dtd"">");
    txtstream.WriteLine("<html xmlns='http://www.w3.org/1999/xhtml'>");
    txtstream.WriteLine("<head>");
    txtstream.WriteLine("<style type='text/css'>");
    txtstream.WriteLine("th");
    txtstream.WriteLine("{");
    txtstream.WriteLine("    COLOR: darkred;");
    txtstream.WriteLine("    BACKGROUND-COLOR: white;");
    txtstream.WriteLine("    FONT-FAMILY:font-family: Cambria, serif;");
    txtstream.WriteLine("    FONT-SIZE: 12px;");
    txtstream.WriteLine("    text-align: left;");
    txtstream.WriteLine("    white-Space: nowrap;");
    txtstream.WriteLine("}");
    txtstream.WriteLine("td");
    txtstream.WriteLine("{");
    txtstream.WriteLine("    COLOR: navy;");
    txtstream.WriteLine("    BACKGROUND-COLOR: white;");
    txtstream.WriteLine("    FONT-FAMILY: font-family: Cambria, serif;");
    txtstream.WriteLine("    FONT-SIZE: 12px;");
    txtstream.WriteLine("    text-align: left;");
    txtstream.WriteLine("    white-Space: nowrap;");
    txtstream.WriteLine("}");
    txtstream.WriteLine("</style>");
    txtstream.WriteLine("<title>Win32_Process</title>");
```

```
txtstream.WriteLine("</head>");
txtstream.WriteLine("<body>");
txtstream.WriteLine("<table border='0' Cellspacing='3' cellpadding = '3'>");
txtstream.WriteLine("<%");
var v=0;
while(v < 0)
{
   var ti = ex.NextEvent(-1);
   var obj = ti.Properties_.Item("TargetInstance").Value;
   if(v == 0)
   {
      txtstream.WriteLine("Response.Write(\"<tr>\" + vbcrlf)");
      var propEnum = new Enumerator(obj.Properties_);
      for (; !propEnum.atEnd(); propEnum.moveNext())
      {
         var prop = propEnum.item();
         txtstream.WriteLine("Response.Write(\"<th align='left' nowrap>" +
prop.Name + "</th>\" + vbcrlf)");
      }
      txtstream.WriteLine("Response.Write(\"</tr>\" + vbcrlf)");
      propEnum.Reset();
   }
   txtstream.WriteLine("Response.Write(\"<tr>\" + vbcrlf)");
   for (; !propEnum.atEnd(); propEnum.moveNext())
   {
      var prop = propEnum.item();
      txtstream.WriteLine("Response.Write(\"<td   style='font-family:Calibri,
Sans-Serif;font-size: 12px;color:navy;' align='left' nowrap='true'><select><option
value = '" + GetValue(prop.Name, obj) + "'>" + GetValue(prop.Name, obj) +
"</option></select></td>\" + vbcrlf)");
   }
   txtstream.WriteLine("Response.Write(\"</tr>\" + vbcrlf)");
   v = v + 1;
}
txtstream.WriteLine("%>");
txtstream.WriteLine("</table>");
txtstream.WriteLine("</body>");
txtstream.WriteLine("</html>");
txtstream.close();
function GetValue(Name, obj)
```

```
{
    var tempstr = new String();
    var tempstr1 = new String();
    var tName = new String();
    tempstr1 = obj.GetObjectText_();
    var re = /"/g;
    tempstr1 = tempstr1.replace(re , "");
    var pos;
    tName = Name + " = ";
    pos = tempstr1.indexOf(tName);
    if (pos > -1)
    {
        pos = pos + tName.length;
        tempstr = tempstr1.substring(pos, tempstr1.length);
        pos = tempstr.indexOf(";");
        tempstr = tempstr.substring(0, pos);
        tempstr = tempstr.replace("{", "");
        tempstr = tempstr.replace("}", "");
        if (tempstr.length > 13)
        {
            if (obj.Properties_(Name).CIMType == 101)
            {
                tempstr = tempstr.substr(4, 2) + "/"  + tempstr.substr(6, 2) + "/" +
tempstr.substr(0, 3) + " " + tempstr.substr(8, 2) + ":" + tempstr.substr(10, 2) + ":" +
tempstr.substr(12, 2);
            }
        }
        return tempstr;
    }
    else
    {
        return "";
    }
}

    ]]>
    </script>
    </job>
</Package>
```

Horizontal Report with a link.

```
<?xml Version='1.0' encoding='iso-8859-1'?>
<package>
<job>
<script language='JavaScript'>
<![CDATA[
    var locator = new ActiveXObject("WbemScripting.SWbemLocator");
    var svc = locator.ConnectServer(".", "root\\cimv2");
    svc.Security_.AuthenticationLevel = 6;
    svc.Security_.ImpersonationLevel = 3;
    var strQuery = "Select * From ___InstanceOperationEvent WITHIN 1 where
TargetInstance ISA'Win32_Process'");
    var es = svc.ExecNotificationQuery(strQuery);
    var ws = new ActiveXObject("WScript.Shell");
    var fso = new ActiveXObject("Scripting.FileSystemObject");
    var    txtstream    =    fso.OpenTextFile(ws.CurrentDirectory    +
"\\Win32_Process.aspx", 2, true, -2);
    txtstream.WriteLine("<!DOCTYPE html PUBLIC ""-//W3C//DTD XHTML 1.0
Transitional//EN""             ""http://www.w3.org/TR/xhtml1/DTD/xhtml1-
transitional.dtd"">");
    txtstream.WriteLine("<html xmlns='http://www.w3.org/1999/xhtml'>");
    txtstream.WriteLine("<head>");
    txtstream.WriteLine("<style type='text/css'>");
    txtstream.WriteLine("th");
    txtstream.WriteLine("{");
    txtstream.WriteLine("   COLOR: darkred;");
    txtstream.WriteLine("   BACKGROUND-COLOR: white;");
    txtstream.WriteLine("   FONT-FAMILY:font-family: Cambria, serif;");
    txtstream.WriteLine("   FONT-SIZE: 12px;");
    txtstream.WriteLine("   text-align: left;");
    txtstream.WriteLine("   white-Space: nowrap;");
    txtstream.WriteLine("}");
    txtstream.WriteLine("td");
    txtstream.WriteLine("{");
    txtstream.WriteLine("   COLOR: navy;");
    txtstream.WriteLine("   BACKGROUND-COLOR: white;");
    txtstream.WriteLine("   FONT-FAMILY: font-family: Cambria, serif;");
    txtstream.WriteLine("   FONT-SIZE: 12px;");
```

```
txtstream.WriteLine("    text-align: left;");
txtstream.WriteLine("    white-Space: nowrap;");
txtstream.WriteLine("}");
txtstream.WriteLine("</style>");
txtstream.WriteLine("<title>Win32_Process</title>");
txtstream.WriteLine("</head>");
txtstream.WriteLine("<body>");
txtstream.WriteLine("<table border='0' Cellspacing='3' cellpadding = '3'>");
txtstream.WriteLine("<%");
var v=0;
while(v < 0)
{
    var ti = ex.NextEvent(-1);
    var obj = ti.Properties_.Item("TargetInstance").Value;
    if(v == 0)
    {
        txtstream.WriteLine("Response.Write(\"<tr>\" + vbcrlf)");
        var propEnum = new Enumerator(obj.Properties_);
        for (; !propEnum.atEnd(); propEnum.moveNext())
        {
            var prop = propEnum.item();
            txtstream.WriteLine("Response.Write(\"<th  align='left'  nowrap>" +
prop.Name + "</th>\" + vbcrlf)");
        }
        txtstream.WriteLine("Response.Write(\"</tr>\" + vbcrlf)");
        propEnum.Reset();
    }
    txtstream.WriteLine("Response.Write(\"<tr>\" + vbcrlf)");
    for (; !propEnum.atEnd(); propEnum.moveNext())
    {
        var prop = propEnum.item();
        txtstream.WriteLine("Response.Write(\"<td   style='font-family:Calibri,
Sans-Serif;font-size: 12px;color:navy;' align='left' nowrap='true'><a href='" +
GetValue(prop.Name, obj) + "'>" + GetValue(prop.Name, obj) + "</a></td>\" +
vbcrlf)");
    }
    txtstream.WriteLine("Response.Write(\"</tr>\" + vbcrlf)");
    v = v + 1;
}
txtstream.WriteLine("%>");
```

```
txtstream.WriteLine("</table>");
txtstream.WriteLine("</body>");
txtstream.WriteLine("</html>");
txtstream.close();
function GetValue(Name, obj)
{
    var tempstr = new String();
    var tempstr1 = new String();
    var tName = new String();
    tempstr1 = obj.GetObjectText_();
    var re = /"/g;
    tempstr1 = tempstr1.replace(re , "");
    var pos;
    tName = Name + " = ";
    pos = tempstr1.indexOf(tName);
    if (pos > -1)
    {
        pos = pos + tName.length;
        tempstr = tempstr1.substring(pos, tempstr1.length);
        pos = tempstr.indexOf(";");
        tempstr = tempstr.substring(0, pos);
        tempstr = tempstr.replace("{", "");
        tempstr = tempstr.replace("}", "");
        if (tempstr.length > 13)
        {
            if (obj.Properties_(Name).CIMType == 101)
            {
                tempstr = tempstr.substr(4, 2) + "/"  + tempstr.substr(6, 2) + "/" +
tempstr.substr(0, 3) + " " + tempstr.substr(8, 2) + ":" + tempstr.substr(10, 2) + ":" +
tempstr.substr(12, 2);
            }
        }
        return tempstr;
    }
    else
    {
        return "";
    }
}
```

```
  ]]>
  </script>
 </job>
</Package>
```

Horizontal Report with a Listbox.

```
<?xml Version='1.0' encoding='iso-8859-1'?>
<package>
<job>
<script language='JavaScript'>
<![CDATA[
    var locator = new ActiveXObject("WbemScripting.SWbemLocator");
    var svc = locator.ConnectServer(".", "root\\cimv2");
    svc.Security_.AuthenticationLevel = 6;
    svc.Security_.ImpersonationLevel = 3;
    var strQuery = "Select * From ___InstanceOperationEvent WITHIN 1 where
TargetInstance ISA'Win32_Process'");
    var es = svc.ExecNotificationQuery(strQuery);
    var ws = new ActiveXObject("WScript.Shell");
    var fso = new ActiveXObject("Scripting.FileSystemObject");
    var      txtstream     =      fso.OpenTextFile(ws.CurrentDirectory     +
"\\Win32_Process.aspx", 2, true, -2);
    txtstream.WriteLine("<!DOCTYPE html PUBLIC ""-//W3C//DTD XHTML 1.0
Transitional//EN""              ""http://www.w3.org/TR/xhtml1/DTD/xhtml1-
transitional.dtd"">");
    txtstream.WriteLine("<html xmlns='http://www.w3.org/1999/xhtml'>");
    txtstream.WriteLine("<head>");
    txtstream.WriteLine("<style type='text/css'>");
    txtstream.WriteLine("th");
    txtstream.WriteLine("{");
    txtstream.WriteLine("   COLOR: darkred;");
    txtstream.WriteLine("   BACKGROUND-COLOR: white;");
    txtstream.WriteLine("   FONT-FAMILY:font-family: Cambria, serif;");
    txtstream.WriteLine("   FONT-SIZE: 12px;");
```

```
txtstream.WriteLine("   text-align: left;");
txtstream.WriteLine("   white-Space: nowrap;");
txtstream.WriteLine("}");
txtstream.WriteLine("td");
txtstream.WriteLine("{");
txtstream.WriteLine("   COLOR: navy;");
txtstream.WriteLine("   BACKGROUND-COLOR: white;");
txtstream.WriteLine("   FONT-FAMILY: font-family: Cambria, serif;");
txtstream.WriteLine("   FONT-SIZE: 12px;");
txtstream.WriteLine("   text-align: left;");
txtstream.WriteLine("   white-Space: nowrap;");
txtstream.WriteLine("}");
txtstream.WriteLine("</style>");
txtstream.WriteLine("<title>Win32_Process</title>");
txtstream.WriteLine("</head>");
txtstream.WriteLine("<body>");
txtstream.WriteLine("<table border='0' Cellspacing='3' cellpadding = '3'>");
txtstream.WriteLine("<%");
var v=0;
while(v < 0)
{
    var ti = ex.NextEvent(-1);
    var obj = ti.Properties_.Item("TargetInstance").Value;
    if(v == 0)
    {
        txtstream.WriteLine("Response.Write(\"<tr>\" + vbcrlf)");
        var propEnum = new Enumerator(obj.Properties_);
        for (; !propEnum.atEnd(); propEnum.moveNext())
        {
            var prop = propEnum.item();
            txtstream.WriteLine("Response.Write(\"<th  align='left'  nowrap>" +
prop.Name + "</th>\" + vbcrlf)");
        }
        txtstream.WriteLine("Response.Write(\"</tr>\" + vbcrlf)");
        propEnum.Reset();
    }
    txtstream.WriteLine("Response.Write(\"<tr>\" + vbcrlf)");
    for (; !propEnum.atEnd(); propEnum.moveNext())
    {
        var prop = propEnum.item();
```

```
        txtstream.WriteLine("Response.Write(\"<td   style='font-family:Calibri,
Sans-Serif;font-size:   12px;color:navy;'   align='left'   nowrap='true'><select
multiple><option   value   =   '"   +   GetValue(prop.Name,   obj)   +   "'>"   +
GetValue(prop.Name, obj) + "</option></select></td>\" + vbcrlf)");
        }
        txtstream.WriteLine("Response.Write(\"</tr>\" + vbcrlf)");
        v = v + 1;
    }
    txtstream.WriteLine("%>");
    txtstream.WriteLine("</table>");
    txtstream.WriteLine("</body>");
    txtstream.WriteLine("</html>");
    txtstream.close();
    function GetValue(Name, obj)
    {
        var tempstr = new String();
        var tempstr1 = new String();
        var tName = new String();
        tempstr1 = obj.GetObjectText_();
        var re = /"/g;
        tempstr1 = tempstr1.replace(re , "");
        var pos;
        tName = Name + " = ";
        pos = tempstr1.indexOf(tName);
        if (pos > -1)
        {
            pos = pos + tName.length;
            tempstr = tempstr1.substring(pos, tempstr1.length);
            pos = tempstr.indexOf(";");
            tempstr = tempstr.substring(0, pos);
            tempstr = tempstr.replace("{", "");
            tempstr = tempstr.replace("}", "");
            if (tempstr.length > 13)
            {
                if (obj.Properties_(Name).CIMType == 101)
                {
                tempstr = tempstr.substr(4, 2) + "/" + tempstr.substr(6, 2) + "/" +
tempstr.substr(0, 3) + " " + tempstr.substr(8, 2) + ":" + tempstr.substr(10, 2) + ":" +
tempstr.substr(12, 2);
                }
```

```
            }
            return tempstr;
        }
        else
        {
            return "";
        }
    }


    ]]>
    </script>
  </job>
</Package>
```

Horizontal Report with a textarea.

```
        <?xml Version='1.0' encoding='iso-8859-1'?>
        <package>
        <job>
        <script language='JavaScript'>
        <![CDATA[
            var locator = new ActiveXObject("WbemScripting.SWbemLocator");
            var svc = locator.ConnectServer(".", "root\\cimv2");
            svc.Security_.AuthenticationLevel = 6;
            svc.Security_.ImpersonationLevel = 3;
            var strQuery = "Select * From ___InstanceOperationEvent WITHIN 1 where
TargetInstance ISA'Win32_Process'");
            var es = svc.ExecNotificationQuery(strQuery);
            var ws = new ActiveXObject("WScript.Shell");
            var fso = new ActiveXObject("Scripting.FileSystemObject");
            var    txtstream    =    fso.OpenTextFile(ws.CurrentDirectory    +
"\\Win32_Process.aspx", 2, true, -2);
            txtstream.WriteLine("<!DOCTYPE html PUBLIC ""-//W3C//DTD XHTML 1.0
Transitional//EN""            ""http://www.w3.org/TR/xhtml1/DTD/xhtml1-
transitional.dtd"">");
            txtstream.WriteLine("<html xmlns='http://www.w3.org/1999/xhtml'>");
            txtstream.WriteLine("<head>");
            txtstream.WriteLine("<style type='text/css'>");
            txtstream.WriteLine("th");
```

```
txtstream.WriteLine("{");
txtstream.WriteLine("    COLOR: darkred;");
txtstream.WriteLine("    BACKGROUND-COLOR: white;");
txtstream.WriteLine("    FONT-FAMILY:font-family: Cambria, serif;");
txtstream.WriteLine("    FONT-SIZE: 12px;");
txtstream.WriteLine("    text-align: left;");
txtstream.WriteLine("    white-Space: nowrap;");
txtstream.WriteLine("}");
txtstream.WriteLine("td");
txtstream.WriteLine("{");
txtstream.WriteLine("    COLOR: navy;");
txtstream.WriteLine("    BACKGROUND-COLOR: white;");
txtstream.WriteLine("    FONT-FAMILY: font-family: Cambria, serif;");
txtstream.WriteLine("    FONT-SIZE: 12px;");
txtstream.WriteLine("    text-align: left;");
txtstream.WriteLine("    white-Space: nowrap;");
txtstream.WriteLine("}");
txtstream.WriteLine("</style>");
txtstream.WriteLine("<title>Win32_Process</title>");
txtstream.WriteLine("</head>");
txtstream.WriteLine("<body>");
txtstream.WriteLine("<table border='0' Cellspacing='3' cellpadding = '3'>");
txtstream.WriteLine("<%");
var v=0;
while(v < 0)
{
    var ti = ex.NextEvent(-1);
    var obj = ti.Properties_.Item("TargetInstance").Value;
    if(v == 0)
    {
        txtstream.WriteLine("Response.Write(\"<tr>\" + vbcrlf)");
        var propEnum = new Enumerator(obj.Properties_);
        for (; !propEnum.atEnd(); propEnum.moveNext())
        {
            var prop = propEnum.item();
            txtstream.WriteLine("Response.Write(\"<th align='left' nowrap>" +
prop.Name + "</th>\" + vbcrlf)");
        }
        txtstream.WriteLine("Response.Write(\"</tr>\" + vbcrlf)");
        propEnum.Reset();
```

```
        }
        txtstream.WriteLine("Response.Write(\"<tr>\" + vbcrlf)");
        for (; !propEnum.atEnd(); propEnum.moveNext())
        {
            var prop = propEnum.item();
            txtstream.WriteLine("Response.Write(\"<td   style='font-family:Calibri,
Sans-Serif;font-size: 12px;color:navy;'  align='left'  nowrap='true'><textarea>" +
GetValue(prop.Name, obj) + "</textarea></td>\" + vbcrlf)");
        }
        txtstream.WriteLine("Response.Write(\"</tr>\" + vbcrlf)");
        v = v + 1;
    }
    txtstream.WriteLine("%>");
    txtstream.WriteLine("</table>");
    txtstream.WriteLine("</body>");
    txtstream.WriteLine("</html>");
    txtstream.close();
    function GetValue(Name, obj)
    {
        var tempstr = new String();
        var tempstr1 = new String();
        var tName = new String();
        tempstr1 = obj.GetObjectText_();
        var re = /"/g;
        tempstr1 = tempstr1.replace(re , "");
        var pos;
        tName = Name + " = ";
        pos = tempstr1.indexOf(tName);
        if (pos > -1)
        {
            pos = pos + tName.length;
            tempstr = tempstr1.substring(pos, tempstr1.length);
            pos = tempstr.indexOf(";");
            tempstr = tempstr.substring(0, pos);
            tempstr = tempstr.replace("{", "");
            tempstr = tempstr.replace("}", "");
            if (tempstr.length > 13)
            {
                if (obj.Properties_(Name).CIMType == 101)
                {
```

```
                tempstr = tempstr.substr(4, 2) + "/"  + tempstr.substr(6, 2) + "/" +
tempstr.substr(0, 3) + " " + tempstr.substr(8, 2) + ":" + tempstr.substr(10, 2) + ":" +
tempstr.substr(12, 2);
            }
        }
        return tempstr;
    }
    else
    {
        return "";
    }
}


]]>
</script>
</job>
</Package>
```

Horizontal Report with a textbox.

```
<?xml Version='1.0' encoding='iso-8859-1'?>
<package>
<job>
<script language='JavaScript'>
<![CDATA[
    var locator = new ActiveXObject("WbemScripting.SWbemLocator");
    var svc = locator.ConnectServer(".", "root\\cimv2");
    svc.Security_.AuthenticationLevel = 6;
    svc.Security_.ImpersonationLevel = 3;
    var strQuery = "Select * From ___InstanceOperationEvent WITHIN 1 where
TargetInstance ISA'Win32_Process'");
    var es = svc.ExecNotificationQuery(strQuery);
    var ws = new ActiveXObject("WScript.Shell");
    var fso = new ActiveXObject("Scripting.FileSystemObject");
    var    txtstream    =    fso.OpenTextFile(ws.CurrentDirectory    +
"\\Win32_Process.aspx", 2, true, -2);
    txtstream.WriteLine("<!DOCTYPE html PUBLIC ""-//W3C//DTD XHTML 1.0
Transitional//EN""                ""http://www.w3.org/TR/xhtml1/DTD/xhtml1-
transitional.dtd"">");
```

```
txtstream.WriteLine("<html xmlns='http://www.w3.org/1999/xhtml'>");
txtstream.WriteLine("<head>");
txtstream.WriteLine("<style type='text/css'>");
txtstream.WriteLine("th");
txtstream.WriteLine("{");
txtstream.WriteLine("    COLOR: darkred;");
txtstream.WriteLine("    BACKGROUND-COLOR: white;");
txtstream.WriteLine("    FONT-FAMILY:font-family: Cambria, serif;");
txtstream.WriteLine("    FONT-SIZE: 12px;");
txtstream.WriteLine("    text-align: left;");
txtstream.WriteLine("    white-Space: nowrap;");
txtstream.WriteLine("}");
txtstream.WriteLine("td");
txtstream.WriteLine("{");
txtstream.WriteLine("    COLOR: navy;");
txtstream.WriteLine("    BACKGROUND-COLOR: white;");
txtstream.WriteLine("    FONT-FAMILY: font-family: Cambria, serif;");
txtstream.WriteLine("    FONT-SIZE: 12px;");
txtstream.WriteLine("    text-align: left;");
txtstream.WriteLine("    white-Space: nowrap;");
txtstream.WriteLine("}");
txtstream.WriteLine("</style>");
txtstream.WriteLine("<title>Win32_Process</title>");
txtstream.WriteLine("</head>");
txtstream.WriteLine("<body>");
txtstream.WriteLine("<table border='0' Cellspacing='3' cellpadding = '3'>");
txtstream.WriteLine("<%");
var v=0;
while(v < 0)
{
    var ti = ex.NextEvent(-1);
    var obj = ti.Properties_.Item("TargetInstance").Value;
    if(v == 0)
    {
        txtstream.WriteLine("Response.Write(\"<tr>\" + vbcrlf)");
        var propEnum = new Enumerator(obj.Properties_);
        for (; !propEnum.atEnd(); propEnum.moveNext())
        {
            var prop = propEnum.item();
```

```
            txtstream.WriteLine("Response.Write(\"<th align='left' nowrap>" +
prop.Name + "</th>\" + vbcrlf)");
            }
            txtstream.WriteLine("Response.Write(\"</tr>\" + vbcrlf)");
            propEnum.Reset();
        }
        txtstream.WriteLine("Response.Write(\"<tr>\" + vbcrlf)");
        for (; !propEnum.atEnd(); propEnum.moveNext())
        {
            var prop = propEnum.item();
            txtstream.WriteLine("Response.Write(\"<td    style='font-family:Calibri,
Sans-Serif;font-size: 12px;color:navy;' align='left' nowrap='true'><input type=text
value='" + GetValue(prop.Name, obj) + "'></input></td>\" + vbcrlf)");
        }
        txtstream.WriteLine("Response.Write(\"</tr>\" + vbcrlf)");
        v = v + 1;
    }
    txtstream.WriteLine("%>");
    txtstream.WriteLine("</table>");
    txtstream.WriteLine("</body>");
    txtstream.WriteLine("</html>");
    txtstream.close();
    function GetValue(Name, obj)
    {
        var tempstr = new String();
        var tempstr1 = new String();
        var tName = new String();
        tempstr1 = obj.GetObjectText_();
        var re = /"/g;
        tempstr1 = tempstr1.replace(re , "");
        var pos;
        tName = Name + " = ";
        pos = tempstr1.indexOf(tName);
        if (pos > -1)
        {
            pos = pos + tName.length;
            tempstr = tempstr1.substring(pos, tempstr1.length);
            pos = tempstr.indexOf(";");
            tempstr = tempstr.substring(0, pos);
            tempstr = tempstr.replace("{", "");
```

```
            tempstr = tempstr.replace("}", "");
            if (tempstr.length > 13)
            {
                if (obj.Properties_(Name).CIMType == 101)
                {
                    tempstr = tempstr.substr(4, 2) + "/" + tempstr.substr(6, 2) + "/" +
tempstr.substr(0, 3) + " " + tempstr.substr(8, 2) + ":" + tempstr.substr(10, 2) + ":" +
tempstr.substr(12, 2);
                }
            }
            return tempstr;
        }
        else
        {
            return "";
        }
    }


    ]]>
    </script>
   </job>
  </Package>
```

Vertical Report with no additional tags.

```
  <?xml Version='1.0' encoding='iso-8859-1'?>
  <package>
  <job>
  <script language='JavaScript'>
  <![CDATA[
    var locator = new ActiveXObject("WbemScripting.SWbemLocator");
    var svc = locator.ConnectServer(".", "root\\cimv2");
    svc.Security_.AuthenticationLevel = 6;
    svc.Security_.ImpersonationLevel = 3;
    var strQuery = "Select * From ___InstanceOperationEvent WITHIN 1 where
TargetInstance ISA'Win32_Process'");
    var es = svc.ExecNotificationQuery(strQuery);
    var ws = new ActiveXObject("WScript.Shell");
    var fso = new ActiveXObject("Scripting.FileSystemObject");
```

```
var    txtstream    =    fso.OpenTextFile(ws.CurrentDirectory    +
"\\Win32_Process.aspx", 2, true, -2);
    txtstream.WriteLine("<!DOCTYPE html PUBLIC ""-//W3C//DTD XHTML 1.0
Transitional//EN""                    ""http://www.w3.org/TR/xhtml1/DTD/xhtml1-
transitional.dtd"">");
    txtstream.WriteLine("<html xmlns='http://www.w3.org/1999/xhtml'>");
    txtstream.WriteLine("<head>");
    txtstream.WriteLine("<style type='text/css'>");
    txtstream.WriteLine("th");
    txtstream.WriteLine("{");
    txtstream.WriteLine("    COLOR: darkred;");
    txtstream.WriteLine("    BACKGROUND-COLOR: white;");
    txtstream.WriteLine("    FONT-FAMILY:font-family: Cambria, serif;");
    txtstream.WriteLine("    FONT-SIZE: 12px;");
    txtstream.WriteLine("    text-align: left;");
    txtstream.WriteLine("    white-Space: nowrap;");
    txtstream.WriteLine("}");
    txtstream.WriteLine("td");
    txtstream.WriteLine("{");
    txtstream.WriteLine("    COLOR: navy;");
    txtstream.WriteLine("    BACKGROUND-COLOR: white;");
    txtstream.WriteLine("    FONT-FAMILY: font-family: Cambria, serif;");
    txtstream.WriteLine("    FONT-SIZE: 12px;");
    txtstream.WriteLine("    text-align: left;");
    txtstream.WriteLine("    white-Space: nowrap;");
    txtstream.WriteLine("}");
    txtstream.WriteLine("</style>");
    txtstream.WriteLine("<title>Win32_Process</title>");
    txtstream.WriteLine("</head>");
    txtstream.WriteLine("<body>");
    txtstream.WriteLine("<table border='0' Cellspacing='3' cellpadding = '3'>");

    var Names;
    var Cols;
    var Rows;
    var x = 0;

    var v = 0;
    while(v < 0)
    {
```

```
var ti = ex.NextEvent(-1);
var obj = ti.Properties_.Item("TargetInstance").Value;
if(v == 0)
{
    Names = new Array[obj.Properties_.Count];
    Cols = new Array[obj.Properties_.Count];
    Rows = new Array[4];
    var propEnum = new Enumerator(obj.Properties_);
    for (; !propEnum.atEnd(); propEnum.moveNext())
    {
        var prop = propEnum.item();
        Names[x] = prop.Name;
        Cols[x] = GetValue(prop.Name, obj);
        x = x + 1;
    }
    Rows[v] = Cols;
    x = 0;
    v = v + 1;
}
else
{
    var propEnum = new Enumerator(obj.Properties_);
    for (; !propEnum.atEnd(); propEnum.moveNext())
    {
        var prop = propEnum.item();
        Cols[x] = GetValue(prop.Name, obj);
        x = x + 1;
    }
    Rows[v] = Cols;
    x = 0;
    v = v + 1;
}
}
txtstream.WriteLine("<%");
for(var a = 0;a < Names.Count; a++)
{
    txtstream.WriteLine("Response.Write(\"<tr><th align='left' nowrap>" +
Names[a] + "</th>\" + vbcrlf)");
    for(var b = 0;b < Rows.Count; b++)
    {
```

```javascript
                    var C = Rows[b];
                    txtstream.WriteLine("Response.Write(\"<td   style='font-family:Calibri,
Sans-Serif;font-size: 12px;color:navy;' align='left' nowrap='nowrap'>" + C[x] +
"</td>\" + vbcrlf)");
                }
                txtstream.WriteLine("Response.Write(\"</tr>\" + vbcrlf)");
            }
            txtstream.WriteLine("%>");
            txtstream.WriteLine("</table>");
            txtstream.WriteLine("</body>");
            txtstream.WriteLine("</html>");
            txtstream.close();
            function GetValue(Name, obj)
            {
                var tempstr = new String();
                var tempstr1 = new String();
                var tName = new String();
                tempstr1 = obj.GetObjectText_();
                var re = /"/g;
                tempstr1 = tempstr1.replace(re , "");
                var pos;
                tName = Name + " = ";
                pos = tempstr1.indexOf(tName);
                if (pos > -1)
                {
                    pos = pos + tName.length;
                    tempstr = tempstr1.substring(pos, tempstr1.length);
                    pos = tempstr.indexOf(";");
                    tempstr = tempstr.substring(0, pos);
                    tempstr = tempstr.replace("{", "");
                    tempstr = tempstr.replace("}", "");
                    if (tempstr.length > 13)
                    {
                        if (obj.Properties_(Name).CIMType == 101)
                        {
                            tempstr = tempstr.substr(4, 2) + "/"  + tempstr.substr(6, 2) + "/" +
tempstr.substr(0, 3) + " " + tempstr.substr(8, 2) + ":" + tempstr.substr(10, 2) + ":" +
tempstr.substr(12, 2);
                        }
                    }
```

```
        return tempstr;
      }
      else
      {
        return "";
      }
    }


    ]]>
    </script>
  </job>
</Package>
```

Vertical Report with a Combobox.

```
<?xml Version='1.0' encoding='iso-8859-1'?>
<package>
<job>
<script language='JavaScript'>
<![CDATA[
    var locator = new ActiveXObject("WbemScripting.SWbemLocator");
    var svc = locator.ConnectServer(".", "root\\cimv2");
    svc.Security_.AuthenticationLevel = 6;
    svc.Security_.ImpersonationLevel = 3;
    var strQuery = "Select * From ___InstanceOperationEvent WITHIN 1 where
TargetInstance ISA'Win32_Process'");
    var es = svc.ExecNotificationQuery(strQuery);
    var ws = new ActiveXObject("WScript.Shell");
    var fso = new ActiveXObject("Scripting.FileSystemObject");
    var    txtstream    =    fso.OpenTextFile(ws.CurrentDirectory    +
"\\Win32_Process.aspx", 2, true, -2);
    txtstream.WriteLine("<!DOCTYPE html PUBLIC ""-//W3C//DTD XHTML 1.0
Transitional//EN""              ""http://www.w3.org/TR/xhtml1/DTD/xhtml1-
transitional.dtd""">");
    txtstream.WriteLine("<html xmlns='http://www.w3.org/1999/xhtml'>");
    txtstream.WriteLine("<head>");
    txtstream.WriteLine("<style type='text/css'>");
    txtstream.WriteLine("th");
    txtstream.WriteLine("{");
```

```
txtstream.WriteLine("    COLOR: darkred;");
txtstream.WriteLine("    BACKGROUND-COLOR: white;");
txtstream.WriteLine("    FONT-FAMILY:font-family: Cambria, serif;");
txtstream.WriteLine("    FONT-SIZE: 12px;");
txtstream.WriteLine("    text-align: left;");
txtstream.WriteLine("    white-Space: nowrap;");
txtstream.WriteLine("}");
txtstream.WriteLine("td");
txtstream.WriteLine("{");
txtstream.WriteLine("    COLOR: navy;");
txtstream.WriteLine("    BACKGROUND-COLOR: white;");
txtstream.WriteLine("    FONT-FAMILY: font-family: Cambria, serif;");
txtstream.WriteLine("    FONT-SIZE: 12px;");
txtstream.WriteLine("    text-align: left;");
txtstream.WriteLine("    white-Space: nowrap;");
txtstream.WriteLine("}");
txtstream.WriteLine("</style>");
txtstream.WriteLine("<title>Win32_Process</title>");
txtstream.WriteLine("</head>");
txtstream.WriteLine("<body>");
txtstream.WriteLine("<table border='0' Cellspacing='3' cellpadding = '3'>");

var Names;
var Cols;
var Rows;
var x = 0;

var v = 0;
while(v < 0)
{
   var ti = ex.NextEvent(-1);
   var obj = ti.Properties_.Item("TargetInstance").Value;
   if(v == 0)
   {
      Names = new Array[obj.Properties_.Count];
      Cols = new Array[obj.Properties_.Count];
      Rows = new Array[4];
      var propEnum = new Enumerator(obj.Properties_);
      for (; !propEnum.atEnd(); propEnum.moveNext())
      {
```

```
        var prop = propEnum.item();
        Names[x] = prop.Name;
        Cols[x] = GetValue(prop.Name, obj);
        x = x + 1;
      }
      Rows[v] = Cols;
      x = 0;
      v = v + 1;
    }
    else
    {
      var propEnum = new Enumerator(obj.Properties_);
      for (; !propEnum.atEnd(); propEnum.moveNext())
      {
        var prop = propEnum.item();
        Cols[x] = GetValue(prop.Name, obj);
        x = x + 1;
      }
      Rows[v] = Cols;
      x = 0;
      v = v + 1;
    }
  }
  txtstream.WriteLine("<%");
  for(var a = 0;a < Names.Count; a++)
  {
      txtstream.WriteLine("Response.Write(\"<tr><th align='left' nowrap>" +
Names[a] + "</th>\" + vbcrlf)");
      for(var b = 0;b < Rows.Count; b++)
      {
        var C = Rows[b];
        txtstream.WriteLine("Response.Write(\"<td   style='font-family:Calibri,
Sans-Serif;font-size: 12px;color:navy;' align='left' nowrap='true'><select><option
value = """ + C[x] + """>" + C[x] + "</option></select></td>\" + vbcrlf)");
      }
      txtstream.WriteLine("Response.Write(\"</tr>\" + vbcrlf)");
  }
  txtstream.WriteLine("%>");
  txtstream.WriteLine("</table>");
  txtstream.WriteLine("</body>");
```

```
txtstream.WriteLine("</html>");
txtstream.close();
function GetValue(Name, obj)
{
    var tempstr = new String();
    var tempstr1 = new String();
    var tName = new String();
    tempstr1 = obj.GetObjectText_();
    var re = /"/g;
    tempstr1 = tempstr1.replace(re , "");
    var pos;
    tName = Name + " = ";
    pos = tempstr1.indexOf(tName);
    if (pos > -1)
    {
        pos = pos + tName.length;
        tempstr = tempstr1.substring(pos, tempstr1.length);
        pos = tempstr.indexOf(";");
        tempstr = tempstr.substring(0, pos);
        tempstr = tempstr.replace("{", "");
        tempstr = tempstr.replace("}", "");
        if (tempstr.length > 13)
        {
            if (obj.Properties_(Name).CIMType == 101)
            {
                tempstr = tempstr.substr(4, 2) + "/"  + tempstr.substr(6, 2) + "/" +
tempstr.substr(0, 3) + " " + tempstr.substr(8, 2) + ":" + tempstr.substr(10, 2) + ":" +
tempstr.substr(12, 2);
            }
        }
        return tempstr;
    }
    else
    {
        return "";
    }
}

]]>
</script>
```

```
    </job>
  </Package>
```

Vertical Report with a link.

```
    <?xml Version='1.0' encoding='iso-8859-1'?>
    <package>
    <job>
    <script language='JavaScript'>
    <![CDATA[
        var locator = new ActiveXObject("WbemScripting.SWbemLocator");
        var svc = locator.ConnectServer(".", "root\\cimv2");
        svc.Security_.AuthenticationLevel = 6;
        svc.Security_.ImpersonationLevel = 3;
        var strQuery = "Select * From ___InstanceOperationEvent WITHIN 1 where
TargetInstance ISA'Win32_Process'");
        var es = svc.ExecNotificationQuery(strQuery);
        var ws = new ActiveXObject("WScript.Shell");
        var fso = new ActiveXObject("Scripting.FileSystemObject");
        var     txtstream     =     fso.OpenTextFile(ws.CurrentDirectory     +
"\\Win32_Process.aspx", 2, true, -2);
        txtstream.WriteLine("<!DOCTYPE html PUBLIC ""-//W3C//DTD XHTML 1.0
Transitional//EN""                ""http://www.w3.org/TR/xhtml1/DTD/xhtml1-
transitional.dtd"">");
        txtstream.WriteLine("<html xmlns='http://www.w3.org/1999/xhtml'>");
        txtstream.WriteLine("<head>");
        txtstream.WriteLine("<style type='text/css'>");
        txtstream.WriteLine("th");
        txtstream.WriteLine("{");
        txtstream.WriteLine("    COLOR: darkred;");
        txtstream.WriteLine("    BACKGROUND-COLOR: white;");
        txtstream.WriteLine("    FONT-FAMILY:font-family: Cambria, serif;");
        txtstream.WriteLine("    FONT-SIZE: 12px;");
        txtstream.WriteLine("    text-align: left;");
        txtstream.WriteLine("    white-Space: nowrap;");
        txtstream.WriteLine("}");
        txtstream.WriteLine("td");
        txtstream.WriteLine("{");
        txtstream.WriteLine("    COLOR: navy;");
```

```
txtstream.WriteLine("    BACKGROUND-COLOR: white;");
txtstream.WriteLine("    FONT-FAMILY: font-family: Cambria, serif;");
txtstream.WriteLine("    FONT-SIZE: 12px;");
txtstream.WriteLine("    text-align: left;");
txtstream.WriteLine("    white-Space: nowrap;");
txtstream.WriteLine("}");
txtstream.WriteLine("</style>");
txtstream.WriteLine("<title>Win32_Process</title>");
txtstream.WriteLine("</head>");
txtstream.WriteLine("<body>");
txtstream.WriteLine("<table border='0' Cellspacing='3' cellpadding = '3'>");

var Names;
var Cols;
var Rows;
var x = 0;

var v = 0;
while(v < 0)
{
    var ti = ex.NextEvent(-1);
    var obj = ti.Properties_.Item("TargetInstance").Value;
    if(v == 0)
    {
        Names = new Array[obj.Properties_.Count];
        Cols = new Array[obj.Properties_.Count];
        Rows = new Array[4];
        var propEnum = new Enumerator(obj.Properties_);
        for (; !propEnum.atEnd(); propEnum.moveNext())
        {
            var prop = propEnum.item();
            Names[x] = prop.Name;
            Cols[x] = GetValue(prop.Name, obj);
            x = x + 1;
        }
        Rows[v] = Cols;
        x = 0;
        v = v + 1;
    }
    else
```

```javascript
        {
            var propEnum = new Enumerator(obj.Properties_);
            for (; !propEnum.atEnd(); propEnum.moveNext())
            {
                var prop = propEnum.item();
                Cols[x] = GetValue(prop.Name, obj);
                x = x + 1;
            }
            Rows[v] = Cols;
            x = 0;
            v = v + 1;
        }
    }
    txtstream.WriteLine("<%");
    for(var a = 0;a < Names.Count; a++)
    {
        txtstream.WriteLine("Response.Write(\"<tr><th align='left' nowrap>" +
Names[a] + "</th>\" + vbcrlf)");
        for(var b = 0;b < Rows.Count; b++)
        {
            var C = Rows[b];
            txtstream.WriteLine("Response.Write(\"<td   style='font-family:Calibri,
Sans-Serif;font-size: 12px;color:navy;' align='left' nowrap='true'><a href='" + C[x]
+ "'>" + C[x] + "</a></td>\" + vbcrlf)");
        }
        txtstream.WriteLine("Response.Write(\"</tr>\" + vbcrlf)");
    }
    txtstream.WriteLine("%>");
    txtstream.WriteLine("</table>");
    txtstream.WriteLine("</body>");
    txtstream.WriteLine("</html>");
    txtstream.close();
    function GetValue(Name, obj)
    {
        var tempstr = new String();
        var tempstr1 = new String();
        var tName = new String();
        tempstr1 = obj.GetObjectText_();
        var re = /"/g;
        tempstr1 = tempstr1.replace(re , "");
```

```
        var pos;
        tName = Name + " = ";
        pos = tempstr1.indexOf(tName);
        if (pos > -1)
        {
            pos = pos + tName.length;
            tempstr = tempstr1.substring(pos, tempstr1.length);
            pos = tempstr.indexOf(";");
            tempstr = tempstr.substring(0, pos);
            tempstr = tempstr.replace("{", "");
            tempstr = tempstr.replace("}", "");
            if (tempstr.length > 13)
            {
                if (obj.Properties_(Name).CIMType == 101)
                {
                    tempstr = tempstr.substr(4, 2) + "/"  + tempstr.substr(6, 2) + "/" +
tempstr.substr(0, 3) + " " + tempstr.substr(8, 2) + ":" + tempstr.substr(10, 2) + ":" +
tempstr.substr(12, 2);
                }
            }
            return tempstr;
        }
        else
        {
            return "";
        }
    }


    ]]>
    </script>
  </job>
</Package>
```

Vertical Report with a Listbox.

```javascript
<?xml Version='1.0' encoding='iso-8859-1'?>
<package>
<job>
<script language='JavaScript'>
<![CDATA[
    var locator = new ActiveXObject("WbemScripting.SWbemLocator");
    var svc = locator.ConnectServer(".", "root\\cimv2");
    svc.Security_.AuthenticationLevel = 6;
    svc.Security_.ImpersonationLevel = 3;
    var strQuery = "Select * From ___InstanceOperationEvent WITHIN 1 where
TargetInstance ISA'Win32_Process'");
    var es = svc.ExecNotificationQuery(strQuery);
    var ws = new ActiveXObject("WScript.Shell");
    var fso = new ActiveXObject("Scripting.FileSystemObject");
    var       txtstream       =       fso.OpenTextFile(ws.CurrentDirectory       +
"\\Win32_Process.aspx", 2, true, -2);
    txtstream.WriteLine("<!DOCTYPE html PUBLIC ""-//W3C//DTD XHTML 1.0
Transitional//EN""                   ""http://www.w3.org/TR/xhtml1/DTD/xhtml1-
transitional.dtd"">");
    txtstream.WriteLine("<html xmlns='http://www.w3.org/1999/xhtml'>");
    txtstream.WriteLine("<head>");
    txtstream.WriteLine("<style type='text/css'>");
    txtstream.WriteLine("th");
    txtstream.WriteLine("{");
    txtstream.WriteLine("    COLOR: darkred;");
    txtstream.WriteLine("    BACKGROUND-COLOR: white;");
    txtstream.WriteLine("    FONT-FAMILY:font-family: Cambria, serif;");
    txtstream.WriteLine("    FONT-SIZE: 12px;");
    txtstream.WriteLine("    text-align: left;");
    txtstream.WriteLine("    white-Space: nowrap;");
    txtstream.WriteLine("}");
    txtstream.WriteLine("td");
    txtstream.WriteLine("{");
    txtstream.WriteLine("    COLOR: navy;");
    txtstream.WriteLine("    BACKGROUND-COLOR: white;");
    txtstream.WriteLine("    FONT-FAMILY: font-family: Cambria, serif;");
    txtstream.WriteLine("    FONT-SIZE: 12px;");
```

```
txtstream.WriteLine("    text-align: left;");
txtstream.WriteLine("    white-Space: nowrap;");
txtstream.WriteLine("}");
txtstream.WriteLine("</style>");
txtstream.WriteLine("<title>Win32_Process</title>");
txtstream.WriteLine("</head>");
txtstream.WriteLine("<body>");
txtstream.WriteLine("<table border='0' Cellspacing='3' cellpadding = '3'>");

var Names;
var Cols;
var Rows;
var x = 0;

var v = 0;
while(v < 0)
{
    var ti = ex.NextEvent(-1);
    var obj = ti.Properties_.Item("TargetInstance").Value;
    if(v == 0)
    {
        Names = new Array[obj.Properties_.Count];
        Cols = new Array[obj.Properties_.Count];
        Rows = new Array[4];
        var propEnum = new Enumerator(obj.Properties_);
        for (; !propEnum.atEnd(); propEnum.moveNext())
        {
            var prop = propEnum.item();
            Names[x] = prop.Name;
            Cols[x] = GetValue(prop.Name, obj);
            x = x + 1;
        }
        Rows[v] = Cols;
        x = 0;
        v = v + 1;
    }
    else
    {
        var propEnum = new Enumerator(obj.Properties_);
        for (; !propEnum.atEnd(); propEnum.moveNext())
```

```
        {
            var prop = propEnum.item();
            Cols[x] = GetValue(prop.Name, obj);
            x = x + 1;
        }
        Rows[v] = Cols;
        x = 0;
        v = v + 1;
    }
}
txtstream.WriteLine("<%");
for(var a = 0;a < Names.Count; a++)
{
    txtstream.WriteLine("Response.Write(\"<tr><th align='left' nowrap>" +
Names[a] + "</th>\" + vbcrlf)");
    for(var b = 0;b < Rows.Count; b++)
    {
        var C = Rows[b];
        txtstream.WriteLine("Response.Write(\"<td   style='font-family:Calibri,
Sans-Serif;font-size:    12px;color:navy;'    align='left'    nowrap='true'><select
multiple><option value = """ + C[x] + """>" + C[x] + "</option></select></td>\" +
vbcrlf)");
    }
    txtstream.WriteLine("Response.Write(\"</tr>\" + vbcrlf)");
}
txtstream.WriteLine("%>");
txtstream.WriteLine("</table>");
txtstream.WriteLine("</body>");
txtstream.WriteLine("</html>");
txtstream.close();
function GetValue(Name, obj)
{
    var tempstr = new String();
    var tempstr1 = new String();
    var tName = new String();
    tempstr1 = obj.GetObjectText_();
    var re = /"/g;
    tempstr1 = tempstr1.replace(re , "");
    var pos;
    tName = Name + " = ";
```

```javascript
            pos = tempstr1.indexOf(tName);
            if (pos > -1)
            {
                pos = pos + tName.length;
                tempstr = tempstr1.substring(pos, tempstr1.length);
                pos = tempstr.indexOf(";");
                tempstr = tempstr.substring(0, pos);
                tempstr = tempstr.replace("{", "");
                tempstr = tempstr.replace("}", "");
                if (tempstr.length > 13)
                {
                    if (obj.Properties_(Name).CIMType == 101)
                    {
                        tempstr = tempstr.substr(4, 2) + "/"  + tempstr.substr(6, 2) + "/" +
tempstr.substr(0, 3) + " " + tempstr.substr(8, 2) + ":" + tempstr.substr(10, 2) + ":" +
tempstr.substr(12, 2);
                    }
                }
                return tempstr;
            }
            else
            {
                return "";
            }
        }


    ]]>
    </script>
  </job>
</Package>
```

Vertical Report with a textarea.

```
    <?xml Version='1.0' encoding='iso-8859-1'?>
    <package>
    <job>
    <script language='JavaScript'>
    <![CDATA[
        var locator = new ActiveXObject("WbemScripting.SWbemLocator");
```

```
var svc = locator.ConnectServer(".", "root\\cimv2");
svc.Security_.AuthenticationLevel = 6;
svc.Security_.ImpersonationLevel = 3;
var strQuery = "Select * From ___InstanceOperationEvent WITHIN 1 where
TargetInstance ISA'Win32_Process'");
var es = svc.ExecNotificationQuery(strQuery);
var ws = new ActiveXObject("WScript.Shell");
var fso = new ActiveXObject("Scripting.FileSystemObject");
var        txtstream      =       fso.OpenTextFile(ws.CurrentDirectory      +
"\\Win32_Process.aspx", 2, true, -2);
txtstream.WriteLine("<!DOCTYPE html PUBLIC ""-//W3C//DTD XHTML 1.0
Transitional//EN""                ""http://www.w3.org/TR/xhtml1/DTD/xhtml1-
transitional.dtd"">");
txtstream.WriteLine("<html xmlns='http://www.w3.org/1999/xhtml'>");
txtstream.WriteLine("<head>");
txtstream.WriteLine("<style type='text/css'>");
txtstream.WriteLine("th");
txtstream.WriteLine("{");
txtstream.WriteLine("   COLOR: darkred;");
txtstream.WriteLine("   BACKGROUND-COLOR: white;");
txtstream.WriteLine("   FONT-FAMILY:font-family: Cambria, serif;");
txtstream.WriteLine("   FONT-SIZE: 12px;");
txtstream.WriteLine("   text-align: left;");
txtstream.WriteLine("   white-Space: nowrap;");
txtstream.WriteLine("}");
txtstream.WriteLine("td");
txtstream.WriteLine("{");
txtstream.WriteLine("   COLOR: navy;");
txtstream.WriteLine("   BACKGROUND-COLOR: white;");
txtstream.WriteLine("   FONT-FAMILY: font-family: Cambria, serif;");
txtstream.WriteLine("   FONT-SIZE: 12px;");
txtstream.WriteLine("   text-align: left;");
txtstream.WriteLine("   white-Space: nowrap;");
txtstream.WriteLine("}");
txtstream.WriteLine("</style>");
txtstream.WriteLine("<title>Win32_Process</title>");
txtstream.WriteLine("</head>");
txtstream.WriteLine("<body>");
txtstream.WriteLine("<table border='0' Cellspacing='3' cellpadding = '3'>");
```

```
var Names;
var Cols;
var Rows;
var x = 0;

var v = 0;
while(v < 0)
{
    var ti = ex.NextEvent(-1);
    var obj = ti.Properties_.Item("TargetInstance").Value;
    if(v == 0)
    {
        Names = new Array[obj.Properties_.Count];
        Cols = new Array[obj.Properties_.Count];
        Rows = new Array[4];
        var propEnum = new Enumerator(obj.Properties_);
        for (; !propEnum.atEnd(); propEnum.moveNext())
        {
            var prop = propEnum.item();
            Names[x] = prop.Name;
            Cols[x] = GetValue(prop.Name, obj);
            x = x + 1;
        }
        Rows[v] = Cols;
        x = 0;
        v = v + 1;
    }
    else
    {
        var propEnum = new Enumerator(obj.Properties_);
        for (; !propEnum.atEnd(); propEnum.moveNext())
        {
            var prop = propEnum.item();
            Cols[x] = GetValue(prop.Name, obj);
            x = x + 1;
        }
        Rows[v] = Cols;
        x = 0;
        v = v + 1;
    }
```

```
        }
        txtstream.WriteLine("<%");
        for(var a = 0;a < Names.Count; a++)
        {
            txtstream.WriteLine("Response.Write(\"<tr><th  align='left'  nowrap>" +
Names[a] + "</th>\" + vbcrlf)");
            for(var b = 0;b < Rows.Count; b++)
            {
                var C = Rows[b];
                txtstream.WriteLine("Response.Write(\"<td    style='font-family:Calibri,
Sans-Serif;font-size:  12px;color:navy;'  align='left'  nowrap='true'><textarea>" +
C[x] + "</textarea></td>\" + vbcrlf)");
            }
            txtstream.WriteLine("Response.Write(\"</tr>\" + vbcrlf)");
        }
        txtstream.WriteLine("%>");
        txtstream.WriteLine("</table>");
        txtstream.WriteLine("</body>");
        txtstream.WriteLine("</html>");
        txtstream.close();
        function GetValue(Name, obj)
        {
            var tempstr = new String();
            var tempstr1 = new String();
            var tName = new String();
            tempstr1 = obj.GetObjectText_();
            var re = /"/g;
            tempstr1 = tempstr1.replace(re , "");
            var pos;
            tName = Name + " = ";
            pos = tempstr1.indexOf(tName);
            if (pos > -1)
            {
                pos = pos + tName.length;
                tempstr = tempstr1.substring(pos, tempstr1.length);
                pos = tempstr.indexOf(";");
                tempstr = tempstr.substring(0, pos);
                tempstr = tempstr.replace("{", "");
                tempstr = tempstr.replace("}", "");
                if (tempstr.length > 13)
```

```javascript
        {
            if (obj.Properties_(Name).CIMType == 101)
            {
                tempstr = tempstr.substr(4, 2) + "/" + tempstr.substr(6, 2) + "/" +
tempstr.substr(0, 3) + " " + tempstr.substr(8, 2) + ":" + tempstr.substr(10, 2) + ":" +
tempstr.substr(12, 2);
            }
        }
        return tempstr;
    }
    else
    {
        return "";
    }
}


]]>
    </script>
  </job>
</Package>
```

Vertical Report with a textbox.

```javascript
<?xml Version='1.0' encoding='iso-8859-1'?>
<package>
<job>
<script language='JavaScript'>
<![CDATA[
    var locator = new ActiveXObject("WbemScripting.SWbemLocator");
    var svc = locator.ConnectServer(".", "root\\cimv2");
    svc.Security_.AuthenticationLevel = 6;
    svc.Security_.ImpersonationLevel = 3;
    var strQuery = "Select * From ___InstanceOperationEvent WITHIN 1 where
TargetInstance ISA'Win32_Process'");
    var es = svc.ExecNotificationQuery(strQuery);
    var ws = new ActiveXObject("WScript.Shell");
    var fso = new ActiveXObject("Scripting.FileSystemObject");
    var     txtstream     =     fso.OpenTextFile(ws.CurrentDirectory     +
"\\Win32_Process.aspx", 2, true, -2);
```

```
txtstream.WriteLine("<!DOCTYPE html PUBLIC ""-//W3C//DTD XHTML 1.0
Transitional//EN"" ""http://www.w3.org/TR/xhtml1/DTD/xhtml1-
transitional.dtd"">");
txtstream.WriteLine("<html xmlns='http://www.w3.org/1999/xhtml'>");
txtstream.WriteLine("<head>");
txtstream.WriteLine("<style type='text/css'>");
txtstream.WriteLine("th");
txtstream.WriteLine("{");
txtstream.WriteLine("   COLOR: darkred;");
txtstream.WriteLine("   BACKGROUND-COLOR: white;");
txtstream.WriteLine("   FONT-FAMILY:font-family: Cambria, serif;");
txtstream.WriteLine("   FONT-SIZE: 12px;");
txtstream.WriteLine("   text-align: left;");
txtstream.WriteLine("   white-Space: nowrap;");
txtstream.WriteLine("}");
txtstream.WriteLine("td");
txtstream.WriteLine("{");
txtstream.WriteLine("   COLOR: navy;");
txtstream.WriteLine("   BACKGROUND-COLOR: white;");
txtstream.WriteLine("   FONT-FAMILY: font-family: Cambria, serif;");
txtstream.WriteLine("   FONT-SIZE: 12px;");
txtstream.WriteLine("   text-align: left;");
txtstream.WriteLine("   white-Space: nowrap;");
txtstream.WriteLine("}");
txtstream.WriteLine("</style>");
txtstream.WriteLine("<title>Win32_Process</title>");
txtstream.WriteLine("</head>");
txtstream.WriteLine("<body>");
txtstream.WriteLine("<table border='0' Cellspacing='3' cellpadding = '3'>");

var Names;
var Cols;
var Rows;
var x = 0;

var v = 0;
while(v < 0)
{
   var ti = ex.NextEvent(-1);
   var obj = ti.Properties_.Item("TargetInstance").Value;
```

```
if(v == 0)
{
    Names = new Array[obj.Properties_.Count];
    Cols = new Array[obj.Properties_.Count];
    Rows = new Array[4];
    var propEnum = new Enumerator(obj.Properties_);
    for (; !propEnum.atEnd(); propEnum.moveNext())
    {
        var prop = propEnum.item();
        Names[x] = prop.Name;
        Cols[x] = GetValue(prop.Name, obj);
        x = x + 1;
    }
    Rows[v] = Cols;
    x = 0;
    v = v + 1;
}
else
{
    var propEnum = new Enumerator(obj.Properties_);
    for (; !propEnum.atEnd(); propEnum.moveNext())
    {
        var prop = propEnum.item();
        Cols[x] = GetValue(prop.Name, obj);
        x = x + 1;
    }
    Rows[v] = Cols;
    x = 0;
    v = v + 1;
}
}
txtstream.WriteLine("<%");
for(var a = 0;a < Names.Count; a++)
{
    txtstream.WriteLine("Response.Write(\"<tr><th align='left' nowrap>" +
Names[a] + "</th>\" + vbcrlf)");
    for(var b = 0;b < Rows.Count; b++)
    {
        var C = Rows[b];
```

```javascript
            txtstream.WriteLine("Response.Write(\"<td    style='font-family:Calibri,
Sans-Serif;font-size: 12px;color:navy;' align='left' nowrap='true'><input type=text
value=\"\"\" + C[x] + "\"\"\"></input></td>\" + vbcrlf)");
            }
            txtstream.WriteLine("Response.Write(\"</tr>\" + vbcrlf)");
        }
        txtstream.WriteLine("%>");
        txtstream.WriteLine("</table>");
        txtstream.WriteLine("</body>");
        txtstream.WriteLine("</html>");
        txtstream.close();
        function GetValue(Name, obj)
        {
            var tempstr = new String();
            var tempstr1 = new String();
            var tName = new String();
            tempstr1 = obj.GetObjectText_();
            var re = /"/g;
            tempstr1 = tempstr1.replace(re , "");
            var pos;
            tName = Name + " = ";
            pos = tempstr1.indexOf(tName);
            if (pos > -1)
            {
                pos = pos + tName.length;
                tempstr = tempstr1.substring(pos, tempstr1.length);
                pos = tempstr.indexOf(";");
                tempstr = tempstr.substring(0, pos);
                tempstr = tempstr.replace("{", "");
                tempstr = tempstr.replace("}", "");
                if (tempstr.length > 13)
                {
                    if (obj.Properties_(Name).CIMType == 101)
                    {
                        tempstr = tempstr.substr(4, 2) + "/"  + tempstr.substr(6, 2) + "/" +
tempstr.substr(0, 3) + " " + tempstr.substr(8, 2) + ":" + tempstr.substr(10, 2) + ":" +
tempstr.substr(12, 2);
                    }
                }
                return tempstr;
```

```
      }
      else
      {
          return "";
      }
  }

  ]]>
  </script>
 </job>
</Package>
```

ASPX Tables

Horizontal Table with no additional tags.

```
<?xml Version='1.0' encoding='iso-8859-1'?>
<package>
<job>
<script language='JavaScript'>
<![CDATA[
   var locator = new ActiveXObject("WbemScripting.SWbemLocator");
   var svc = locator.ConnectServer(".", "root\\cimv2");
   svc.Security_.AuthenticationLevel = 6;
   svc.Security_.ImpersonationLevel = 3;
   var strQuery = "Select * From ___InstanceOperationEvent WITHIN 1 where
TargetInstance ISA'Win32_Process'");
   var es = svc.ExecNotificationQuery(strQuery);
   var ws = new ActiveXObject("WScript.Shell");
   var fso = new ActiveXObject("Scripting.FileSystemObject");
   var      txtstream      =      fso.OpenTextFile(ws.CurrentDirectory      +
"\\Win32_Process.aspx", 2, true, -2);
   txtstream.WriteLine("<!DOCTYPE html PUBLIC ""-//W3C//DTD XHTML 1.0
Transitional//EN""                ""http://www.w3.org/TR/xhtml1/DTD/xhtml1-
transitional.dtd"">");
   txtstream.WriteLine("<html xmlns='http://www.w3.org/1999/xhtml'>");
   txtstream.WriteLine("<head>");
   txtstream.WriteLine("<style type='text/css'>");
   txtstream.WriteLine("th");
   txtstream.WriteLine("{");
   txtstream.WriteLine("    COLOR: darkred;");
   txtstream.WriteLine("    BACKGROUND-COLOR: white;");
   txtstream.WriteLine("    FONT-FAMILY:font-family: Cambria, serif;");
   txtstream.WriteLine("    FONT-SIZE: 12px;");
```

```
txtstream.WriteLine("    text-align: left;");
txtstream.WriteLine("    white-Space: nowrap;");
txtstream.WriteLine("}");
txtstream.WriteLine("td");
txtstream.WriteLine("{");
txtstream.WriteLine("    COLOR: navy;");
txtstream.WriteLine("    BACKGROUND-COLOR: white;");
txtstream.WriteLine("    FONT-FAMILY: font-family: Cambria, serif;");
txtstream.WriteLine("    FONT-SIZE: 12px;");
txtstream.WriteLine("    text-align: left;");
txtstream.WriteLine("    white-Space: nowrap;");
txtstream.WriteLine("}");
txtstream.WriteLine("</style>");
txtstream.WriteLine("<title>Win32_Process</title>");
txtstream.WriteLine("</head>");
txtstream.WriteLine("<body>");
txtstream.WriteLine("<table border='1' Cellspacing='3' cellpadding = '3'>");
txtstream.WriteLine("<%");
var v=0;
while(v < 0)
{
    var ti = ex.NextEvent(-1);
    var obj = ti.Properties_.Item("TargetInstance").Value;
    if(v == 0)
    {
        txtstream.WriteLine("Response.Write(\"<tr>\" + vbcrlf)");
        var propEnum = new Enumerator(obj.Properties_);
        for (; !propEnum.atEnd(); propEnum.moveNext())
        {
            var prop = propEnum.item();
            txtstream.WriteLine("Response.Write(\"<th align='left' nowrap>" +
prop.Name + "</th>\" + vbcrlf)");
        }
        txtstream.WriteLine("Response.Write(\"</tr>\" + vbcrlf)");
        propEnum.Reset();
    }
    txtstream.WriteLine("Response.Write(\"<tr>\" + vbcrlf)");
    for (; !propEnum.atEnd(); propEnum.moveNext())
    {
        var prop = propEnum.item();
```

```
            txtstream.WriteLine("Response.Write(\"<td   style='font-family:Calibri,
Sans-Serif;font-size:   12px;color:navy;'   align='left'   nowrap='nowrap'>"   +
GetValue(prop.Name, obj) + "</td>\" + vbcrlf)");
        }
        txtstream.WriteLine("Response.Write(\"</tr>\" + vbcrlf)");
        v = v + 1;
    }
    txtstream.WriteLine("%>");
    txtstream.WriteLine("</table>");
    txtstream.WriteLine("</body>");
    txtstream.WriteLine("</html>");
    txtstream.close();
    function GetValue(Name, obj)
    {
        var tempstr = new String();
        var tempstr1 = new String();
        var tName = new String();
        tempstr1 = obj.GetObjectText_();
        var re = /"/g;
        tempstr1 = tempstr1.replace(re , "");
        var pos;
        tName = Name + " = ";
        pos = tempstr1.indexOf(tName);
        if (pos > -1)
        {
            pos = pos + tName.length;
            tempstr = tempstr1.substring(pos, tempstr1.length);
            pos = tempstr.indexOf(";");
            tempstr = tempstr.substring(0, pos);
            tempstr = tempstr.replace("{", "");
            tempstr = tempstr.replace("}", "");
            if (tempstr.length > 13)
            {
                if (obj.Properties_(Name).CIMType == 101)
                {
                    tempstr = tempstr.substr(4, 2) + "/" + tempstr.substr(6, 2) + "/" +
tempstr.substr(0, 3) + " " + tempstr.substr(8, 2) + ":" + tempstr.substr(10, 2) + ":" +
tempstr.substr(12, 2);
                }
            }
```

```
      return tempstr;
    }
    else
    {
      return "";
    }
  }

  ]]>
  </script>
 </job>
</Package>
```

Horizontal Table with a Combobox.

```
<?xml Version='1.0' encoding='iso-8859-1'?>
<package>
<job>
<script language='JavaScript'>
<![CDATA[
   var locator = new ActiveXObject("WbemScripting.SWbemLocator");
   var svc = locator.ConnectServer(".", "root\\cimv2");
   svc.Security_.AuthenticationLevel = 6;
   svc.Security_.ImpersonationLevel = 3;
   var strQuery = "Select * From ___InstanceOperationEvent WITHIN 1 where
TargetInstance ISA'Win32_Process'");
   var es = svc.ExecNotificationQuery(strQuery);
   var ws = new ActiveXObject("WScript.Shell");
   var fso = new ActiveXObject("Scripting.FileSystemObject");
   var       txtstream     =       fso.OpenTextFile(ws.CurrentDirectory       +
"\\Win32_Process.aspx", 2, true, -2);
   txtstream.WriteLine("<!DOCTYPE html PUBLIC ""-//W3C//DTD XHTML 1.0
Transitional//EN"""              ""http://www.w3.org/TR/xhtml1/DTD/xhtml1-
transitional.dtd""">");
   txtstream.WriteLine("<html xmlns='http://www.w3.org/1999/xhtml'>");
   txtstream.WriteLine("<head>");
   txtstream.WriteLine("<style type='text/css'>");
   txtstream.WriteLine("th");
   txtstream.WriteLine("{");
```

```
txtstream.WriteLine("   COLOR: darkred;");
txtstream.WriteLine("   BACKGROUND-COLOR: white;");
txtstream.WriteLine("   FONT-FAMILY:font-family: Cambria, serif;");
txtstream.WriteLine("   FONT-SIZE: 12px;");
txtstream.WriteLine("   text-align: left;");
txtstream.WriteLine("   white-Space: nowrap;");
txtstream.WriteLine("}");
txtstream.WriteLine("td");
txtstream.WriteLine("{");
txtstream.WriteLine("   COLOR: navy;");
txtstream.WriteLine("   BACKGROUND-COLOR: white;");
txtstream.WriteLine("   FONT-FAMILY: font-family: Cambria, serif;");
txtstream.WriteLine("   FONT-SIZE: 12px;");
txtstream.WriteLine("   text-align: left;");
txtstream.WriteLine("   white-Space: nowrap;");
txtstream.WriteLine("}");
txtstream.WriteLine("</style>");
txtstream.WriteLine("<title>Win32_Process</title>");
txtstream.WriteLine("</head>");
txtstream.WriteLine("<body>");
txtstream.WriteLine("<table border='1' Cellspacing='3' cellpadding = '3'>");
txtstream.WriteLine("<%");
var v=0;
while(v < 0)
{
    var ti = ex.NextEvent(-1);
    var obj = ti.Properties_.Item("TargetInstance").Value;
    if(v == 0)
    {
        txtstream.WriteLine("Response.Write(\"<tr>\" + vbcrlf)");
        var propEnum = new Enumerator(obj.Properties_);
        for (; !propEnum.atEnd(); propEnum.moveNext())
        {
            var prop = propEnum.item();
            txtstream.WriteLine("Response.Write(\"<th align='left' nowrap>" +
prop.Name + "</th>\" + vbcrlf)");
        }
        txtstream.WriteLine("Response.Write(\"</tr>\" + vbcrlf)");
        propEnum.Reset();
    }
```

```
txtstream.WriteLine("Response.Write(\"<tr>\" + vbcrlf)");
for (; !propEnum.atEnd(); propEnum.moveNext())
{
    var prop = propEnum.item();
    txtstream.WriteLine("Response.Write(\"<td   style='font-family:Calibri,
Sans-Serif;font-size: 12px;color:navy;' align='left' nowrap='true'><select><option
value = '" + GetValue(prop.Name, obj) + "'>" + GetValue(prop.Name, obj) +
"</option></select></td>\" + vbcrlf)");
}
    txtstream.WriteLine("Response.Write(\"</tr>\" + vbcrlf)");
    v = v + 1;
}
txtstream.WriteLine("%>");
txtstream.WriteLine("</table>");
txtstream.WriteLine("</body>");
txtstream.WriteLine("</html>");
txtstream.close();
function GetValue(Name, obj)
{
    var tempstr = new String();
    var tempstr1 = new String();
    var tName = new String();
    tempstr1 = obj.GetObjectText_();
    var re = /"/g;
    tempstr1 = tempstr1.replace(re , "");
    var pos;
    tName = Name + " = ";
    pos = tempstr1.indexOf(tName);
    if (pos > -1)
    {
        pos = pos + tName.length;
        tempstr = tempstr1.substring(pos, tempstr1.length);
        pos = tempstr.indexOf(";");
        tempstr = tempstr.substring(0, pos);
        tempstr = tempstr.replace("{", "");
        tempstr = tempstr.replace("}", "");
        if (tempstr.length > 13)
        {
            if (obj.Properties_(Name).CIMType == 101)
            {
```

```
            tempstr = tempstr.substr(4, 2) + "/"  + tempstr.substr(6, 2) + "/" +
tempstr.substr(0, 3) + " " + tempstr.substr(8, 2) + ":" + tempstr.substr(10, 2) + ":" +
tempstr.substr(12, 2);
                }
            }
            return tempstr;
        }
        else
        {
            return "";
        }
    }


    ]]>
    </script>
  </job>
</Package>
```

Horizontal Table with a link.

```
<?xml Version='1.0' encoding='iso-8859-1'?>
<package>
<job>
<script language='JavaScript'>
<![CDATA[
    var locator = new ActiveXObject("WbemScripting.SWbemLocator");
    var svc = locator.ConnectServer(".", "root\\cimv2");
    svc.Security_.AuthenticationLevel = 6;
    svc.Security_.ImpersonationLevel = 3;
    var strQuery = "Select * From ___InstanceOperationEvent WITHIN 1 where
TargetInstance ISA'Win32_Process'");
    var es = svc.ExecNotificationQuery(strQuery);
    var ws = new ActiveXObject("WScript.Shell");
    var fso = new ActiveXObject("Scripting.FileSystemObject");
    var    txtstream    =    fso.OpenTextFile(ws.CurrentDirectory    +
"\\Win32_Process.aspx", 2, true, -2);
    txtstream.WriteLine("<!DOCTYPE html PUBLIC ""-//W3C//DTD XHTML 1.0
Transitional//EN""         ""http://www.w3.org/TR/xhtml1/DTD/xhtml1-
transitional.dtd"">");
```

```
txtstream.WriteLine("<html xmlns='http://www.w3.org/1999/xhtml'>");
txtstream.WriteLine("<head>");
txtstream.WriteLine("<style type='text/css'>");
txtstream.WriteLine("th");
txtstream.WriteLine("{");
txtstream.WriteLine("    COLOR: darkred;");
txtstream.WriteLine("    BACKGROUND-COLOR: white;");
txtstream.WriteLine("    FONT-FAMILY:font-family: Cambria, serif;");
txtstream.WriteLine("    FONT-SIZE: 12px;");
txtstream.WriteLine("    text-align: left;");
txtstream.WriteLine("    white-Space: nowrap;");
txtstream.WriteLine("}");
txtstream.WriteLine("td");
txtstream.WriteLine("{");
txtstream.WriteLine("    COLOR: navy;");
txtstream.WriteLine("    BACKGROUND-COLOR: white;");
txtstream.WriteLine("    FONT-FAMILY: font-family: Cambria, serif;");
txtstream.WriteLine("    FONT-SIZE: 12px;");
txtstream.WriteLine("    text-align: left;");
txtstream.WriteLine("    white-Space: nowrap;");
txtstream.WriteLine("}");
txtstream.WriteLine("</style>");
txtstream.WriteLine("<title>Win32_Process</title>");
txtstream.WriteLine("</head>");
txtstream.WriteLine("<body>");
txtstream.WriteLine("<table border='1' Cellspacing='3' cellpadding = '3'>");
txtstream.WriteLine("<%");
var v=0;
while(v < 0)
{
    var ti = ex.NextEvent(-1);
    var obj = ti.Properties_.Item("TargetInstance").Value;
    if(v == 0)
    {
        txtstream.WriteLine("Response.Write(\"<tr>\" + vbcrlf)");
        var propEnum = new Enumerator(obj.Properties_);
        for (; !propEnum.atEnd(); propEnum.moveNext())
        {
            var prop = propEnum.item();
```

```
            txtstream.WriteLine("Response.Write(\"<th align='left' nowrap>" +
prop.Name + "</th>\" + vbcrlf)");
        }
        txtstream.WriteLine("Response.Write(\"</tr>\" + vbcrlf)");
        propEnum.Reset();
    }
    txtstream.WriteLine("Response.Write(\"<tr>\" + vbcrlf)");
    for (; !propEnum.atEnd(); propEnum.moveNext())
    {
        var prop = propEnum.item();
        txtstream.WriteLine("Response.Write(\"<td    style='font-family:Calibri,
Sans-Serif;font-size: 12px;color:navy;' align='left' nowrap='true'><a href='" +
GetValue(prop.Name, obj) + "'>" + GetValue(prop.Name, obj) + "</a></td>\" +
vbcrlf)");
    }
    txtstream.WriteLine("Response.Write(\"</tr>\" + vbcrlf)");
    v = v + 1;
}
txtstream.WriteLine("%>");
txtstream.WriteLine("</table>");
txtstream.WriteLine("</body>");
txtstream.WriteLine("</html>");
txtstream.close();
function GetValue(Name, obj)
{
    var tempstr = new String();
    var tempstr1 = new String();
    var tName = new String();
    tempstr1 = obj.GetObjectText_();
    var re = /"/g;
    tempstr1 = tempstr1.replace(re , "");
    var pos;
    tName = Name + " = ";
    pos = tempstr1.indexOf(tName);
    if (pos > -1)
    {
        pos = pos + tName.length;
        tempstr = tempstr1.substring(pos, tempstr1.length);
        pos = tempstr.indexOf(";");
        tempstr = tempstr.substring(0, pos);
```

```javascript
                tempstr = tempstr.replace("{", "");
                tempstr = tempstr.replace("}", "");
                if (tempstr.length > 13)
                {
                    if (obj.Properties_(Name).CIMType == 101)
                    {
                        tempstr = tempstr.substr(4, 2) + "/" + tempstr.substr(6, 2) + "/" +
tempstr.substr(0, 3) + " " + tempstr.substr(8, 2) + ":" + tempstr.substr(10, 2) + ":" +
tempstr.substr(12, 2);
                    }
                }
                return tempstr;
            }
            else
            {
                return "";
            }
        }


    ]]>
    </script>
   </job>
  </Package>
```

Horizontal Table with a Listbox.

```xml
<?xml Version='1.0' encoding='iso-8859-1'?>
<package>
<job>
<script language='JavaScript'>
<![CDATA[
   var locator = new ActiveXObject("WbemScripting.SWbemLocator");
   var svc = locator.ConnectServer(".", "root\\cimv2");
   svc.Security_.AuthenticationLevel = 6;
   svc.Security_.ImpersonationLevel = 3;
```

```
var strQuery = "Select * From ___InstanceOperationEvent WITHIN 1 where
TargetInstance ISA'Win32_Process'");
var es = svc.ExecNotificationQuery(strQuery);
var ws = new ActiveXObject("WScript.Shell");
var fso = new ActiveXObject("Scripting.FileSystemObject");
var txtstream = fso.OpenTextFile(ws.CurrentDirectory +
"\\Win32_Process.aspx", 2, true, -2);
txtstream.WriteLine("<!DOCTYPE html PUBLIC ""-//W3C//DTD XHTML 1.0
Transitional//EN"" ""http://www.w3.org/TR/xhtml1/DTD/xhtml1-
transitional.dtd"">");
txtstream.WriteLine("<html xmlns='http://www.w3.org/1999/xhtml'>");
txtstream.WriteLine("<head>");
txtstream.WriteLine("<style type='text/css'>");
txtstream.WriteLine("th");
txtstream.WriteLine("{");
txtstream.WriteLine("   COLOR: darkred;");
txtstream.WriteLine("   BACKGROUND-COLOR: white;");
txtstream.WriteLine("   FONT-FAMILY:font-family: Cambria, serif;");
txtstream.WriteLine("   FONT-SIZE: 12px;");
txtstream.WriteLine("   text-align: left;");
txtstream.WriteLine("   white-Space: nowrap;");
txtstream.WriteLine("}");
txtstream.WriteLine("td");
txtstream.WriteLine("{");
txtstream.WriteLine("   COLOR: navy;");
txtstream.WriteLine("   BACKGROUND-COLOR: white;");
txtstream.WriteLine("   FONT-FAMILY: font-family: Cambria, serif;");
txtstream.WriteLine("   FONT-SIZE: 12px;");
txtstream.WriteLine("   text-align: left;");
txtstream.WriteLine("   white-Space: nowrap;");
txtstream.WriteLine("}");
txtstream.WriteLine("</style>");
txtstream.WriteLine("<title>Win32_Process</title>");
txtstream.WriteLine("</head>");
txtstream.WriteLine("<body>");
txtstream.WriteLine("<table border='1' Cellspacing='3' cellpadding = '3'>");
txtstream.WriteLine("<%");
var v=0;
while(v < 0)
{
```

```
var ti = ex.NextEvent(-1);
var obj = ti.Properties_.Item("TargetInstance").Value;
if(v == 0)
{
    txtstream.WriteLine("Response.Write(\"<tr>\" + vbcrlf)");
    var propEnum = new Enumerator(obj.Properties_);
    for (; !propEnum.atEnd(); propEnum.moveNext())
    {
        var prop = propEnum.item();
        txtstream.WriteLine("Response.Write(\"<th align='left' nowrap>" +
prop.Name + "</th>\" + vbcrlf)");
    }
    txtstream.WriteLine("Response.Write(\"</tr>\" + vbcrlf)");
    propEnum.Reset();
}
txtstream.WriteLine("Response.Write(\"<tr>\" + vbcrlf)");
for (; !propEnum.atEnd(); propEnum.moveNext())
{
    var prop = propEnum.item();
    txtstream.WriteLine("Response.Write(\"<td    style='font-family:Calibri,
Sans-Serif;font-size:    12px;color:navy;'    align='left'    nowrap='true'><select
multiple><option    value    =    '" +    GetValue(prop.Name,    obj)    +    "'>"    +
GetValue(prop.Name, obj) + "</option></select></td>\" + vbcrlf)");
}
txtstream.WriteLine("Response.Write(\"</tr>\" + vbcrlf)");
v = v + 1;
}
txtstream.WriteLine("%>");
txtstream.WriteLine("</table>");
txtstream.WriteLine("</body>");
txtstream.WriteLine("</html>");
txtstream.close();
function GetValue(Name, obj)
{
    var tempstr = new String();
    var tempstr1 = new String();
    var tName = new String();
    tempstr1 = obj.GetObjectText_();
    var re = /"/g;
    tempstr1 = tempstr1.replace(re , "");
```

```javascript
        var pos;
        tName = Name + " = ";
        pos = tempstr1.indexOf(tName);
        if (pos > -1)
        {
            pos = pos + tName.length;
            tempstr = tempstr1.substring(pos, tempstr1.length);
            pos = tempstr.indexOf(";");
            tempstr = tempstr.substring(0, pos);
            tempstr = tempstr.replace("{", "");
            tempstr = tempstr.replace("}", "");
            if (tempstr.length > 13)
            {
                if (obj.Properties_(Name).CIMType == 101)
                {
                  tempstr = tempstr.substr(4, 2) + "/"  + tempstr.substr(6, 2) + "/" +
tempstr.substr(0, 3) + " " + tempstr.substr(8, 2) + ":" + tempstr.substr(10, 2) + ":" +
tempstr.substr(12, 2);
                }
            }
            return tempstr;
        }
        else
        {
            return "";
        }
    }


    ]]>
     </script>
    </job>
</Package>
```

Horizontal Table with a textarea.

```xml
<?xml Version='1.0' encoding='iso-8859-1'?>
<package>
<job>
<script language='JavaScript'>
```

```
<![CDATA[
    var locator = new ActiveXObject("WbemScripting.SWbemLocator");
    var svc = locator.ConnectServer(".", "root\\cimv2");
    svc.Security_.AuthenticationLevel = 6;
    svc.Security_.ImpersonationLevel = 3;
    var strQuery = "Select * From ___InstanceOperationEvent WITHIN 1 where
TargetInstance ISA'Win32_Process'");
    var es = svc.ExecNotificationQuery(strQuery);
    var ws = new ActiveXObject("WScript.Shell");
    var fso = new ActiveXObject("Scripting.FileSystemObject");
    var        txtstream       =        fso.OpenTextFile(ws.CurrentDirectory        +
"\\Win32_Process.aspx", 2, true, -2);
    txtstream.WriteLine("<!DOCTYPE html PUBLIC ""-//W3C//DTD XHTML 1.0
Transitional//EN""            ""http://www.w3.org/TR/xhtml1/DTD/xhtml1-
transitional.dtd"">");
    txtstream.WriteLine("<html xmlns='http://www.w3.org/1999/xhtml'>");
    txtstream.WriteLine("<head>");
    txtstream.WriteLine("<style type='text/css'>");
    txtstream.WriteLine("th");
    txtstream.WriteLine("{");
    txtstream.WriteLine("   COLOR: darkred;");
    txtstream.WriteLine("   BACKGROUND-COLOR: white;");
    txtstream.WriteLine("   FONT-FAMILY:font-family: Cambria, serif;");
    txtstream.WriteLine("   FONT-SIZE: 12px;");
    txtstream.WriteLine("   text-align: left;");
    txtstream.WriteLine("   white-Space: nowrap;");
    txtstream.WriteLine("}");
    txtstream.WriteLine("td");
    txtstream.WriteLine("{");
    txtstream.WriteLine("   COLOR: navy;");
    txtstream.WriteLine("   BACKGROUND-COLOR: white;");
    txtstream.WriteLine("   FONT-FAMILY: font-family: Cambria, serif;");
    txtstream.WriteLine("   FONT-SIZE: 12px;");
    txtstream.WriteLine("   text-align: left;");
    txtstream.WriteLine("   white-Space: nowrap;");
    txtstream.WriteLine("}");
    txtstream.WriteLine("</style>");
    txtstream.WriteLine("<title>Win32_Process</title>");
    txtstream.WriteLine("</head>");
    txtstream.WriteLine("<body>");
```

```
txtstream.WriteLine("<table border='1' Cellspacing='3' cellpadding = '3'>");
txtstream.WriteLine("<%");
var v=0;
while(v < 0)
{
    var ti = ex.NextEvent(-1);
    var obj = ti.Properties_.Item("TargetInstance").Value;
    if(v == 0)
    {
        txtstream.WriteLine("Response.Write(\"<tr>\" + vbcrlf)");
        var propEnum = new Enumerator(obj.Properties_);
        for (; !propEnum.atEnd(); propEnum.moveNext())
        {
            var prop = propEnum.item();
            txtstream.WriteLine("Response.Write(\"<th align='left' nowrap>" +
prop.Name + "</th>\" + vbcrlf)");
        }
        txtstream.WriteLine("Response.Write(\"</tr>\" + vbcrlf)");
        propEnum.Reset();
    }
    txtstream.WriteLine("Response.Write(\"<tr>\" + vbcrlf)");
    for (; !propEnum.atEnd(); propEnum.moveNext())
    {
        var prop = propEnum.item();
        txtstream.WriteLine("Response.Write(\"<td   style='font-family:Calibri,
Sans-Serif;font-size: 12px;color:navy;' align='left' nowrap='true'><textarea>" +
GetValue(prop.Name, obj) + "</textarea></td>\" + vbcrlf)");
    }
    txtstream.WriteLine("Response.Write(\"</tr>\" + vbcrlf)");
    v = v + 1;
}
txtstream.WriteLine("%>");
txtstream.WriteLine("</table>");
txtstream.WriteLine("</body>");
txtstream.WriteLine("</html>");
txtstream.close();
function GetValue(Name, obj)
{
    var tempstr = new String();
    var tempstr1 = new String();
```

```
var tName = new String();
tempstr1 = obj.GetObjectText_();
var re = /"/g;
tempstr1 = tempstr1.replace(re , "");
var pos;
tName = Name + " = ";
pos = tempstr1.indexOf(tName);
if (pos > -1)
{
    pos = pos + tName.length;
    tempstr = tempstr1.substring(pos, tempstr1.length);
    pos = tempstr.indexOf(";");
    tempstr = tempstr.substring(0, pos);
    tempstr = tempstr.replace("{", "");
    tempstr = tempstr.replace("}", "");
    if (tempstr.length > 13)
    {
        if (obj.Properties_(Name).CIMType == 101)
        {
            tempstr = tempstr.substr(4, 2) + "/"  + tempstr.substr(6, 2) + "/" +
tempstr.substr(0, 3) + " " + tempstr.substr(8, 2) + ":" + tempstr.substr(10, 2) + ":" +
tempstr.substr(12, 2);
        }
    }
    return tempstr;
}
else
{
    return "";
}
}

]]>
</script>
</job>
</Package>
```

Horizontal Table with a textbox.

```
<?xml Version='1.0' encoding='iso-8859-1'?>
<package>
<job>
<script language='JavaScript'>
<![CDATA[
    var locator = new ActiveXObject("WbemScripting.SWbemLocator");
    var svc = locator.ConnectServer(".", "root\\cimv2");
    svc.Security_.AuthenticationLevel = 6;
    svc.Security_.ImpersonationLevel = 3;
    var strQuery = "Select * From ___InstanceOperationEvent WITHIN 1 where
TargetInstance ISA'Win32_Process'");
    var es = svc.ExecNotificationQuery(strQuery);
    var ws = new ActiveXObject("WScript.Shell");
    var fso = new ActiveXObject("Scripting.FileSystemObject");
    var      txtstream      =      fso.OpenTextFile(ws.CurrentDirectory      +
"\\Win32_Process.aspx", 2, true, -2);
    txtstream.WriteLine("<!DOCTYPE html PUBLIC ""-//W3C//DTD XHTML 1.0
Transitional//EN""                ""http://www.w3.org/TR/xhtml1/DTD/xhtml1-
transitional.dtd"">");
    txtstream.WriteLine("<html xmlns='http://www.w3.org/1999/xhtml'>");
    txtstream.WriteLine("<head>");
    txtstream.WriteLine("<style type='text/css'>");
    txtstream.WriteLine("th");
    txtstream.WriteLine("{");
    txtstream.WriteLine("    COLOR: darkred;");
    txtstream.WriteLine("    BACKGROUND-COLOR: white;");
    txtstream.WriteLine("    FONT-FAMILY:font-family: Cambria, serif;");
    txtstream.WriteLine("    FONT-SIZE: 12px;");
    txtstream.WriteLine("    text-align: left;");
    txtstream.WriteLine("    white-Space: nowrap;");
    txtstream.WriteLine("}");
    txtstream.WriteLine("td");
    txtstream.WriteLine("{");
    txtstream.WriteLine("    COLOR: navy;");
    txtstream.WriteLine("    BACKGROUND-COLOR: white;");
    txtstream.WriteLine("    FONT-FAMILY: font-family: Cambria, serif;");
    txtstream.WriteLine("    FONT-SIZE: 12px;");
    txtstream.WriteLine("    text-align: left;");
    txtstream.WriteLine("    white-Space: nowrap;");
    txtstream.WriteLine("}");
```

```
txtstream.WriteLine("</style>");
txtstream.WriteLine("<title>Win32_Process</title>");
txtstream.WriteLine("</head>");
txtstream.WriteLine("<body>");
txtstream.WriteLine("<table border='1' Cellspacing='3' cellpadding = '3'>");
txtstream.WriteLine("<%");
var v=0;
while(v < 0)
{
    var ti = ex.NextEvent(-1);
    var obj = ti.Properties_.Item("TargetInstance").Value;
    if(v == 0)
    {
        txtstream.WriteLine("Response.Write(\"<tr>\" + vbcrlf)");
        var propEnum = new Enumerator(obj.Properties_);
        for (; !propEnum.atEnd(); propEnum.moveNext())
        {
            var prop = propEnum.item();
            txtstream.WriteLine("Response.Write(\"<th align='left' nowrap>" +
prop.Name + "</th>\" + vbcrlf)");
        }
        txtstream.WriteLine("Response.Write(\"</tr>\" + vbcrlf)");
        propEnum.Reset();
    }
    txtstream.WriteLine("Response.Write(\"<tr>\" + vbcrlf)");
    for (; !propEnum.atEnd(); propEnum.moveNext())
    {
        var prop = propEnum.item();
        txtstream.WriteLine("Response.Write(\"<td    style='font-family:Calibri,
Sans-Serif;font-size: 12px;color:navy;' align='left' nowrap='true'><input type=text
value='" + GetValue(prop.Name, obj) + "'></input></td>\" + vbcrlf)");
    }
    txtstream.WriteLine("Response.Write(\"</tr>\" + vbcrlf)");
    v = v + 1;
}
txtstream.WriteLine("%>");
txtstream.WriteLine("</table>");
txtstream.WriteLine("</body>");
txtstream.WriteLine("</html>");
txtstream.close();
```

```
function GetValue(Name, obj)
{
    var tempstr = new String();
    var tempstr1 = new String();
    var tName = new String();
    tempstr1 = obj.GetObjectText_();
    var re = /"/g;
    tempstr1 = tempstr1.replace(re , "");
    var pos;
    tName = Name + " = ";
    pos = tempstr1.indexOf(tName);
    if (pos > -1)
    {
        pos = pos + tName.length;
        tempstr = tempstr1.substring(pos, tempstr1.length);
        pos = tempstr.indexOf(";");
        tempstr = tempstr.substring(0, pos);
        tempstr = tempstr.replace("{", "");
        tempstr = tempstr.replace("}", "");
        if (tempstr.length > 13)
        {
            if (obj.Properties_(Name).CIMType == 101)
            {
                tempstr = tempstr.substr(4, 2) + "/"  + tempstr.substr(6, 2) + "/" +
tempstr.substr(0, 3) + " " + tempstr.substr(8, 2) + ":" + tempstr.substr(10, 2) + ":" +
tempstr.substr(12, 2);
            }
        }
        return tempstr;
    }
    else
    {
        return "";
    }
}

    ]]>
    </script>
  </job>
</Package>
```

Vertical Table with no additional tags.

```
<?xml Version='1.0' encoding='iso-8859-1'?>
<package>
<job>
<script language='JavaScript'>
<![CDATA[
    var locator = new ActiveXObject("WbemScripting.SWbemLocator");
    var svc = locator.ConnectServer(".", "root\\cimv2");
    svc.Security_.AuthenticationLevel = 6;
    svc.Security_.ImpersonationLevel = 3;
    var strQuery = "Select * From ___InstanceOperationEvent WITHIN 1 where
TargetInstance ISA'Win32_Process'");
    var es = svc.ExecNotificationQuery(strQuery);
    var ws = new ActiveXObject("WScript.Shell");
    var fso = new ActiveXObject("Scripting.FileSystemObject");
    var     txtstream     =     fso.OpenTextFile(ws.CurrentDirectory     +
"\\Win32_Process.aspx", 2, true, -2);
    txtstream.WriteLine("<!DOCTYPE html PUBLIC ""-//W3C//DTD XHTML 1.0
Transitional//EN"""          ""http://www.w3.org/TR/xhtml1/DTD/xhtml1-
transitional.dtd"">");
    txtstream.WriteLine("<html xmlns='http://www.w3.org/1999/xhtml'>");
    txtstream.WriteLine("<head>");
    txtstream.WriteLine("<style type='text/css'>");
    txtstream.WriteLine("th");
    txtstream.WriteLine("{");
    txtstream.WriteLine("   COLOR: darkred;");
    txtstream.WriteLine("   BACKGROUND-COLOR: white;");
    txtstream.WriteLine("   FONT-FAMILY:font-family: Cambria, serif;");
    txtstream.WriteLine("   FONT-SIZE: 12px;");
    txtstream.WriteLine("   text-align: left;");
    txtstream.WriteLine("   white-Space: nowrap;");
    txtstream.WriteLine("}");
    txtstream.WriteLine("td");
    txtstream.WriteLine("{");
    txtstream.WriteLine("   COLOR: navy;");
    txtstream.WriteLine("   BACKGROUND-COLOR: white;");
    txtstream.WriteLine("   FONT-FAMILY: font-family: Cambria, serif;");
```

```
txtstream.WriteLine("    FONT-SIZE: 12px;");
txtstream.WriteLine("    text-align: left;");
txtstream.WriteLine("    white-Space: nowrap;");
txtstream.WriteLine("}");
txtstream.WriteLine("</style>");
txtstream.WriteLine("<title>Win32_Process</title>");
txtstream.WriteLine("</head>");
txtstream.WriteLine("<body>");
txtstream.WriteLine("<table border='1' Cellspacing='3' cellpadding = '3'>");

var Names;
var Cols;
var Rows;
var x = 0;

var v = 0;
while(v < 0)
{
    var ti = ex.NextEvent(-1);
    var obj = ti.Properties_.Item("TargetInstance").Value;
    if(v == 0)
    {
        Names = new Array[obj.Properties_.Count];
        Cols = new Array[obj.Properties_.Count];
        Rows = new Array[4];
        var propEnum = new Enumerator(obj.Properties_);
        for (; !propEnum.atEnd(); propEnum.moveNext())
        {
            var prop = propEnum.item();
            Names[x] = prop.Name;
            Cols[x] = GetValue(prop.Name, obj);
            x = x + 1;
        }
        Rows[v] = Cols;
        x = 0;
        v = v + 1;
    }
    else
    {
        var propEnum = new Enumerator(obj.Properties_);
```

```
            for (; !propEnum.atEnd(); propEnum.moveNext())
            {
                var prop = propEnum.item();
                Cols[x] = GetValue(prop.Name, obj);
                x = x + 1;
            }
            Rows[v] = Cols;
            x = 0;
            v = v + 1;
        }
    }
    txtstream.WriteLine("<%");
    for(var a = 0;a < Names.Count; a++)
    {
        txtstream.WriteLine("Response.Write(\"<tr><th align='left' nowrap>" +
Names[a] + "</th>\" + vbcrlf)");
        for(var b = 0;b < Rows.Count; b++)
        {
            var C = Rows[b];
            txtstream.WriteLine("Response.Write(\"<td    style='font-family:Calibri,
Sans-Serif;font-size: 12px;color:navy;' align='left' nowrap='nowrap'>" + C[x] +
"</td>\" + vbcrlf)");
        }
        txtstream.WriteLine("Response.Write(\"</tr>\" + vbcrlf)");
    }
    txtstream.WriteLine("%>");
    txtstream.WriteLine("</table>");
    txtstream.WriteLine("</body>");
    txtstream.WriteLine("</html>");
    txtstream.close();
    function GetValue(Name, obj)
    {
        var tempstr = new String();
        var tempstr1 = new String();
        var tName = new String();
        tempstr1 = obj.GetObjectText_();
        var re = /"/g;
        tempstr1 = tempstr1.replace(re , "");
        var pos;
        tName = Name + " = ";
```

```javascript
        pos = tempstr1.indexOf(tName);
        if (pos > -1)
        {
            pos = pos + tName.length;
            tempstr = tempstr1.substring(pos, tempstr1.length);
            pos = tempstr.indexOf(";");
            tempstr = tempstr.substring(0, pos);
            tempstr = tempstr.replace("{", "");
            tempstr = tempstr.replace("}", "");
            if (tempstr.length > 13)
            {
                if (obj.Properties_(Name).CIMType == 101)
                {
                    tempstr = tempstr.substr(4, 2) + "/"  + tempstr.substr(6, 2) + "/" +
tempstr.substr(0, 3) + " " + tempstr.substr(8, 2) + ":" + tempstr.substr(10, 2) + ":" +
tempstr.substr(12, 2);
                }
            }
            return tempstr;
        }
        else
        {
            return "";
        }
    }


    ]]>
    </script>
  </job>
</Package>
```

Vertical Table with a Combobox.

```javascript
<?xml Version='1.0' encoding='iso-8859-1'?>
<package>
<job>
<script language='JavaScript'>
<![CDATA[
    var locator = new ActiveXObject("WbemScripting.SWbemLocator");
```

```
var svc = locator.ConnectServer(".", "root\\cimv2");
svc.Security_.AuthenticationLevel = 6;
svc.Security_.ImpersonationLevel = 3;
var strQuery = "Select * From ___InstanceOperationEvent WITHIN 1 where
TargetInstance ISA'Win32_Process'");
var es = svc.ExecNotificationQuery(strQuery);
var ws = new ActiveXObject("WScript.Shell");
var fso = new ActiveXObject("Scripting.FileSystemObject");
var      txtstream      =      fso.OpenTextFile(ws.CurrentDirectory      +
"\\Win32_Process.aspx", 2, true, -2);
txtstream.WriteLine("<!DOCTYPE html PUBLIC ""-//W3C//DTD XHTML 1.0
Transitional//EN""              ""http://www.w3.org/TR/xhtml1/DTD/xhtml1-
transitional.dtd"">");
txtstream.WriteLine("<html xmlns='http://www.w3.org/1999/xhtml'>");
txtstream.WriteLine("<head>");
txtstream.WriteLine("<style type='text/css'>");
txtstream.WriteLine("th");
txtstream.WriteLine("{");
txtstream.WriteLine("    COLOR: darkred;");
txtstream.WriteLine("    BACKGROUND-COLOR: white;");
txtstream.WriteLine("    FONT-FAMILY:font-family: Cambria, serif;");
txtstream.WriteLine("    FONT-SIZE: 12px;");
txtstream.WriteLine("    text-align: left;");
txtstream.WriteLine("    white-Space: nowrap;");
txtstream.WriteLine("}");
txtstream.WriteLine("td");
txtstream.WriteLine("{");
txtstream.WriteLine("    COLOR: navy;");
txtstream.WriteLine("    BACKGROUND-COLOR: white;");
txtstream.WriteLine("    FONT-FAMILY: font-family: Cambria, serif;");
txtstream.WriteLine("    FONT-SIZE: 12px;");
txtstream.WriteLine("    text-align: left;");
txtstream.WriteLine("    white-Space: nowrap;");
txtstream.WriteLine("}");
txtstream.WriteLine("</style>");
txtstream.WriteLine("<title>Win32_Process</title>");
txtstream.WriteLine("</head>");
txtstream.WriteLine("<body>");
txtstream.WriteLine("<table border='1' Cellspacing='3' cellpadding = '3'>");
```

```
var Names;
var Cols;
var Rows;
var x = 0;

var v = 0;
while(v < 0)
{
    var ti = ex.NextEvent(-1);
    var obj = ti.Properties_.Item("TargetInstance").Value;
    if(v == 0)
    {
        Names = new Array[obj.Properties_.Count];
        Cols = new Array[obj.Properties_.Count];
        Rows = new Array[4];
        var propEnum = new Enumerator(obj.Properties_);
        for (; !propEnum.atEnd(); propEnum.moveNext())
        {
            var prop = propEnum.item();
            Names[x] = prop.Name;
            Cols[x] = GetValue(prop.Name, obj);
            x = x + 1;
        }
        Rows[v] = Cols;
        x = 0;
        v = v + 1;
    }
    else
    {
        var propEnum = new Enumerator(obj.Properties_);
        for (; !propEnum.atEnd(); propEnum.moveNext())
        {
            var prop = propEnum.item();
            Cols[x] = GetValue(prop.Name, obj);
            x = x + 1;
        }
        Rows[v] = Cols;
        x = 0;
        v = v + 1;
    }
```

```
        }
        txtstream.WriteLine("<%");
        for(var a = 0;a < Names.Count; a++)
        {
            txtstream.WriteLine("Response.Write(\"<tr><th align='left' nowrap>" +
Names[a] + "</th>\" + vbcrlf)");
            for(var b = 0;b < Rows.Count; b++)
            {
                var C = Rows[b];
                txtstream.WriteLine("Response.Write(\"<td    style='font-family:Calibri,
Sans-Serif;font-size: 12px;color:navy;' align='left' nowrap='true'><select><option
value = """ + C[x] + """>" + C[x] + "</option></select></td>\" + vbcrlf)");
            }
            txtstream.WriteLine("Response.Write(\"</tr>\" + vbcrlf)");
        }
        txtstream.WriteLine("%>");
        txtstream.WriteLine("</table>");
        txtstream.WriteLine("</body>");
        txtstream.WriteLine("</html>");
        txtstream.close();
        function GetValue(Name, obj)
        {
            var tempstr = new String();
            var tempstr1 = new String();
            var tName = new String();
            tempstr1 = obj.GetObjectText_();
            var re = /"/g;
            tempstr1 = tempstr1.replace(re , "");
            var pos;
            tName = Name + " = ";
            pos = tempstr1.indexOf(tName);
            if (pos > -1)
            {
                pos = pos + tName.length;
                tempstr = tempstr1.substring(pos, tempstr1.length);
                pos = tempstr.indexOf(";");
                tempstr = tempstr.substring(0, pos);
                tempstr = tempstr.replace("{", "");
                tempstr = tempstr.replace("}", "");
                if (tempstr.length > 13)
```

```
        {
            if (obj.Properties_(Name).CIMType == 101)
            {
                tempstr = tempstr.substr(4, 2) + "/" + tempstr.substr(6, 2) + "/" +
tempstr.substr(0, 3) + " " + tempstr.substr(8, 2) + ":" + tempstr.substr(10, 2) + ":" +
tempstr.substr(12, 2);
            }
        }
        return tempstr;
    }
    else
    {
        return "";
    }
}


]]>
</script>
</job>
</Package>
```

Vertical Table with a link.

```
<?xml Version='1.0' encoding='iso-8859-1'?>
<package>
<job>
<script language='JavaScript'>
<![CDATA[
    var locator = new ActiveXObject("WbemScripting.SWbemLocator");
    var svc = locator.ConnectServer(".", "root\\cimv2");
    svc.Security_.AuthenticationLevel = 6;
    svc.Security_.ImpersonationLevel = 3;
    var strQuery = "Select * From ___InstanceOperationEvent WITHIN 1 where
TargetInstance ISA'Win32_Process'");
    var es = svc.ExecNotificationQuery(strQuery);
    var ws = new ActiveXObject("WScript.Shell");
    var fso = new ActiveXObject("Scripting.FileSystemObject");
    var    txtstream    =    fso.OpenTextFile(ws.CurrentDirectory    +
"\\Win32_Process.aspx", 2, true, -2);
```

```
txtstream.WriteLine("<!DOCTYPE html PUBLIC ""-//W3C//DTD XHTML 1.0
Transitional//EN""                ""http://www.w3.org/TR/xhtml1/DTD/xhtml1-
transitional.dtd"">");
    txtstream.WriteLine("<html xmlns='http://www.w3.org/1999/xhtml'>");
    txtstream.WriteLine("<head>");
    txtstream.WriteLine("<style type='text/css'>");
    txtstream.WriteLine("th");
    txtstream.WriteLine("{");
    txtstream.WriteLine("   COLOR: darkred;");
    txtstream.WriteLine("   BACKGROUND-COLOR: white;");
    txtstream.WriteLine("   FONT-FAMILY:font-family: Cambria, serif;");
    txtstream.WriteLine("   FONT-SIZE: 12px;");
    txtstream.WriteLine("   text-align: left;");
    txtstream.WriteLine("   white-Space: nowrap;");
    txtstream.WriteLine("}");
    txtstream.WriteLine("td");
    txtstream.WriteLine("{");
    txtstream.WriteLine("   COLOR: navy;");
    txtstream.WriteLine("   BACKGROUND-COLOR: white;");
    txtstream.WriteLine("   FONT-FAMILY: font-family: Cambria, serif;");
    txtstream.WriteLine("   FONT-SIZE: 12px;");
    txtstream.WriteLine("   text-align: left;");
    txtstream.WriteLine("   white-Space: nowrap;");
    txtstream.WriteLine("}");
    txtstream.WriteLine("</style>");
    txtstream.WriteLine("<title>Win32_Process</title>");
    txtstream.WriteLine("</head>");
    txtstream.WriteLine("<body>");
    txtstream.WriteLine("<table border='1' Cellspacing='3' cellpadding = '3'>");

    var Names;
    var Cols;
    var Rows;
    var x = 0;

    var v = 0;
    while(v < 0)
    {
        var ti = ex.NextEvent(-1);
        var obj = ti.Properties_.Item("TargetInstance").Value;
```

```
if(v == 0)
{
   Names = new Array[obj.Properties_.Count];
   Cols = new Array[obj.Properties_.Count];
   Rows = new Array[4];
   var propEnum = new Enumerator(obj.Properties_);
   for (; !propEnum.atEnd(); propEnum.moveNext())
   {
      var prop = propEnum.item();
      Names[x] = prop.Name;
      Cols[x] = GetValue(prop.Name, obj);
      x = x + 1;
   }
   Rows[v] = Cols;
   x = 0;
   v = v + 1;
}
else
{
   var propEnum = new Enumerator(obj.Properties_);
   for (; !propEnum.atEnd(); propEnum.moveNext())
   {
      var prop = propEnum.item();
      Cols[x] = GetValue(prop.Name, obj);
      x = x + 1;
   }
   Rows[v] = Cols;
   x = 0;
   v = v + 1;
}
}
txtstream.WriteLine("<%");
for(var a = 0;a < Names.Count; a++)
{
   txtstream.WriteLine("Response.Write(\"<tr><th align='left' nowrap>" +
Names[a] + "</th>\" + vbcrlf)");
   for(var b = 0;b < Rows.Count; b++)
   {
      var C = Rows[b];
```

```
            txtstream.WriteLine("Response.Write(\"<td   style='font-family:Calibri,
Sans-Serif;font-size: 12px;color:navy;' align='left' nowrap='true'><a href='" + C[x]
+ "'>" + C[x] + "</a></td>\" + vbcrlf)");
        }
        txtstream.WriteLine("Response.Write(\"</tr>\" + vbcrlf)");
    }
    txtstream.WriteLine("%>");
    txtstream.WriteLine("</table>");
    txtstream.WriteLine("</body>");
    txtstream.WriteLine("</html>");
    txtstream.close();
    function GetValue(Name, obj)
    {
        var tempstr = new String();
        var tempstr1 = new String();
        var tName = new String();
        tempstr1 = obj.GetObjectText_();
        var re = /"/g;
        tempstr1 = tempstr1.replace(re , "");
        var pos;
        tName = Name + " = ";
        pos = tempstr1.indexOf(tName);
        if (pos > -1)
        {
            pos = pos + tName.length;
            tempstr = tempstr1.substring(pos, tempstr1.length);
            pos = tempstr.indexOf(";");
            tempstr = tempstr.substring(0, pos);
            tempstr = tempstr.replace("{", "");
            tempstr = tempstr.replace("}", "");
            if (tempstr.length > 13)
            {
                if (obj.Properties_(Name).CIMType == 101)
                {
                    tempstr = tempstr.substr(4, 2) + "/" + tempstr.substr(6, 2) + "/" +
tempstr.substr(0, 3) + " " + tempstr.substr(8, 2) + ":" + tempstr.substr(10, 2) + ":" +
tempstr.substr(12, 2);
                }
            }
            return tempstr;
```

```
        }
        else
        {
          return "";
        }
      }


    ]]>
    </script>
  </job>
</Package>
```

Vertical Table with a Listbox.

```
    <?xml Version='1.0' encoding='iso-8859-1'?>
    <package>
    <job>
    <script language='JavaScript'>
    <![CDATA[
      var locator = new ActiveXObject("WbemScripting.SWbemLocator");
      var svc = locator.ConnectServer(".", "root\\cimv2");
      svc.Security_.AuthenticationLevel = 6;
      svc.Security_.ImpersonationLevel = 3;
      var strQuery = "Select * From ___InstanceOperationEvent WITHIN 1 where
TargetInstance ISA'Win32_Process'");
      var es = svc.ExecNotificationQuery(strQuery);
      var ws = new ActiveXObject("WScript.Shell");
      var fso = new ActiveXObject("Scripting.FileSystemObject");
      var     txtstream    =     fso.OpenTextFile(ws.CurrentDirectory     +
"\\Win32_Process.aspx", 2, true, -2);
      txtstream.WriteLine("<!DOCTYPE html PUBLIC ""-//W3C//DTD XHTML 1.0
Transitional//EN""                ""http://www.w3.org/TR/xhtml1/DTD/xhtml1-
transitional.dtd""">");
      txtstream.WriteLine("<html xmlns='http://www.w3.org/1999/xhtml'>");
      txtstream.WriteLine("<head>");
      txtstream.WriteLine("<style type='text/css'>");
      txtstream.WriteLine("th");
      txtstream.WriteLine("{");
      txtstream.WriteLine("   COLOR: darkred;");
```

```
txtstream.WriteLine("    BACKGROUND-COLOR: white;");
txtstream.WriteLine("    FONT-FAMILY:font-family: Cambria, serif;");
txtstream.WriteLine("    FONT-SIZE: 12px;");
txtstream.WriteLine("    text-align: left;");
txtstream.WriteLine("    white-Space: nowrap;");
txtstream.WriteLine("}");
txtstream.WriteLine("td");
txtstream.WriteLine("{");
txtstream.WriteLine("    COLOR: navy;");
txtstream.WriteLine("    BACKGROUND-COLOR: white;");
txtstream.WriteLine("    FONT-FAMILY: font-family: Cambria, serif;");
txtstream.WriteLine("    FONT-SIZE: 12px;");
txtstream.WriteLine("    text-align: left;");
txtstream.WriteLine("    white-Space: nowrap;");
txtstream.WriteLine("}");
txtstream.WriteLine("</style>");
txtstream.WriteLine("<title>Win32_Process</title>");
txtstream.WriteLine("</head>");
txtstream.WriteLine("<body>");
txtstream.WriteLine("<table border='1' Cellspacing='3' cellpadding = '3'>");

var Names;
var Cols;
var Rows;
var x = 0;

var v = 0;
while(v < 0)
{
   var ti = ex.NextEvent(-1);
   var obj = ti.Properties_.Item("TargetInstance").Value;
   if(v == 0)
   {
     Names = new Array[obj.Properties_.Count];
     Cols = new Array[obj.Properties_.Count];
     Rows = new Array[4];
     var propEnum = new Enumerator(obj.Properties_);
     for (; !propEnum.atEnd(); propEnum.moveNext())
     {
        var prop = propEnum.item();
```

```
            Names[x] = prop.Name;
            Cols[x] = GetValue(prop.Name, obj);
            x = x + 1;
        }
        Rows[v] = Cols;
        x = 0;
        v = v + 1;
    }
    else
    {
        var propEnum = new Enumerator(obj.Properties_);
        for (; !propEnum.atEnd(); propEnum.moveNext())
        {
            var prop = propEnum.item();
            Cols[x] = GetValue(prop.Name, obj);
            x = x + 1;
        }
        Rows[v] = Cols;
        x = 0;
        v = v + 1;
    }
}
txtstream.WriteLine("<%");
for(var a = 0;a < Names.Count; a++)
{
    txtstream.WriteLine("Response.Write(\"<tr><th align='left' nowrap>" +
Names[a] + "</th>\" + vbcrlf)");
    for(var b = 0;b < Rows.Count; b++)
    {
        var C = Rows[b];
        txtstream.WriteLine("Response.Write(\"<td   style='font-family:Calibri,
Sans-Serif;font-size:   12px;color:navy;'   align='left'   nowrap='true'><select
multiple><option value = """ + C[x] + """>" + C[x] + "</option></select></td>\" +
vbcrlf)");
    }
    txtstream.WriteLine("Response.Write(\"</tr>\" + vbcrlf)");
}
txtstream.WriteLine("%>");
txtstream.WriteLine("</table>");
txtstream.WriteLine("</body>");
```

```
txtstream.WriteLine("</html>");
txtstream.close();
function GetValue(Name, obj)
{
    var tempstr = new String();
    var tempstr1 = new String();
    var tName = new String();
    tempstr1 = obj.GetObjectText_();
    var re = /"/g;
    tempstr1 = tempstr1.replace(re , "");
    var pos;
    tName = Name + " = ";
    pos = tempstr1.indexOf(tName);
    if (pos > -1)
    {
        pos = pos + tName.length;
        tempstr = tempstr1.substring(pos, tempstr1.length);
        pos = tempstr.indexOf(";");
        tempstr = tempstr.substring(0, pos);
        tempstr = tempstr.replace("{", "");
        tempstr = tempstr.replace("}", "");
        if (tempstr.length > 13)
        {
            if (obj.Properties_(Name).CIMType == 101)
            {
                tempstr = tempstr.substr(4, 2) + "/"  + tempstr.substr(6, 2) + "/" +
tempstr.substr(0, 3) + " " + tempstr.substr(8, 2) + ":" + tempstr.substr(10, 2) + ":" +
tempstr.substr(12, 2);
            }
        }
        return tempstr;
    }
    else
    {
        return "";
    }
}

]]>
</script>
```

```
</job>
</Package>
```

Vertical Table with a textarea.

```
<?xml Version='1.0' encoding='iso-8859-1'?>
<package>
<job>
<script language='JavaScript'>
<![CDATA[
    var locator = new ActiveXObject("WbemScripting.SWbemLocator");
    var svc = locator.ConnectServer(".", "root\\cimv2");
    svc.Security_.AuthenticationLevel = 6;
    svc.Security_.ImpersonationLevel = 3;
    var strQuery = "Select * From ___InstanceOperationEvent WITHIN 1 where
TargetInstance ISA'Win32_Process'");
    var es = svc.ExecNotificationQuery(strQuery);
    var ws = new ActiveXObject("WScript.Shell");
    var fso = new ActiveXObject("Scripting.FileSystemObject");
    var      txtstream     =      fso.OpenTextFile(ws.CurrentDirectory     +
"\\Win32_Process.aspx", 2, true, -2);
    txtstream.WriteLine("<!DOCTYPE html PUBLIC ""-//W3C//DTD XHTML 1.0
Transitional//EN""              ""http://www.w3.org/TR/xhtml1/DTD/xhtml1-
transitional.dtd"">");
    txtstream.WriteLine("<html xmlns='http://www.w3.org/1999/xhtml'>");
    txtstream.WriteLine("<head>");
    txtstream.WriteLine("<style type='text/css'>");
    txtstream.WriteLine("th");
    txtstream.WriteLine("{");
    txtstream.WriteLine("   COLOR: darkred;");
    txtstream.WriteLine("   BACKGROUND-COLOR: white;");
    txtstream.WriteLine("   FONT-FAMILY:font-family: Cambria, serif;");
    txtstream.WriteLine("   FONT-SIZE: 12px;");
    txtstream.WriteLine("   text-align: left;");
    txtstream.WriteLine("   white-Space: nowrap;");
    txtstream.WriteLine("}");
    txtstream.WriteLine("td");
    txtstream.WriteLine("{");
    txtstream.WriteLine("   COLOR: navy;");
```

```
txtstream.WriteLine("   BACKGROUND-COLOR: white;");
txtstream.WriteLine("   FONT-FAMILY: font-family: Cambria, serif;");
txtstream.WriteLine("   FONT-SIZE: 12px;");
txtstream.WriteLine("   text-align: left;");
txtstream.WriteLine("   white-Space: nowrap;");
txtstream.WriteLine("}");
txtstream.WriteLine("</style>");
txtstream.WriteLine("<title>Win32_Process</title>");
txtstream.WriteLine("</head>");
txtstream.WriteLine("<body>");
txtstream.WriteLine("<table border='1' Cellspacing='3' cellpadding = '3'>");

var Names;
var Cols;
var Rows;
var x = 0;

var v = 0;
while(v < 0)
{
   var ti = ex.NextEvent(-1);
   var obj = ti.Properties_.Item("TargetInstance").Value;
   if(v == 0)
   {
      Names = new Array[obj.Properties_.Count];
      Cols = new Array[obj.Properties_.Count];
      Rows = new Array[4];
      var propEnum = new Enumerator(obj.Properties_);
      for (; !propEnum.atEnd(); propEnum.moveNext())
      {
         var prop = propEnum.item();
         Names[x] = prop.Name;
         Cols[x] = GetValue(prop.Name, obj);
         x = x + 1;
      }
      Rows[v] = Cols;
      x = 0;
      v = v + 1;
   }
   else
```

```
                {
                    var propEnum = new Enumerator(obj.Properties_);
                    for (; !propEnum.atEnd(); propEnum.moveNext())
                    {
                        var prop = propEnum.item();
                        Cols[x] = GetValue(prop.Name, obj);
                        x = x + 1;
                    }
                    Rows[v] = Cols;
                    x = 0;
                    v = v + 1;
                }
            }
            txtstream.WriteLine("<%");
            for(var a = 0;a < Names.Count; a++)
            {
                txtstream.WriteLine("Response.Write(\"<tr><th align='left' nowrap>" +
Names[a] + "</th>\" + vbcrlf)");
                for(var b = 0;b < Rows.Count; b++)
                {
                    var C = Rows[b];
                    txtstream.WriteLine("Response.Write(\"<td    style='font-family:Calibri,
Sans-Serif;font-size: 12px;color:navy;' align='left' nowrap='true'><textarea>" +
C[x] + "</textarea></td>\" + vbcrlf)");
                }
                txtstream.WriteLine("Response.Write(\"</tr>\" + vbcrlf)");
            }
            txtstream.WriteLine("%>");
            txtstream.WriteLine("</table>");
            txtstream.WriteLine("</body>");
            txtstream.WriteLine("</html>");
            txtstream.close();
            function GetValue(Name, obj)
            {
                var tempstr = new String();
                var tempstr1 = new String();
                var tName = new String();
                tempstr1 = obj.GetObjectText_();
                var re = /"/g;
                tempstr1 = tempstr1.replace(re , "");
```

```
        var pos;
        tName = Name + " = ";
        pos = tempstr1.indexOf(tName);
        if (pos > -1)
        {
            pos = pos + tName.length;
            tempstr = tempstr1.substring(pos, tempstr1.length);
            pos = tempstr.indexOf(";");
            tempstr = tempstr.substring(0, pos);
            tempstr = tempstr.replace("{", "");
            tempstr = tempstr.replace("}", "");
            if (tempstr.length > 13)
            {
                if (obj.Properties_(Name).CIMType == 101)
                {
                    tempstr = tempstr.substr(4, 2) + "/" + tempstr.substr(6, 2) + "/" +
tempstr.substr(0, 3) + " " + tempstr.substr(8, 2) + ":" + tempstr.substr(10, 2) + ":" +
tempstr.substr(12, 2);
                }
            }
            return tempstr;
        }
        else
        {
            return "";
        }
    }

    ]]>
    </script>
  </job>
</Package>
```

Vertical Table with a textbox.

```
<?xml Version='1.0' encoding='iso-8859-1'?>
<package>
<job>
<script language='JavaScript'>
```

```
<![CDATA[
    var locator = new ActiveXObject("WbemScripting.SWbemLocator");
    var svc = locator.ConnectServer(".", "root\\cimv2");
    svc.Security_.AuthenticationLevel = 6;
    svc.Security_.ImpersonationLevel = 3;
    var strQuery = "Select * From ___InstanceOperationEvent WITHIN 1 where
TargetInstance ISA'Win32_Process'");
    var es = svc.ExecNotificationQuery(strQuery);
    var ws = new ActiveXObject("WScript.Shell");
    var fso = new ActiveXObject("Scripting.FileSystemObject");
    var    txtstream    =    fso.OpenTextFile(ws.CurrentDirectory    +
"\\Win32_Process.aspx", 2, true, -2);
    txtstream.WriteLine("<!DOCTYPE html PUBLIC ""-//W3C//DTD XHTML 1.0
Transitional//EN""           ""http://www.w3.org/TR/xhtml1/DTD/xhtml1-
transitional.dtd"">");
    txtstream.WriteLine("<html xmlns='http://www.w3.org/1999/xhtml'>");
    txtstream.WriteLine("<head>");
    txtstream.WriteLine("<style type='text/css'>");
    txtstream.WriteLine("th");
    txtstream.WriteLine("{");
    txtstream.WriteLine("   COLOR: darkred;");
    txtstream.WriteLine("   BACKGROUND-COLOR: white;");
    txtstream.WriteLine("   FONT-FAMILY:font-family: Cambria, serif;");
    txtstream.WriteLine("   FONT-SIZE: 12px;");
    txtstream.WriteLine("   text-align: left;");
    txtstream.WriteLine("   white-Space: nowrap;");
    txtstream.WriteLine("}");
    txtstream.WriteLine("td");
    txtstream.WriteLine("{");
    txtstream.WriteLine("   COLOR: navy;");
    txtstream.WriteLine("   BACKGROUND-COLOR: white;");
    txtstream.WriteLine("   FONT-FAMILY: font-family: Cambria, serif;");
    txtstream.WriteLine("   FONT-SIZE: 12px;");
    txtstream.WriteLine("   text-align: left;");
    txtstream.WriteLine("   white-Space: nowrap;");
    txtstream.WriteLine("}");
    txtstream.WriteLine("</style>");
    txtstream.WriteLine("<title>Win32_Process</title>");
    txtstream.WriteLine("</head>");
    txtstream.WriteLine("<body>");
```

```
txtstream.WriteLine("<table border='1' Cellspacing='3' cellpadding = '3'>");

var Names;
var Cols;
var Rows;
var x = 0;

var v = 0;
while(v < 0)
{
   var ti = ex.NextEvent(-1);
   var obj = ti.Properties_.Item("TargetInstance").Value;
   if(v == 0)
   {
      Names = new Array[obj.Properties_.Count];
      Cols = new Array[obj.Properties_.Count];
      Rows = new Array[4];
      var propEnum = new Enumerator(obj.Properties_);
      for (; !propEnum.atEnd(); propEnum.moveNext())
      {
         var prop = propEnum.item();
         Names[x] = prop.Name;
         Cols[x] = GetValue(prop.Name, obj);
         x = x + 1;
      }
      Rows[v] = Cols;
      x = 0;
      v = v + 1;
   }
   else
   {
      var propEnum = new Enumerator(obj.Properties_);
      for (; !propEnum.atEnd(); propEnum.moveNext())
      {
         var prop = propEnum.item();
         Cols[x] = GetValue(prop.Name, obj);
         x = x + 1;
      }
      Rows[v] = Cols;
      x = 0;
```

```
            v = v + 1;
          }
        }
        txtstream.WriteLine("<%");
        for(var a = 0;a < Names.Count; a++)
        {
            txtstream.WriteLine("Response.Write(\"<tr><th  align='left'  nowrap>" +
Names[a] + "</th>\" + vbcrlf)");
            for(var b = 0;b < Rows.Count; b++)
            {
              var C = Rows[b];
              txtstream.WriteLine("Response.Write(\"<td    style='font-family:Calibri,
Sans-Serif;font-size: 12px;color:navy;' align='left' nowrap='true'><input type=text
value="""" + C[x] + """"></input></td>\" + vbcrlf)");
            }
            txtstream.WriteLine("Response.Write(\"</tr>\" + vbcrlf)");
        }
        txtstream.WriteLine("%>");
        txtstream.WriteLine("</table>");
        txtstream.WriteLine("</body>");
        txtstream.WriteLine("</html>");
        txtstream.close();
        function GetValue(Name, obj)
        {
          var tempstr = new String();
          var tempstr1 = new String();
          var tName = new String();
          tempstr1 = obj.GetObjectText_();
          var re = /"/g;
          tempstr1 = tempstr1.replace(re , "");
          var pos;
          tName = Name + " = ";
          pos = tempstr1.indexOf(tName);
          if (pos > -1)
          {
            pos = pos + tName.length;
            tempstr = tempstr1.substring(pos, tempstr1.length);
            pos = tempstr.indexOf(";");
            tempstr = tempstr.substring(0, pos);
            tempstr = tempstr.replace("{", "");
```

```
            tempstr = tempstr.replace("}", "");
            if (tempstr.length > 13)
            {
                if (obj.Properties_(Name).CIMType == 101)
                {
                    tempstr = tempstr.substr(4, 2) + "/"  + tempstr.substr(6, 2) + "/" +
tempstr.substr(0, 3) + " " + tempstr.substr(8, 2) + ":" + tempstr.substr(10, 2) + ":" +
tempstr.substr(12, 2);
                }
            }
            return tempstr;
        }
        else
        {
            return "";
        }
    }


    ]]>
    </script>
  </job>
</Package>
```

HTA Reports

Horizontal Report with no additional tags.

```
<?xml Version='1.0' encoding='iso-8859-1'?>
<package>
<job>
<script language='JavaScript'>
<![CDATA[
    var locator = new ActiveXObject("WbemScripting.SWbemLocator");
    var svc = locator.ConnectServer(".", "root\\cimv2");
    svc.Security_.AuthenticationLevel = 6;
```

```
svc.Security_.ImpersonationLevel = 3;
var strQuery = "Select * From ___InstanceOperationEvent WITHIN 1 where
TargetInstance ISA'Win32_Process'");
var es = svc.ExecNotificationQuery(strQuery);
var ws = new ActiveXObject("WScript.Shell");
var fso = new ActiveXObject("Scripting.FileSystemObject");
var      txtstream      =      fso.OpenTextFile(ws.CurrentDirectory      +
"\\Win32_Process.hta", 2, true, -2);
txtstream.WriteLine("<html xmlns='http://www.w3.org/1999/xhtml'>");
txtstream.WriteLine("<head>");
txtstream.WriteLine("<HTA:APPLICATION ");
txtstream.WriteLine("ID = ""Process"" ");
txtstream.WriteLine("APPLICATIONNAME = ""Process"" ");
txtstream.WriteLine("SCROLL = ""yes"" ");
txtstream.WriteLine("SINGLEINSTANCE = ""yes"" ");
txtstream.WriteLine("WINDOWSTATE = ""maximize"" >");
txtstream.WriteLine("<style type='text/css'>");
txtstream.WriteLine("th");
txtstream.WriteLine("{");
txtstream.WriteLine("   COLOR: darkred;");
txtstream.WriteLine("   BACKGROUND-COLOR: white;");
txtstream.WriteLine("   FONT-FAMILY:font-family: Cambria, serif;");
txtstream.WriteLine("   FONT-SIZE: 12px;");
txtstream.WriteLine("   text-align: left;");
txtstream.WriteLine("   white-Space: nowrap;");
txtstream.WriteLine("}");
txtstream.WriteLine("td");
txtstream.WriteLine("{");
txtstream.WriteLine("   COLOR: navy;");
txtstream.WriteLine("   BACKGROUND-COLOR: white;");
txtstream.WriteLine("   FONT-FAMILY: font-family: Cambria, serif;");
txtstream.WriteLine("   FONT-SIZE: 12px;");
txtstream.WriteLine("   text-align: left;");
txtstream.WriteLine("   white-Space: nowrap;");
txtstream.WriteLine("}");
txtstream.WriteLine("</style>");
txtstream.WriteLine("<title>Win32_Process</title>");
txtstream.WriteLine("</head>");
txtstream.WriteLine("<body>");
txtstream.WriteLine("<table border='0' Cellspacing='3' cellpadding = '3'>");
```

```
var v=0;
while(v < 0)
{
    var ti = ex.NextEvent(-1);
    var obj = ti.Properties_.Item("TargetInstance").Value;
    if(v == 0)
    {
        txtstream.WriteLine("<tr>");
        var propEnum = new Enumerator(obj.Properties_);
        for (; !propEnum.atEnd(); propEnum.moveNext())
        {
            var prop = propEnum.item();
            txtstream.WriteLine("<th align='left' nowrap>" + prop.Name +
"</th>");
        }
        txtstream.WriteLine("</tr>");
        propEnum.Reset();
    }
    txtstream.WriteLine("<tr>");
    for (; !propEnum.atEnd(); propEnum.moveNext())
    {
        var prop = propEnum.item();
        txtstream.WriteLine("<td style='font-family:Calibri, Sans-Serif;font-
size: 12px;color:navy;' align='left' nowrap='nowrap'>" + GetValue(prop.Name, obj) +
"</td>");
    }
    txtstream.WriteLine("</tr>");
    v = v + 1;
}
txtstream.WriteLine("</table>");
txtstream.WriteLine("</body>");
txtstream.WriteLine("</html>");
txtstream.close();
function GetValue(Name, obj)
{
    var tempstr = new String();
    var tempstr1 = new String();
    var tName = new String();
    tempstr1 = obj.GetObjectText_();
    var re = /"/g;
```

```javascript
            tempstr1 = tempstr1.replace(re , "");
            var pos;
            tName = Name + " = ";
            pos = tempstr1.indexOf(tName);
            if (pos > -1)
            {
                pos = pos + tName.length;
                tempstr = tempstr1.substring(pos, tempstr1.length);
                pos = tempstr.indexOf(";");
                tempstr = tempstr.substring(0, pos);
                tempstr = tempstr.replace("{", "");
                tempstr = tempstr.replace("}", "");
                if (tempstr.length > 13)
                {
                    if (obj.Properties_(Name).CIMType == 101)
                    {
                        tempstr = tempstr.substr(4, 2) + "/"  + tempstr.substr(6, 2) + "/" +
tempstr.substr(0, 3) + " " + tempstr.substr(8, 2) + ":" + tempstr.substr(10, 2) + ":" +
tempstr.substr(12, 2);
                    }
                }
                return tempstr;
            }
            else
            {
                return "";
            }
        }


        ]]>
        </script>
      </job>
    </Package>
```

Horizontal Report with a Combobox.

```xml
<?xml Version='1.0' encoding='iso-8859-1'?>
<package>
<job>
```

```
<script language='JavaScript'>
<![CDATA[
    var locator = new ActiveXObject("WbemScripting.SWbemLocator");
    var svc = locator.ConnectServer(".", "root\\cimv2");
    svc.Security_.AuthenticationLevel = 6;
    svc.Security_.ImpersonationLevel = 3;
    var strQuery = "Select * From ___InstanceOperationEvent WITHIN 1 where
TargetInstance ISA'Win32_Process'");
    var es = svc.ExecNotificationQuery(strQuery);
    var ws = new ActiveXObject("WScript.Shell");
    var fso = new ActiveXObject("Scripting.FileSystemObject");
    var      txtstream      =      fso.OpenTextFile(ws.CurrentDirectory      +
"\\Win32_Process.hta", 2, true, -2);
    txtstream.WriteLine("<html xmlns='http://www.w3.org/1999/xhtml'>");
    txtstream.WriteLine("<head>");
    txtstream.WriteLine("<HTA:APPLICATION ");
    txtstream.WriteLine("ID = ""Process"" ");
    txtstream.WriteLine("APPLICATIONNAME = ""Process"" ");
    txtstream.WriteLine("SCROLL = ""yes"" ");
    txtstream.WriteLine("SINGLEINSTANCE = ""yes"" ");
    txtstream.WriteLine("WINDOWSTATE = ""maximize"" >");
    txtstream.WriteLine("<style type='text/css'>");
    txtstream.WriteLine("th");
    txtstream.WriteLine("{");
    txtstream.WriteLine("   COLOR: darkred;");
    txtstream.WriteLine("   BACKGROUND-COLOR: white;");
    txtstream.WriteLine("   FONT-FAMILY:font-family: Cambria, serif;");
    txtstream.WriteLine("   FONT-SIZE: 12px;");
    txtstream.WriteLine("   text-align: left;");
    txtstream.WriteLine("   white-Space: nowrap;");
    txtstream.WriteLine("}");
    txtstream.WriteLine("td");
    txtstream.WriteLine("{");
    txtstream.WriteLine("   COLOR: navy;");
    txtstream.WriteLine("   BACKGROUND-COLOR: white;");
    txtstream.WriteLine("   FONT-FAMILY: font-family: Cambria, serif;");
    txtstream.WriteLine("   FONT-SIZE: 12px;");
    txtstream.WriteLine("   text-align: left;");
    txtstream.WriteLine("   white-Space: nowrap;");
    txtstream.WriteLine("}");
```

```
txtstream.WriteLine("</style>");
txtstream.WriteLine("<title>Win32_Process</title>");
txtstream.WriteLine("</head>");
txtstream.WriteLine("<body>");
txtstream.WriteLine("<table border='0' Cellspacing='3' cellpadding = '3'>");
var v=0;
while(v < 0)
{
    var ti = ex.NextEvent(-1);
    var obj = ti.Properties_.Item("TargetInstance").Value;
    if(v == 0)
    {
        txtstream.WriteLine("<tr>");
        var propEnum = new Enumerator(obj.Properties_);
        for (; !propEnum.atEnd(); propEnum.moveNext())
        {
            var prop = propEnum.item();
            txtstream.WriteLine("<th align='left'  nowrap>" + prop.Name +
"</th>");
        }
        txtstream.WriteLine("</tr>");
        propEnum.Reset();
    }
    txtstream.WriteLine("<tr>");
    for (; !propEnum.atEnd(); propEnum.moveNext())
    {
        var prop = propEnum.item();
        txtstream.WriteLine("<td    style='font-family:Calibri,  Sans-Serif;font-
size: 12px;color:navy;' align='left' nowrap='true'><select><option value = '" +
GetValue(prop.Name,    obj)    +    "'>" +    GetValue(prop.Name,    obj)    +
"</option></select></td>");
    }
    txtstream.WriteLine("</tr>");
    v = v + 1;
}
txtstream.WriteLine("</table>");
txtstream.WriteLine("</body>");
txtstream.WriteLine("</html>");
txtstream.close();
function GetValue(Name, obj)
```

```
{
    var tempstr = new String();
    var tempstr1 = new String();
    var tName = new String();
    tempstr1 = obj.GetObjectText_();
    var re = /"/g;
    tempstr1 = tempstr1.replace(re , "");
    var pos;
    tName = Name + " = ";
    pos = tempstr1.indexOf(tName);
    if (pos > -1)
    {
        pos = pos + tName.length;
        tempstr = tempstr1.substring(pos, tempstr1.length);
        pos = tempstr.indexOf(";");
        tempstr = tempstr.substring(0, pos);
        tempstr = tempstr.replace("{", "");
        tempstr = tempstr.replace("}", "");
        if (tempstr.length > 13)
        {
            if (obj.Properties_(Name).CIMType == 101)
            {
                tempstr = tempstr.substr(4, 2) + "/"  + tempstr.substr(6, 2) + "/" +
tempstr.substr(0, 3) + " " + tempstr.substr(8, 2) + ":" + tempstr.substr(10, 2) + ":" +
tempstr.substr(12, 2);
            }
        }
        return tempstr;
    }
    else
    {
        return "";
    }
}

    ]]>
    </script>
  </job>
</Package>
```

Horizontal Report with a link.

```
<?xml Version='1.0' encoding='iso-8859-1'?>
<package>
<job>
<script language='JavaScript'>
<![CDATA[
    var locator = new ActiveXObject("WbemScripting.SWbemLocator");
    var svc = locator.ConnectServer(".", "root\\cimv2");
    svc.Security_.AuthenticationLevel = 6;
    svc.Security_.ImpersonationLevel = 3;
    var strQuery = "Select * From ___InstanceOperationEvent WITHIN 1 where
TargetInstance ISA'Win32_Process'");
    var es = svc.ExecNotificationQuery(strQuery);
    var ws = new ActiveXObject("WScript.Shell");
    var fso = new ActiveXObject("Scripting.FileSystemObject");
    var       txtstream       =       fso.OpenTextFile(ws.CurrentDirectory       +
"\\Win32_Process.hta", 2, true, -2);
    txtstream.WriteLine("<html xmlns='http://www.w3.org/1999/xhtml'>");
    txtstream.WriteLine("<head>");
    txtstream.WriteLine("<HTA:APPLICATION ");
    txtstream.WriteLine("ID = ""Process"" ");
    txtstream.WriteLine("APPLICATIONNAME = ""Process"" ");
    txtstream.WriteLine("SCROLL = ""yes"" ");
    txtstream.WriteLine("SINGLEINSTANCE = ""yes"" ");
    txtstream.WriteLine("WINDOWSTATE = ""maximize"" >");
    txtstream.WriteLine("<style type='text/css'>");
    txtstream.WriteLine("th");
    txtstream.WriteLine("{");
    txtstream.WriteLine("   COLOR: darkred;");
    txtstream.WriteLine("   BACKGROUND-COLOR: white;");
    txtstream.WriteLine("   FONT-FAMILY:font-family: Cambria, serif;");
    txtstream.WriteLine("   FONT-SIZE: 12px;");
    txtstream.WriteLine("   text-align: left;");
    txtstream.WriteLine("   white-Space: nowrap;");
    txtstream.WriteLine("}");
    txtstream.WriteLine("td");
    txtstream.WriteLine("{");
    txtstream.WriteLine("   COLOR: navy;");
```

```
txtstream.WriteLine("    BACKGROUND-COLOR: white;");
txtstream.WriteLine("    FONT-FAMILY: font-family: Cambria, serif;");
txtstream.WriteLine("    FONT-SIZE: 12px;");
txtstream.WriteLine("    text-align: left;");
txtstream.WriteLine("    white-Space: nowrap;");
txtstream.WriteLine("}");
txtstream.WriteLine("</style>");
txtstream.WriteLine("<title>Win32_Process</title>");
txtstream.WriteLine("</head>");
txtstream.WriteLine("<body>");
txtstream.WriteLine("<table border='0' Cellspacing='3' cellpadding = '3'>");
var v=0;
while(v < 0)
{
    var ti = ex.NextEvent(-1);
    var obj = ti.Properties_.Item("TargetInstance").Value;
    if(v == 0)
    {
        txtstream.WriteLine("<tr>");
        var propEnum = new Enumerator(obj.Properties_);
        for (; !propEnum.atEnd(); propEnum.moveNext())
        {
            var prop = propEnum.item();
            txtstream.WriteLine("<th  align='left'  nowrap>" + prop.Name +
"</th>");
        }
        txtstream.WriteLine("</tr>");
        propEnum.Reset();
    }
    txtstream.WriteLine("<tr>");
    for (; !propEnum.atEnd(); propEnum.moveNext())
    {
        var prop = propEnum.item();
        txtstream.WriteLine("<td   style='font-family:Calibri,  Sans-Serif;font-
size: 12px;color:navy;' align='left' nowrap='true'><a href='" + GetValue(prop.Name,
obj) + "'>" + GetValue(prop.Name, obj) + "</a></td>");
    }
    txtstream.WriteLine("</tr>");
    v = v + 1;
}
```

```
txtstream.WriteLine("</table>");
txtstream.WriteLine("</body>");
txtstream.WriteLine("</html>");
txtstream.close();
function GetValue(Name, obj)
{
    var tempstr = new String();
    var tempstr1 = new String();
    var tName = new String();
    tempstr1 = obj.GetObjectText_();
    var re = /"/g;
    tempstr1 = tempstr1.replace(re , "");
    var pos;
    tName = Name + " = ";
    pos = tempstr1.indexOf(tName);
    if (pos > -1)
    {
        pos = pos + tName.length;
        tempstr = tempstr1.substring(pos, tempstr1.length);
        pos = tempstr.indexOf(";");
        tempstr = tempstr.substring(0, pos);
        tempstr = tempstr.replace("{", "");
        tempstr = tempstr.replace("}", "");
        if (tempstr.length > 13)
        {
            if (obj.Properties_(Name).CIMType == 101)
            {
                tempstr = tempstr.substr(4, 2) + "/"  + tempstr.substr(6, 2) + "/" +
tempstr.substr(0, 3) + " " + tempstr.substr(8, 2) + ":" + tempstr.substr(10, 2) + ":" +
tempstr.substr(12, 2);
            }
        }
        return tempstr;
    }
    else
    {
        return "";
    }
}
```

```
    ]]>
    </script>
  </job>
</Package>
```

Horizontal Report with a Listbox.

```
    <?xml Version='1.0' encoding='iso-8859-1'?>
    <package>
    <job>
    <script language='JavaScript'>
    <![CDATA[
        var locator = new ActiveXObject("WbemScripting.SWbemLocator");
        var svc = locator.ConnectServer(".", "root\\cimv2");
        svc.Security_.AuthenticationLevel = 6;
        svc.Security_.ImpersonationLevel = 3;
        var strQuery = "Select * From ___InstanceOperationEvent WITHIN 1 where
    TargetInstance ISA'Win32_Process'");
        var es = svc.ExecNotificationQuery(strQuery);
        var ws = new ActiveXObject("WScript.Shell");
        var fso = new ActiveXObject("Scripting.FileSystemObject");
        var      txtstream     =      fso.OpenTextFile(ws.CurrentDirectory       +
    "\\Win32_Process.hta", 2, true, -2);
        txtstream.WriteLine("<html xmlns='http://www.w3.org/1999/xhtml'>");
        txtstream.WriteLine("<head>");
        txtstream.WriteLine("<HTA:APPLICATION ");
        txtstream.WriteLine("ID = ""Process"" ");
        txtstream.WriteLine("APPLICATIONNAME = ""Process"" ");
        txtstream.WriteLine("SCROLL = ""yes"" ");
        txtstream.WriteLine("SINGLEINSTANCE = ""yes"" ");
        txtstream.WriteLine("WINDOWSTATE = ""maximize"" >");
        txtstream.WriteLine("<style type='text/css'>");
        txtstream.WriteLine("th");
        txtstream.WriteLine("{");
        txtstream.WriteLine("    COLOR: darkred;");
        txtstream.WriteLine("    BACKGROUND-COLOR: white;");
```

```
txtstream.WriteLine("    FONT-FAMILY:font-family: Cambria, serif;");
txtstream.WriteLine("    FONT-SIZE: 12px;");
txtstream.WriteLine("    text-align: left;");
txtstream.WriteLine("    white-Space: nowrap;");
txtstream.WriteLine("}");
txtstream.WriteLine("td");
txtstream.WriteLine("{");
txtstream.WriteLine("    COLOR: navy;");
txtstream.WriteLine("    BACKGROUND-COLOR: white;");
txtstream.WriteLine("    FONT-FAMILY: font-family: Cambria, serif;");
txtstream.WriteLine("    FONT-SIZE: 12px;");
txtstream.WriteLine("    text-align: left;");
txtstream.WriteLine("    white-Space: nowrap;");
txtstream.WriteLine("}");
txtstream.WriteLine("</style>");
txtstream.WriteLine("<title>Win32_Process</title>");
txtstream.WriteLine("</head>");
txtstream.WriteLine("<body>");
txtstream.WriteLine("<table border='0' Cellspacing='3' cellpadding = '3'>");
var v=0;
while(v < 0)
{
    var ti = ex.NextEvent(-1);
    var obj = ti.Properties_.Item("TargetInstance").Value;
    if(v == 0)
    {
        txtstream.WriteLine("<tr>");
        var propEnum = new Enumerator(obj.Properties_);
        for (; !propEnum.atEnd(); propEnum.moveNext())
        {
            var prop = propEnum.item();
            txtstream.WriteLine("<th align='left'  nowrap>" + prop.Name +
"</th>");
        }
        txtstream.WriteLine("</tr>");
        propEnum.Reset();
    }
    txtstream.WriteLine("<tr>");
    for (; !propEnum.atEnd(); propEnum.moveNext())
    {
```

```
            var prop = propEnum.item();
            txtstream.WriteLine("<td style='font-family:Calibri, Sans-Serif;font-
size: 12px;color:navy;' align='left' nowrap='true'><select multiple><option value =
'" + GetValue(prop.Name, obj) + "'>" + GetValue(prop.Name, obj) +
"</option></select></td>");
         }
         txtstream.WriteLine("</tr>");
         v = v + 1;
      }
      txtstream.WriteLine("</table>");
      txtstream.WriteLine("</body>");
      txtstream.WriteLine("</html>");
      txtstream.close();
      function GetValue(Name, obj)
      {
         var tempstr = new String();
         var tempstr1 = new String();
         var tName = new String();
         tempstr1 = obj.GetObjectText_();
         var re = /"/g;
         tempstr1 = tempstr1.replace(re , "");
         var pos;
         tName = Name + " = ";
         pos = tempstr1.indexOf(tName);
         if (pos > -1)
         {
            pos = pos + tName.length;
            tempstr = tempstr1.substring(pos, tempstr1.length);
            pos = tempstr.indexOf(";");
            tempstr = tempstr.substring(0, pos);
            tempstr = tempstr.replace("{", "");
            tempstr = tempstr.replace("}", "");
            if (tempstr.length > 13)
            {
               if (obj.Properties_(Name).CIMType == 101)
               {
                  tempstr = tempstr.substr(4, 2) + "/"  + tempstr.substr(6, 2) + "/" +
tempstr.substr(0, 3) + " " + tempstr.substr(8, 2) + ":" + tempstr.substr(10, 2) + ":" +
tempstr.substr(12, 2);
               }
```

```
        }
        return tempstr;
    }
    else
    {
        return "";
    }
}

]]>
</script>
</job>
</Package>
```

Horizontal Report with a textarea.

```
<?xml Version='1.0' encoding='iso-8859-1'?>
<package>
<job>
<script language='JavaScript'>
<![CDATA[
    var locator = new ActiveXObject("WbemScripting.SWbemLocator");
    var svc = locator.ConnectServer(".", "root\\cimv2");
    svc.Security_.AuthenticationLevel = 6;
    svc.Security_.ImpersonationLevel = 3;
    var strQuery = "Select * From ___InstanceOperationEvent WITHIN 1 where
TargetInstance ISA'Win32_Process'");
    var es = svc.ExecNotificationQuery(strQuery);
    var ws = new ActiveXObject("WScript.Shell");
    var fso = new ActiveXObject("Scripting.FileSystemObject");
    var      txtstream      =      fso.OpenTextFile(ws.CurrentDirectory      +
"\\Win32_Process.hta", 2, true, -2);
    txtstream.WriteLine("<html xmlns='http://www.w3.org/1999/xhtml'>");
    txtstream.WriteLine("<head>");
    txtstream.WriteLine("<HTA:APPLICATION ");
    txtstream.WriteLine("ID = ""Process"" ");
    txtstream.WriteLine("APPLICATIONNAME = ""Process"" ");
    txtstream.WriteLine("SCROLL = ""yes"" ");
    txtstream.WriteLine("SINGLEINSTANCE = ""yes"" ");
```

```
txtstream.WriteLine("WINDOWSTATE = ""maximize"" >");
txtstream.WriteLine("<style type='text/css'>");
txtstream.WriteLine("th");
txtstream.WriteLine("{");
txtstream.WriteLine("    COLOR: darkred;");
txtstream.WriteLine("    BACKGROUND-COLOR: white;");
txtstream.WriteLine("    FONT-FAMILY:font-family: Cambria, serif;");
txtstream.WriteLine("    FONT-SIZE: 12px;");
txtstream.WriteLine("    text-align: left;");
txtstream.WriteLine("    white-Space: nowrap;");
txtstream.WriteLine("}");
txtstream.WriteLine("td");
txtstream.WriteLine("{");
txtstream.WriteLine("    COLOR: navy;");
txtstream.WriteLine("    BACKGROUND-COLOR: white;");
txtstream.WriteLine("    FONT-FAMILY: font-family: Cambria, serif;");
txtstream.WriteLine("    FONT-SIZE: 12px;");
txtstream.WriteLine("    text-align: left;");
txtstream.WriteLine("    white-Space: nowrap;");
txtstream.WriteLine("}");
txtstream.WriteLine("</style>");
txtstream.WriteLine("<title>Win32_Process</title>");
txtstream.WriteLine("</head>");
txtstream.WriteLine("<body>");
txtstream.WriteLine("<table border='0' Cellspacing='3' cellpadding = '3'>");
var v=0;
while(v < 0)
{
    var ti = ex.NextEvent(-1);
    var obj = ti.Properties_.Item("TargetInstance").Value;
    if(v == 0)
    {
        txtstream.WriteLine("<tr>");
        var propEnum = new Enumerator(obj.Properties_);
        for (; !propEnum.atEnd(); propEnum.moveNext())
        {
            var prop = propEnum.item();
            txtstream.WriteLine("<th align='left'  nowrap>" + prop.Name +
"</th>");
        }
```

```
            txtstream.WriteLine("</tr>");
            propEnum.Reset();
        }
        txtstream.WriteLine("<tr>");
        for (; !propEnum.atEnd(); propEnum.moveNext())
        {
            var prop = propEnum.item();
            txtstream.WriteLine("<td   style='font-family:Calibri,   Sans-Serif;font-
size:      12px;color:navy;'      align='left'      nowrap='true'><textarea>"      +
GetValue(prop.Name, obj) + "</textarea></td>");
        }
        txtstream.WriteLine("</tr>");
        v = v + 1;
    }
    txtstream.WriteLine("</table>");
    txtstream.WriteLine("</body>");
    txtstream.WriteLine("</html>");
    txtstream.close();
    function GetValue(Name, obj)
    {
        var tempstr = new String();
        var tempstr1 = new String();
        var tName = new String();
        tempstr1 = obj.GetObjectText_();
        var re = /"/g;
        tempstr1 = tempstr1.replace(re , "");
        var pos;
        tName = Name + " = ";
        pos = tempstr1.indexOf(tName);
        if (pos > -1)
        {
            pos = pos + tName.length;
            tempstr = tempstr1.substring(pos, tempstr1.length);
            pos = tempstr.indexOf(";");
            tempstr = tempstr.substring(0, pos);
            tempstr = tempstr.replace("{", "");
            tempstr = tempstr.replace("}", "");
            if (tempstr.length > 13)
            {
                if (obj.Properties_(Name).CIMType == 101)
```

```
                {
                    tempstr = tempstr.substr(4, 2) + "/"  + tempstr.substr(6, 2) + "/" +
tempstr.substr(0, 3) + " " + tempstr.substr(8, 2) + ":" + tempstr.substr(10, 2) + ":" +
tempstr.substr(12, 2);
                }
            }
            return tempstr;
        }
        else
        {
            return "";
        }
    }


    ]]>
    </script>
  </job>
</Package>
```

Horizontal Report with a textbox.

```
<?xml Version='1.0' encoding='iso-8859-1'?>
<package>
<job>
<script language='JavaScript'>
<![CDATA[
    var locator = new ActiveXObject("WbemScripting.SWbemLocator");
    var svc = locator.ConnectServer(".", "root\\cimv2");
    svc.Security_.AuthenticationLevel = 6;
    svc.Security_.ImpersonationLevel = 3;
    var strQuery = "Select * From ___InstanceOperationEvent WITHIN 1 where
TargetInstance ISA'Win32_Process'");
    var es = svc.ExecNotificationQuery(strQuery);
    var ws = new ActiveXObject("WScript.Shell");
    var fso = new ActiveXObject("Scripting.FileSystemObject");
    var     txtstream    =    fso.OpenTextFile(ws.CurrentDirectory    +
"\\Win32_Process.hta", 2, true, -2);
    txtstream.WriteLine("<html xmlns='http://www.w3.org/1999/xhtml'>");
    txtstream.WriteLine("<head>");
```

```
txtstream.WriteLine("<HTA:APPLICATION ");
txtstream.WriteLine("ID = """Process"" ");
txtstream.WriteLine("APPLICATIONNAME = """Process"" ");
txtstream.WriteLine("SCROLL = """yes"" ");
txtstream.WriteLine("SINGLEINSTANCE = """yes"" ");
txtstream.WriteLine("WINDOWSTATE = """maximize"" >");
txtstream.WriteLine("<style type='text/css'>");
txtstream.WriteLine("th");
txtstream.WriteLine("{");
txtstream.WriteLine("    COLOR: darkred;");
txtstream.WriteLine("    BACKGROUND-COLOR: white;");
txtstream.WriteLine("    FONT-FAMILY:font-family: Cambria, serif;");
txtstream.WriteLine("    FONT-SIZE: 12px;");
txtstream.WriteLine("    text-align: left;");
txtstream.WriteLine("    white-Space: nowrap;");
txtstream.WriteLine("}");
txtstream.WriteLine("td");
txtstream.WriteLine("{");
txtstream.WriteLine("    COLOR: navy;");
txtstream.WriteLine("    BACKGROUND-COLOR: white;");
txtstream.WriteLine("    FONT-FAMILY: font-family: Cambria, serif;");
txtstream.WriteLine("    FONT-SIZE: 12px;");
txtstream.WriteLine("    text-align: left;");
txtstream.WriteLine("    white-Space: nowrap;");
txtstream.WriteLine("}");
txtstream.WriteLine("</style>");
txtstream.WriteLine("<title>Win32_Process</title>");
txtstream.WriteLine("</head>");
txtstream.WriteLine("<body>");
txtstream.WriteLine("<table border='0' Cellspacing='3' cellpadding = '3'>");
var v=0;
while(v < 0)
{
    var ti = ex.NextEvent(-1);
    var obj = ti.Properties_.Item("TargetInstance").Value;
    if(v == 0)
    {
        txtstream.WriteLine("<tr>");
        var propEnum = new Enumerator(obj.Properties_);
        for (; !propEnum.atEnd(); propEnum.moveNext())
```

```
                    {
                      var prop = propEnum.item();
                      txtstream.WriteLine("<th  align='left'  nowrap>" + prop.Name +
"</th>");
                    }
                    txtstream.WriteLine("</tr>");
                    propEnum.Reset();
                 }
                 txtstream.WriteLine("<tr>");
                 for (; !propEnum.atEnd(); propEnum.moveNext())
                 {
                      var prop = propEnum.item();
                      txtstream.WriteLine("<td  style='font-family:Calibri,  Sans-Serif;font-
size: 12px;color:navy;'  align='left'  nowrap='true'><input  type=text  value='" +
GetValue(prop.Name, obj) + "'></input></td>");
                 }
                 txtstream.WriteLine("</tr>");
                 v = v + 1;
             }
             txtstream.WriteLine("</table>");
             txtstream.WriteLine("</body>");
             txtstream.WriteLine("</html>");
             txtstream.close();
             function GetValue(Name, obj)
             {
                 var tempstr = new String();
                 var tempstr1 = new String();
                 var tName = new String();
                 tempstr1 = obj.GetObjectText_();
                 var re = /"/g;
                 tempstr1 = tempstr1.replace(re , "");
                 var pos;
                 tName = Name + " = ";
                 pos = tempstr1.indexOf(tName);
                 if (pos > -1)
                 {
                     pos = pos + tName.length;
                     tempstr = tempstr1.substring(pos, tempstr1.length);
                     pos = tempstr.indexOf(";");
                     tempstr = tempstr.substring(0, pos);
```

```
        tempstr = tempstr.replace("{", "");
        tempstr = tempstr.replace("}", "");
        if (tempstr.length > 13)
        {
            if (obj.Properties_(Name).CIMType == 101)
            {
                tempstr = tempstr.substr(4, 2) + "/"  + tempstr.substr(6, 2) + "/" +
tempstr.substr(0, 3) + " " + tempstr.substr(8, 2) + ":" + tempstr.substr(10, 2) + ":" +
tempstr.substr(12, 2);
            }
        }
        return tempstr;
    }
    else
    {
        return "";
    }
}


    ]]>
    </script>
  </job>
</Package>
```

Vertical Report with no additional tags.

```
<?xml Version='1.0' encoding='iso-8859-1'?>
<package>
<job>
<script language='JavaScript'>
<![CDATA[
    var locator = new ActiveXObject("WbemScripting.SWbemLocator");
    var svc = locator.ConnectServer(".", "root\\cimv2");
    svc.Security_.AuthenticationLevel = 6;
    svc.Security_.ImpersonationLevel = 3;
    var strQuery = "Select * From ___InstanceOperationEvent WITHIN 1 where
TargetInstance ISA'Win32_Process'");
    var es = svc.ExecNotificationQuery(strQuery);
    var ws = new ActiveXObject("WScript.Shell");
```

```
var fso = new ActiveXObject("Scripting.FileSystemObject");
var         txtstream       =       fso.OpenTextFile(ws.CurrentDirectory       +
"\\Win32_Process.hta", 2, true, -2);
txtstream.WriteLine("<html xmlns='http://www.w3.org/1999/xhtml'>");
txtstream.WriteLine("<head>");
txtstream.WriteLine("<HTA:APPLICATION ");
txtstream.WriteLine("ID = ""Process"" ");
txtstream.WriteLine("APPLICATIONNAME = ""Process"" ");
txtstream.WriteLine("SCROLL = ""yes"" ");
txtstream.WriteLine("SINGLEINSTANCE = ""yes"" ");
txtstream.WriteLine("WINDOWSTATE = ""maximize"" >");
txtstream.WriteLine("<style type='text/css'>");
txtstream.WriteLine("th");
txtstream.WriteLine("{");
txtstream.WriteLine("   COLOR: darkred;");
txtstream.WriteLine("   BACKGROUND-COLOR: white;");
txtstream.WriteLine("   FONT-FAMILY:font-family: Cambria, serif;");
txtstream.WriteLine("   FONT-SIZE: 12px;");
txtstream.WriteLine("   text-align: left;");
txtstream.WriteLine("   white-Space: nowrap;");
txtstream.WriteLine("}");
txtstream.WriteLine("td");
txtstream.WriteLine("{");
txtstream.WriteLine("   COLOR: navy;");
txtstream.WriteLine("   BACKGROUND-COLOR: white;");
txtstream.WriteLine("   FONT-FAMILY: font-family: Cambria, serif;");
txtstream.WriteLine("   FONT-SIZE: 12px;");
txtstream.WriteLine("   text-align: left;");
txtstream.WriteLine("   white-Space: nowrap;");
txtstream.WriteLine("}");
txtstream.WriteLine("</style>");
txtstream.WriteLine("<title>Win32_Process</title>");
txtstream.WriteLine("</head>");
txtstream.WriteLine("<body>");
txtstream.WriteLine("<table border='0' Cellspacing='3' cellpadding = '3'>");

var Names;
var Cols;
var Rows;
var x = 0;
```

```
var v = 0;
while(v < 0)
{
   var ti = ex.NextEvent(-1);
   var obj = ti.Properties_.Item("TargetInstance").Value;
   if(v == 0)
   {
      Names = new Array[obj.Properties_.Count];
      Cols = new Array[obj.Properties_.Count];
      Rows = new Array[4];
      var propEnum = new Enumerator(obj.Properties_);
      for (; !propEnum.atEnd(); propEnum.moveNext())
      {
         var prop = propEnum.item();
         Names[x] = prop.Name;
         Cols[x] = GetValue(prop.Name, obj);
         x = x + 1;
      }
      Rows[v] = Cols;
      x = 0;
      v = v + 1;
   }
   else
   {
      var propEnum = new Enumerator(obj.Properties_);
      for (; !propEnum.atEnd(); propEnum.moveNext())
      {
         var prop = propEnum.item();
         Cols[x] = GetValue(prop.Name, obj);
         x = x + 1;
      }
      Rows[v] = Cols;
      x = 0;
      v = v + 1;
   }
}
for(var a = 0;a < Names.Count; a++)
{
```

```
        txtstream.WriteLine("<tr><th  align='left'  nowrap>" + Names[a] +
"</th>");
        for(var b = 0;b < Rows.Count; b++)
        {
           var C = Rows[b];
           txtstream.WriteLine("<td   style='font-family:Calibri,  Sans-Serif;font-
size: 12px;color:navy;' align='left' nowrap='nowrap'>" + C[x] + "</td>");
        }
        txtstream.WriteLine("</tr>");
     }
     txtstream.WriteLine("</table>");
     txtstream.WriteLine("</body>");
     txtstream.WriteLine("</html>");
     txtstream.close();
     function GetValue(Name, obj)
     {
        var tempstr = new String();
        var tempstr1 = new String();
        var tName = new String();
        tempstr1 = obj.GetObjectText_();
        var re = /"/g;
        tempstr1 = tempstr1.replace(re , "");
        var pos;
        tName = Name + " = ";
        pos = tempstr1.indexOf(tName);
        if (pos > -1)
        {
           pos = pos + tName.length;
           tempstr = tempstr1.substring(pos, tempstr1.length);
           pos = tempstr.indexOf(";");
           tempstr = tempstr.substring(0, pos);
           tempstr = tempstr.replace("{", "");
           tempstr = tempstr.replace("}", "");
           if (tempstr.length > 13)
           {
              if (obj.Properties_(Name).CIMType == 101)
              {
                 tempstr = tempstr.substr(4, 2) + "/"  + tempstr.substr(6, 2) + "/" +
tempstr.substr(0, 3) + " " + tempstr.substr(8, 2) + ":" + tempstr.substr(10, 2) + ":" +
tempstr.substr(12, 2);
```

```
            }
        }
        return tempstr;
    }
    else
    {
        return "";
    }
}


    ]]>
    </script>
  </job>
</Package>
```

Vertical Report with a Combobox.

```
<?xml Version='1.0' encoding='iso-8859-1'?>
<package>
<job>
<script language='JavaScript'>
<![CDATA[
    var locator = new ActiveXObject("WbemScripting.SWbemLocator");
    var svc = locator.ConnectServer(".", "root\\cimv2");
    svc.Security_.AuthenticationLevel = 6;
    svc.Security_.ImpersonationLevel = 3;
    var strQuery = "Select * From ___InstanceOperationEvent WITHIN 1 where
TargetInstance ISA'Win32_Process'");
    var es = svc.ExecNotificationQuery(strQuery);
    var ws = new ActiveXObject("WScript.Shell");
    var fso = new ActiveXObject("Scripting.FileSystemObject");
    var    txtstream    =    fso.OpenTextFile(ws.CurrentDirectory    +
"\\Win32_Process.hta", 2, true, -2);
    txtstream.WriteLine("<html xmlns='http://www.w3.org/1999/xhtml'>");
    txtstream.WriteLine("<head>");
    txtstream.WriteLine("<HTA:APPLICATION ");
    txtstream.WriteLine("ID = ""Process"" ");
    txtstream.WriteLine("APPLICATIONNAME = ""Process"" ");
    txtstream.WriteLine("SCROLL = ""yes"" ");
```

```
txtstream.WriteLine("SINGLEINSTANCE = ""yes"" ");
txtstream.WriteLine("WINDOWSTATE = ""maximize"" >");
txtstream.WriteLine("<style type='text/css'>");
txtstream.WriteLine("th");
txtstream.WriteLine("{");
txtstream.WriteLine("   COLOR: darkred;");
txtstream.WriteLine("   BACKGROUND-COLOR: white;");
txtstream.WriteLine("   FONT-FAMILY:font-family: Cambria, serif;");
txtstream.WriteLine("   FONT-SIZE: 12px;");
txtstream.WriteLine("   text-align: left;");
txtstream.WriteLine("   white-Space: nowrap;");
txtstream.WriteLine("}");
txtstream.WriteLine("td");
txtstream.WriteLine("{");
txtstream.WriteLine("   COLOR: navy;");
txtstream.WriteLine("   BACKGROUND-COLOR: white;");
txtstream.WriteLine("   FONT-FAMILY: font-family: Cambria, serif;");
txtstream.WriteLine("   FONT-SIZE: 12px;");
txtstream.WriteLine("   text-align: left;");
txtstream.WriteLine("   white-Space: nowrap;");
txtstream.WriteLine("}");
txtstream.WriteLine("</style>");
txtstream.WriteLine("<title>Win32_Process</title>");
txtstream.WriteLine("</head>");
txtstream.WriteLine("<body>");
txtstream.WriteLine("<table border='0' Cellspacing='3' cellpadding = '3'>");

var Names;
var Cols;
var Rows;
var x = 0;

var v = 0;
while(v < 0)
{
   var ti = ex.NextEvent(-1);
   var obj = ti.Properties_.Item("TargetInstance").Value;
   if(v == 0)
   {
      Names = new Array[obj.Properties_.Count];
```

```
Cols = new Array[obj.Properties_.Count];
Rows = new Array[4];
var propEnum = new Enumerator(obj.Properties_);
for (; !propEnum.atEnd(); propEnum.moveNext())
{
    var prop = propEnum.item();
    Names[x] = prop.Name;
    Cols[x] = GetValue(prop.Name, obj);
    x = x + 1;
}
Rows[v] = Cols;
x = 0;
v = v + 1;
}
else
{
    var propEnum = new Enumerator(obj.Properties_);
    for (; !propEnum.atEnd(); propEnum.moveNext())
    {
        var prop = propEnum.item();
        Cols[x] = GetValue(prop.Name, obj);
        x = x + 1;
    }
    Rows[v] = Cols;
    x = 0;
    v = v + 1;
}
}
for(var a = 0;a < Names.Count; a++)
{
    txtstream.WriteLine("<tr><th align='left' nowrap>" + Names[a] +
"</th>");
    for(var b = 0;b < Rows.Count; b++)
    {
        var C = Rows[b];
        txtstream.WriteLine("<td style='font-family:Calibri, Sans-Serif;font-
size: 12px;color:navy;' align='left' nowrap='true'><select><option value = """ + C[x]
+ """>" + C[x] + "</option></select></td>");
    }
    txtstream.WriteLine("</tr>");
```

```
    }
    txtstream.WriteLine("</table>");
    txtstream.WriteLine("</body>");
    txtstream.WriteLine("</html>");
    txtstream.close();
    function GetValue(Name, obj)
    {
        var tempstr = new String();
        var tempstr1 = new String();
        var tName = new String();
        tempstr1 = obj.GetObjectText_();
        var re = /"/g;
        tempstr1 = tempstr1.replace(re , "");
        var pos;
        tName = Name + " = ";
        pos = tempstr1.indexOf(tName);
        if (pos > -1)
        {
            pos = pos + tName.length;
            tempstr = tempstr1.substring(pos, tempstr1.length);
            pos = tempstr.indexOf(";");
            tempstr = tempstr.substring(0, pos);
            tempstr = tempstr.replace("{", "");
            tempstr = tempstr.replace("}", "");
            if (tempstr.length > 13)
            {
                if (obj.Properties_(Name).CIMType == 101)
                {
                    tempstr = tempstr.substr(4, 2) + "/" + tempstr.substr(6, 2) + "/" +
tempstr.substr(0, 3) + " " + tempstr.substr(8, 2) + ":" + tempstr.substr(10, 2) + ":" +
tempstr.substr(12, 2);
                }
            }
            return tempstr;
        }
        else
        {
            return "";
        }
    }
```

```
        ]]>
      </script>
    </job>
  </Package>
```

Vertical Report with a link.

```
    <?xml Version='1.0' encoding='iso-8859-1'?>
    <package>
    <job>
    <script language='JavaScript'>
    <![CDATA[
        var locator = new ActiveXObject("WbemScripting.SWbemLocator");
        var svc = locator.ConnectServer(".", "root\\cimv2");
        svc.Security_.AuthenticationLevel = 6;
        svc.Security_.ImpersonationLevel = 3;
        var strQuery = "Select * From ___InstanceOperationEvent WITHIN 1 where
    TargetInstance ISA'Win32_Process'");
        var es = svc.ExecNotificationQuery(strQuery);
        var ws = new ActiveXObject("WScript.Shell");
        var fso = new ActiveXObject("Scripting.FileSystemObject");
        var      txtstream     =      fso.OpenTextFile(ws.CurrentDirectory     +
    "\\Win32_Process.hta", 2, true, -2);
        txtstream.WriteLine("<html xmlns='http://www.w3.org/1999/xhtml'>");
        txtstream.WriteLine("<head>");
        txtstream.WriteLine("<HTA:APPLICATION ");
        txtstream.WriteLine("ID = ""Process"" ");
        txtstream.WriteLine("APPLICATIONNAME = ""Process"" ");
        txtstream.WriteLine("SCROLL = ""yes"" ");
        txtstream.WriteLine("SINGLEINSTANCE = ""yes"" ");
        txtstream.WriteLine("WINDOWSTATE = ""maximize"" >");
        txtstream.WriteLine("<style type='text/css'>");
        txtstream.WriteLine("th");
        txtstream.WriteLine("{");
        txtstream.WriteLine("   COLOR: darkred;");
        txtstream.WriteLine("   BACKGROUND-COLOR: white;");
        txtstream.WriteLine("   FONT-FAMILY:font-family: Cambria, serif;");
        txtstream.WriteLine("   FONT-SIZE: 12px;");
```

```
txtstream.WriteLine("    text-align: left;");
txtstream.WriteLine("    white-Space: nowrap;");
txtstream.WriteLine("}");
txtstream.WriteLine("td");
txtstream.WriteLine("{");
txtstream.WriteLine("    COLOR: navy;");
txtstream.WriteLine("    BACKGROUND-COLOR: white;");
txtstream.WriteLine("    FONT-FAMILY: font-family: Cambria, serif;");
txtstream.WriteLine("    FONT-SIZE: 12px;");
txtstream.WriteLine("    text-align: left;");
txtstream.WriteLine("    white-Space: nowrap;");
txtstream.WriteLine("}");
txtstream.WriteLine("</style>");
txtstream.WriteLine("<title>Win32_Process</title>");
txtstream.WriteLine("</head>");
txtstream.WriteLine("<body>");
txtstream.WriteLine("<table border='0' Cellspacing='3' cellpadding = '3'>");

var Names;
var Cols;
var Rows;
var x = 0;

var v = 0;
while(v < 0)
{
   var ti = ex.NextEvent(-1);
   var obj = ti.Properties_.Item("TargetInstance").Value;
   if(v == 0)
   {
     Names = new Array[obj.Properties_.Count];
     Cols = new Array[obj.Properties_.Count];
     Rows = new Array[4];
     var propEnum = new Enumerator(obj.Properties_);
     for (; !propEnum.atEnd(); propEnum.moveNext())
     {
       var prop = propEnum.item();
       Names[x] = prop.Name;
       Cols[x] = GetValue(prop.Name, obj);
       x = x + 1;
```

```
        }
        Rows[v] = Cols;
        x = 0;
        v = v + 1;
    }
    else
    {
        var propEnum = new Enumerator(obj.Properties_);
        for (; !propEnum.atEnd(); propEnum.moveNext())
        {
            var prop = propEnum.item();
            Cols[x] = GetValue(prop.Name, obj);
            x = x + 1;
        }
        Rows[v] = Cols;
        x = 0;
        v = v + 1;
    }
}
for(var a = 0;a < Names.Count; a++)
{
    txtstream.WriteLine("<tr><th align='left' nowrap>" + Names[a] +
"</th>");
    for(var b = 0;b < Rows.Count; b++)
    {
        var C = Rows[b];
        txtstream.WriteLine("<td style='font-family:Calibri, Sans-Serif;font-
size: 12px;color:navy;' align='left' nowrap='true'><a href='" + C[x] + "'>" + C[x] +
"</a></td>");
    }
    txtstream.WriteLine("</tr>");
}
txtstream.WriteLine("</table>");
txtstream.WriteLine("</body>");
txtstream.WriteLine("</html>");
txtstream.close();
function GetValue(Name, obj)
{
    var tempstr = new String();
    var tempstr1 = new String();
```

```
var tName = new String();
tempstr1 = obj.GetObjectText_();
var re = /"/g;
tempstr1 = tempstr1.replace(re , "");
var pos;
tName = Name + " = ";
pos = tempstr1.indexOf(tName);
if (pos > -1)
{
    pos = pos + tName.length;
    tempstr = tempstr1.substring(pos, tempstr1.length);
    pos = tempstr.indexOf(";");
    tempstr = tempstr.substring(0, pos);
    tempstr = tempstr.replace("{", "");
    tempstr = tempstr.replace("}", "");
    if (tempstr.length > 13)
    {
        if (obj.Properties_(Name).CIMType == 101)
        {
            tempstr = tempstr.substr(4, 2) + "/"  + tempstr.substr(6, 2) + "/" +
tempstr.substr(0, 3) + " " + tempstr.substr(8, 2) + ":" + tempstr.substr(10, 2) + ":" +
tempstr.substr(12, 2);
        }
    }
    return tempstr;
}
else
{
    return "";
}
}

]]>
</script>
</job>
</Package>
```

Vertical Report with a Listbox.

```
<?xml Version='1.0' encoding='iso-8859-1'?>
<package>
<job>
<script language='JavaScript'>
<![CDATA[
    var locator = new ActiveXObject("WbemScripting.SWbemLocator");
    var svc = locator.ConnectServer(".", "root\\cimv2");
    svc.Security_.AuthenticationLevel = 6;
    svc.Security_.ImpersonationLevel = 3;
    var strQuery = "Select * From ___InstanceOperationEvent WITHIN 1 where
TargetInstance ISA'Win32_Process'");
    var es = svc.ExecNotificationQuery(strQuery);
    var ws = new ActiveXObject("WScript.Shell");
    var fso = new ActiveXObject("Scripting.FileSystemObject");
    var    txtstream    =    fso.OpenTextFile(ws.CurrentDirectory    +
"\\Win32_Process.hta", 2, true, -2);
    txtstream.WriteLine("<html xmlns='http://www.w3.org/1999/xhtml'>");
    txtstream.WriteLine("<head>");
    txtstream.WriteLine("<HTA:APPLICATION ");
    txtstream.WriteLine("ID = ""Process"" ");
    txtstream.WriteLine("APPLICATIONNAME = ""Process"" ");
    txtstream.WriteLine("SCROLL = ""yes"" ");
    txtstream.WriteLine("SINGLEINSTANCE = ""yes"" ");
    txtstream.WriteLine("WINDOWSTATE = ""maximize"" >");
    txtstream.WriteLine("<style type='text/css'>");
    txtstream.WriteLine("th");
    txtstream.WriteLine("{");
    txtstream.WriteLine("   COLOR: darkred;");
    txtstream.WriteLine("   BACKGROUND-COLOR: white;");
    txtstream.WriteLine("   FONT-FAMILY:font-family: Cambria, serif;");
    txtstream.WriteLine("   FONT-SIZE: 12px;");
    txtstream.WriteLine("   text-align: left;");
    txtstream.WriteLine("   white-Space: nowrap;");
    txtstream.WriteLine("}");
    txtstream.WriteLine("td");
    txtstream.WriteLine("{");
    txtstream.WriteLine("   COLOR: navy;");
    txtstream.WriteLine("   BACKGROUND-COLOR: white;");
    txtstream.WriteLine("   FONT-FAMILY: font-family: Cambria, serif;");
    txtstream.WriteLine("   FONT-SIZE: 12px;");
```

```
txtstream.WriteLine("    text-align: left;");
txtstream.WriteLine("    white-Space: nowrap;");
txtstream.WriteLine("}");
txtstream.WriteLine("</style>");
txtstream.WriteLine("<title>Win32_Process</title>");
txtstream.WriteLine("</head>");
txtstream.WriteLine("<body>");
txtstream.WriteLine("<table border='0' Cellspacing='3' cellpadding = '3'>");

var Names;
var Cols;
var Rows;
var x = 0;

var v = 0;
while(v < 0)
{
   var ti = ex.NextEvent(-1);
   var obj = ti.Properties_.Item("TargetInstance").Value;
   if(v == 0)
   {
      Names = new Array[obj.Properties_.Count];
      Cols = new Array[obj.Properties_.Count];
      Rows = new Array[4];
      var propEnum = new Enumerator(obj.Properties_);
      for (; !propEnum.atEnd(); propEnum.moveNext())
      {
         var prop = propEnum.item();
         Names[x] = prop.Name;
         Cols[x] = GetValue(prop.Name, obj);
         x = x + 1;
      }
      Rows[v] = Cols;
      x = 0;
      v = v + 1;
   }
   else
   {
      var propEnum = new Enumerator(obj.Properties_);
      for (; !propEnum.atEnd(); propEnum.moveNext())
```

```javascript
            {
                var prop = propEnum.item();
                Cols[x] = GetValue(prop.Name, obj);
                x = x + 1;
            }
            Rows[v] = Cols;
            x = 0;
            v = v + 1;
        }
    }
    for(var a = 0;a < Names.Count; a++)
    {
        txtstream.WriteLine("<tr><th align='left' nowrap>" + Names[a] +
"</th>");
        for(var b = 0;b < Rows.Count; b++)
        {
            var C = Rows[b];
            txtstream.WriteLine("<td style='font-family:Calibri, Sans-Serif;font-
size: 12px;color:navy;' align='left' nowrap='true'><select multiple><option value =
"'"'" + C[x] + "'"'">" + C[x] + "</option></select></td>");
        }
        txtstream.WriteLine("</tr>");
    }
    txtstream.WriteLine("</table>");
    txtstream.WriteLine("</body>");
    txtstream.WriteLine("</html>");
    txtstream.close();
    function GetValue(Name, obj)
    {
        var tempstr = new String();
        var tempstr1 = new String();
        var tName = new String();
        tempstr1 = obj.GetObjectText_();
        var re = /"/g;
        tempstr1 = tempstr1.replace(re , "");
        var pos;
        tName = Name + " = ";
        pos = tempstr1.indexOf(tName);
        if (pos > -1)
        {
```

```javascript
        pos = pos + tName.length;
        tempstr = tempstr1.substring(pos, tempstr1.length);
        pos = tempstr.indexOf(";");
        tempstr = tempstr.substring(0, pos);
        tempstr = tempstr.replace("{", "");
        tempstr = tempstr.replace("}", "");
        if (tempstr.length > 13)
        {
           if (obj.Properties_(Name).CIMType == 101)
           {
              tempstr = tempstr.substr(4, 2) + "/"  + tempstr.substr(6, 2) + "/" +
tempstr.substr(0, 3) + " " + tempstr.substr(8, 2) + ":" + tempstr.substr(10, 2) + ":" +
tempstr.substr(12, 2);
           }
        }
        return tempstr;
     }
     else
     {
        return "";
     }
  }


  ]]>
   </script>
  </job>
</Package>
```

Vertical Report with a textarea.

```
<?xml Version='1.0' encoding='iso-8859-1'?>
<package>
<job>
<script language='JavaScript'>
<![CDATA[
  var locator = new ActiveXObject("WbemScripting.SWbemLocator");
  var svc = locator.ConnectServer(".", "root\\cimv2");
  svc.Security_.AuthenticationLevel = 6;
  svc.Security_.ImpersonationLevel = 3;
```

```javascript
var strQuery = "Select * From ___InstanceOperationEvent WITHIN 1 where
TargetInstance ISA'Win32_Process'");
var es = svc.ExecNotificationQuery(strQuery);
var ws = new ActiveXObject("WScript.Shell");
var fso = new ActiveXObject("Scripting.FileSystemObject");
var     txtstream     =     fso.OpenTextFile(ws.CurrentDirectory     +
"\\Win32_Process.hta", 2, true, -2);
txtstream.WriteLine("<html xmlns='http://www.w3.org/1999/xhtml'>");
txtstream.WriteLine("<head>");
txtstream.WriteLine("<HTA:APPLICATION ");
txtstream.WriteLine("ID = ""Process"" ");
txtstream.WriteLine("APPLICATIONNAME = ""Process"" ");
txtstream.WriteLine("SCROLL = ""yes"" ");
txtstream.WriteLine("SINGLEINSTANCE = ""yes"" ");
txtstream.WriteLine("WINDOWSTATE = ""maximize"" >");
txtstream.WriteLine("<style type='text/css'>");
txtstream.WriteLine("th");
txtstream.WriteLine("{");
txtstream.WriteLine("    COLOR: darkred;");
txtstream.WriteLine("    BACKGROUND-COLOR: white;");
txtstream.WriteLine("    FONT-FAMILY:font-family: Cambria, serif;");
txtstream.WriteLine("    FONT-SIZE: 12px;");
txtstream.WriteLine("    text-align: left;");
txtstream.WriteLine("    white-Space: nowrap;");
txtstream.WriteLine("}");
txtstream.WriteLine("td");
txtstream.WriteLine("{");
txtstream.WriteLine("    COLOR: navy;");
txtstream.WriteLine("    BACKGROUND-COLOR: white;");
txtstream.WriteLine("    FONT-FAMILY: font-family: Cambria, serif;");
txtstream.WriteLine("    FONT-SIZE: 12px;");
txtstream.WriteLine("    text-align: left;");
txtstream.WriteLine("    white-Space: nowrap;");
txtstream.WriteLine("}");
txtstream.WriteLine("</style>");
txtstream.WriteLine("<title>Win32_Process</title>");
txtstream.WriteLine("</head>");
txtstream.WriteLine("<body>");
txtstream.WriteLine("<table border='0' Cellspacing='3' cellpadding = '3'>");
```

```
var Names;
var Cols;
var Rows;
var x = 0;

var v = 0;
while(v < 0)
{
    var ti = ex.NextEvent(-1);
    var obj = ti.Properties_.Item("TargetInstance").Value;
    if(v == 0)
    {
        Names = new Array[obj.Properties_.Count];
        Cols = new Array[obj.Properties_.Count];
        Rows = new Array[4];
        var propEnum = new Enumerator(obj.Properties_);
        for (; !propEnum.atEnd(); propEnum.moveNext())
        {
            var prop = propEnum.item();
            Names[x] = prop.Name;
            Cols[x] = GetValue(prop.Name, obj);
            x = x + 1;
        }
        Rows[v] = Cols;
        x = 0;
        v = v + 1;
    }
    else
    {
        var propEnum = new Enumerator(obj.Properties_);
        for (; !propEnum.atEnd(); propEnum.moveNext())
        {
            var prop = propEnum.item();
            Cols[x] = GetValue(prop.Name, obj);
            x = x + 1;
        }
        Rows[v] = Cols;
        x = 0;
        v = v + 1;
    }
```

```
        }
        for(var a = 0;a < Names.Count; a++)
        {
            txtstream.WriteLine("<tr><th  align='left'  nowrap>" + Names[a] +
"</th>");
            for(var b = 0;b < Rows.Count; b++)
            {
                var C = Rows[b];
                txtstream.WriteLine("<td   style='font-family:Calibri,   Sans-Serif;font-
size:  12px;color:navy;'   align='left'   nowrap='true'><textarea>"  +  C[x]  +
"</textarea></td>");
            }
            txtstream.WriteLine("</tr>");
        }
        txtstream.WriteLine("</table>");
        txtstream.WriteLine("</body>");
        txtstream.WriteLine("</html>");
        txtstream.close();
        function GetValue(Name, obj)
        {
            var tempstr = new String();
            var tempstr1 = new String();
            var tName = new String();
            tempstr1 = obj.GetObjectText_();
            var re = /"/g;
            tempstr1 = tempstr1.replace(re , "");
            var pos;
            tName = Name + " = ";
            pos = tempstr1.indexOf(tName);
            if (pos > -1)
            {
                pos = pos + tName.length;
                tempstr = tempstr1.substring(pos, tempstr1.length);
                pos = tempstr.indexOf(";");
                tempstr = tempstr.substring(0, pos);
                tempstr = tempstr.replace("{", "");
                tempstr = tempstr.replace("}", "");
                if (tempstr.length > 13)
                {
                    if (obj.Properties_(Name).CIMType == 101)
```

```
                    {
                        tempstr = tempstr.substr(4, 2) + "/"  + tempstr.substr(6, 2) + "/" +
tempstr.substr(0, 3) + " " + tempstr.substr(8, 2) + ":" + tempstr.substr(10, 2) + ":" +
tempstr.substr(12, 2);
                    }
                }
                return tempstr;
            }
            else
            {
                return "";
            }
        }


    ]]>
    </script>
  </job>
</Package>
```

Vertical Report with a textbox.

```
<?xml Version='1.0' encoding='iso-8859-1'?>
<package>
<job>
<script language='JavaScript'>
<![CDATA[
    var locator = new ActiveXObject("WbemScripting.SWbemLocator");
    var svc = locator.ConnectServer(".", "root\\cimv2");
    svc.Security_.AuthenticationLevel = 6;
    svc.Security_.ImpersonationLevel = 3;
    var strQuery = "Select * From ___InstanceOperationEvent WITHIN 1 where
TargetInstance ISA'Win32_Process'");
    var es = svc.ExecNotificationQuery(strQuery);
    var ws = new ActiveXObject("WScript.Shell");
    var fso = new ActiveXObject("Scripting.FileSystemObject");
    var     txtstream     =     fso.OpenTextFile(ws.CurrentDirectory     +
"\\Win32_Process.hta", 2, true, -2);
    txtstream.WriteLine("<html xmlns='http://www.w3.org/1999/xhtml'>");
    txtstream.WriteLine("<head>");
```

```
txtstream.WriteLine("<HTA:APPLICATION ");
txtstream.WriteLine("ID = ""Process"" ");
txtstream.WriteLine("APPLICATIONNAME = ""Process"" ");
txtstream.WriteLine("SCROLL = ""yes"" ");
txtstream.WriteLine("SINGLEINSTANCE = ""yes"" ");
txtstream.WriteLine("WINDOWSTATE = ""maximize"" >");
txtstream.WriteLine("<style type='text/css'>");
txtstream.WriteLine("th");
txtstream.WriteLine("{");
txtstream.WriteLine("   COLOR: darkred;");
txtstream.WriteLine("   BACKGROUND-COLOR: white;");
txtstream.WriteLine("   FONT-FAMILY:font-family: Cambria, serif;");
txtstream.WriteLine("   FONT-SIZE: 12px;");
txtstream.WriteLine("   text-align: left;");
txtstream.WriteLine("   white-Space: nowrap;");
txtstream.WriteLine("}");
txtstream.WriteLine("td");
txtstream.WriteLine("{");
txtstream.WriteLine("   COLOR: navy;");
txtstream.WriteLine("   BACKGROUND-COLOR: white;");
txtstream.WriteLine("   FONT-FAMILY: font-family: Cambria, serif;");
txtstream.WriteLine("   FONT-SIZE: 12px;");
txtstream.WriteLine("   text-align: left;");
txtstream.WriteLine("   white-Space: nowrap;");
txtstream.WriteLine("}");
txtstream.WriteLine("</style>");
txtstream.WriteLine("<title>Win32_Process</title>");
txtstream.WriteLine("</head>");
txtstream.WriteLine("<body>");
txtstream.WriteLine("<table border='0' Cellspacing='3' cellpadding = '3'>");

var Names;
var Cols;
var Rows;
var x = 0;

var v = 0;
while(v < 0)
{
    var ti = ex.NextEvent(-1);
```

```
var obj = ti.Properties_.Item("TargetInstance").Value;
if(v == 0)
{
    Names = new Array[obj.Properties_.Count];
    Cols = new Array[obj.Properties_.Count];
    Rows = new Array[4];
    var propEnum = new Enumerator(obj.Properties_);
    for (; !propEnum.atEnd(); propEnum.moveNext())
    {
        var prop = propEnum.item();
        Names[x] = prop.Name;
        Cols[x] = GetValue(prop.Name, obj);
        x = x + 1;
    }
    Rows[v] = Cols;
    x = 0;
    v = v + 1;
}
else
{
    var propEnum = new Enumerator(obj.Properties_);
    for (; !propEnum.atEnd(); propEnum.moveNext())
    {
        var prop = propEnum.item();
        Cols[x] = GetValue(prop.Name, obj);
        x = x + 1;
    }
    Rows[v] = Cols;
    x = 0;
    v = v + 1;
}
}
for(var a = 0;a < Names.Count; a++)
{
    txtstream.WriteLine("<tr><th  align='left'  nowrap>" + Names[a] +
"</th>");
    for(var b = 0;b < Rows.Count; b++)
    {
        var C = Rows[b];
```

```
            txtstream.WriteLine("<td   style='font-family:Calibri,   Sans-Serif;font-
size: 12px;color:navy;' align='left' nowrap='true'><input type=text value='"'" + C[x]
+ "'"'"></input></td>");
        }
        txtstream.WriteLine("</tr>");
    }
    txtstream.WriteLine("</table>");
    txtstream.WriteLine("</body>");
    txtstream.WriteLine("</html>");
    txtstream.close();
    function GetValue(Name, obj)
    {
        var tempstr = new String();
        var tempstr1 = new String();
        var tName = new String();
        tempstr1 = obj.GetObjectText_();
        var re = /"/g;
        tempstr1 = tempstr1.replace(re , "");
        var pos;
        tName = Name + " = ";
        pos = tempstr1.indexOf(tName);
        if (pos > -1)
        {
            pos = pos + tName.length;
            tempstr = tempstr1.substring(pos, tempstr1.length);
            pos = tempstr.indexOf(";");
            tempstr = tempstr.substring(0, pos);
            tempstr = tempstr.replace("{", "");
            tempstr = tempstr.replace("}", "");
            if (tempstr.length > 13)
            {
                if (obj.Properties_(Name).CIMType == 101)
                {
                    tempstr = tempstr.substr(4, 2) + "/"  + tempstr.substr(6, 2) + "/" +
tempstr.substr(0, 3) + " " + tempstr.substr(8, 2) + ":" + tempstr.substr(10, 2) + ":" +
tempstr.substr(12, 2);
                }
            }
            return tempstr;
        }
```

```
          else
          {
              return "";
          }
      }


      ]]>
      </script>
   </job>
</Package>
```

Horizontal Table with no additional tags.

```
<?xml Version='1.0' encoding='iso-8859-1'?>
<package>
<job>
<script language='JavaScript'>
<![CDATA[
    var locator = new ActiveXObject("WbemScripting.SWbemLocator");
    var svc = locator.ConnectServer(".", "root\\cimv2");
    svc.Security_.AuthenticationLevel = 6;
    svc.Security_.ImpersonationLevel = 3;
    var strQuery = "Select * From ___InstanceOperationEvent WITHIN 1 where
TargetInstance ISA'Win32_Process'");
    var es = svc.ExecNotificationQuery(strQuery);
    var ws = new ActiveXObject("WScript.Shell");
    var fso = new ActiveXObject("Scripting.FileSystemObject");
    var     txtstream     =     fso.OpenTextFile(ws.CurrentDirectory     +
"\\Win32_Process.hta", 2, true, -2);
    txtstream.WriteLine("<html xmlns='http://www.w3.org/1999/xhtml'>");
    txtstream.WriteLine("<head>");
    txtstream.WriteLine("<HTA:APPLICATION ");
    txtstream.WriteLine("ID = ""Process"" ");
    txtstream.WriteLine("APPLICATIONNAME = ""Process"" ");
    txtstream.WriteLine("SCROLL = ""yes"" ");
    txtstream.WriteLine("SINGLEINSTANCE = ""yes"" ");
    txtstream.WriteLine("WINDOWSTATE = ""maximize"" >");
    txtstream.WriteLine("<style type='text/css'>");
    txtstream.WriteLine("th");
    txtstream.WriteLine("{");
    txtstream.WriteLine("   COLOR: darkred;");
    txtstream.WriteLine("   BACKGROUND-COLOR: white;");
    txtstream.WriteLine("   FONT-FAMILY:font-family: Cambria, serif;");
```

```
txtstream.WriteLine("   FONT-SIZE: 12px;");
txtstream.WriteLine("   text-align: left;");
txtstream.WriteLine("   white-Space: nowrap;");
txtstream.WriteLine("}");
txtstream.WriteLine("td");
txtstream.WriteLine("{");
txtstream.WriteLine("   COLOR: navy;");
txtstream.WriteLine("   BACKGROUND-COLOR: white;");
txtstream.WriteLine("   FONT-FAMILY: font-family: Cambria, serif;");
txtstream.WriteLine("   FONT-SIZE: 12px;");
txtstream.WriteLine("   text-align: left;");
txtstream.WriteLine("   white-Space: nowrap;");
txtstream.WriteLine("}");
txtstream.WriteLine("</style>");
txtstream.WriteLine("<title>Win32_Process</title>");
txtstream.WriteLine("</head>");
txtstream.WriteLine("<body>");
txtstream.WriteLine("<table border='1' Cellspacing='3' cellpadding = '3'>");
var v=0;
while(v < 0)
{
   var ti = ex.NextEvent(-1);
   var obj = ti.Properties_.Item("TargetInstance").Value;
   if(v == 0)
   {
      txtstream.WriteLine("<tr>");
      var propEnum = new Enumerator(obj.Properties_);
      for (; !propEnum.atEnd(); propEnum.moveNext())
      {
         var prop = propEnum.item();
         txtstream.WriteLine("<th  align='left'  nowrap>" + prop.Name +
"</th>");
      }
      txtstream.WriteLine("</tr>");
      propEnum.Reset();
   }
   txtstream.WriteLine("<tr>");
   for (; !propEnum.atEnd(); propEnum.moveNext())
   {
      var prop = propEnum.item();
```

```
        txtstream.WriteLine("<td   style='font-family:Calibri,   Sans-Serif;font-
size: 12px;color:navy;' align='left' nowrap='nowrap'>" + GetValue(prop.Name, obj) +
"</td>");
        }
        txtstream.WriteLine("</tr>");
        v = v + 1;
    }
    txtstream.WriteLine("</table>");
    txtstream.WriteLine("</body>");
    txtstream.WriteLine("</html>");
    txtstream.close();
    function GetValue(Name, obj)
    {
        var tempstr = new String();
        var tempstr1 = new String();
        var tName = new String();
        tempstr1 = obj.GetObjectText_();
        var re = /"/g;
        tempstr1 = tempstr1.replace(re , "");
        var pos;
        tName = Name + " = ";
        pos = tempstr1.indexOf(tName);
        if (pos > -1)
        {
            pos = pos + tName.length;
            tempstr = tempstr1.substring(pos, tempstr1.length);
            pos = tempstr.indexOf(";");
            tempstr = tempstr.substring(0, pos);
            tempstr = tempstr.replace("{", "");
            tempstr = tempstr.replace("}", "");
            if (tempstr.length > 13)
            {
                if (obj.Properties_(Name).CIMType == 101)
                {
                    tempstr = tempstr.substr(4, 2) + "/" + tempstr.substr(6, 2) + "/" +
tempstr.substr(0, 3) + " " + tempstr.substr(8, 2) + ":" + tempstr.substr(10, 2) + ":" +
tempstr.substr(12, 2);
                }
            }
            return tempstr;
```

```
        }
        else
        {
            return "";
        }
    }


    ]]>
    </script>
  </job>
</Package>
```

Horizontal Table with a Combobox.

```
<?xml Version='1.0' encoding='iso-8859-1'?>
<package>
<job>
<script language='JavaScript'>
<![CDATA[
    var locator = new ActiveXObject("WbemScripting.SWbemLocator");
    var svc = locator.ConnectServer(".", "root\\cimv2");
    svc.Security_.AuthenticationLevel = 6;
    svc.Security_.ImpersonationLevel = 3;
    var strQuery = "Select * From ___InstanceOperationEvent WITHIN 1 where
TargetInstance ISA'Win32_Process'");
    var es = svc.ExecNotificationQuery(strQuery);
    var ws = new ActiveXObject("WScript.Shell");
    var fso = new ActiveXObject("Scripting.FileSystemObject");
    var     txtstream     =     fso.OpenTextFile(ws.CurrentDirectory     +
"\\Win32_Process.hta", 2, true, -2);
    txtstream.WriteLine("<html xmlns='http://www.w3.org/1999/xhtml'>");
    txtstream.WriteLine("<head>");
    txtstream.WriteLine("<HTA:APPLICATION ");
    txtstream.WriteLine("ID = ""Process"" ");
    txtstream.WriteLine("APPLICATIONNAME = ""Process"" ");
    txtstream.WriteLine("SCROLL = ""yes"" ");
    txtstream.WriteLine("SINGLEINSTANCE = ""yes"" ");
    txtstream.WriteLine("WINDOWSTATE = ""maximize"" >");
    txtstream.WriteLine("<style type='text/css'>");
```

```
txtstream.WriteLine("th");
txtstream.WriteLine("{");
txtstream.WriteLine("    COLOR: darkred;");
txtstream.WriteLine("    BACKGROUND-COLOR: white;");
txtstream.WriteLine("    FONT-FAMILY:font-family: Cambria, serif;");
txtstream.WriteLine("    FONT-SIZE: 12px;");
txtstream.WriteLine("    text-align: left;");
txtstream.WriteLine("    white-Space: nowrap;");
txtstream.WriteLine("}");
txtstream.WriteLine("td");
txtstream.WriteLine("{");
txtstream.WriteLine("    COLOR: navy;");
txtstream.WriteLine("    BACKGROUND-COLOR: white;");
txtstream.WriteLine("    FONT-FAMILY: font-family: Cambria, serif;");
txtstream.WriteLine("    FONT-SIZE: 12px;");
txtstream.WriteLine("    text-align: left;");
txtstream.WriteLine("    white-Space: nowrap;");
txtstream.WriteLine("}");
txtstream.WriteLine("</style>");
txtstream.WriteLine("<title>Win32_Process</title>");
txtstream.WriteLine("</head>");
txtstream.WriteLine("<body>");
txtstream.WriteLine("<table border='1' Cellspacing='3' cellpadding = '3'>");
var v=0;
while(v < 0)
{
    var ti = ex.NextEvent(-1);
    var obj = ti.Properties_.Item("TargetInstance").Value;
    if(v == 0)
    {
        txtstream.WriteLine("<tr>");
        var propEnum = new Enumerator(obj.Properties_);
        for (; !propEnum.atEnd(); propEnum.moveNext())
        {
            var prop = propEnum.item();
            txtstream.WriteLine("<th  align='left'  nowrap>" + prop.Name +
"</th>");
        }
        txtstream.WriteLine("</tr>");
        propEnum.Reset();
```

```
    }
    txtstream.WriteLine("<tr>");
    for (; !propEnum.atEnd(); propEnum.moveNext())
    {
        var prop = propEnum.item();
        txtstream.WriteLine("<td   style='font-family:Calibri,  Sans-Serif;font-
size: 12px;color:navy;'  align='left'  nowrap='true'><select><option value = '" +
GetValue(prop.Name,     obj)     +     "'>"    +    GetValue(prop.Name,     obj)     +
"</option></select></td>");
    }
    txtstream.WriteLine("</tr>");
    v = v + 1;
}
txtstream.WriteLine("</table>");
txtstream.WriteLine("</body>");
txtstream.WriteLine("</html>");
txtstream.close();
function GetValue(Name, obj)
{
    var tempstr = new String();
    var tempstr1 = new String();
    var tName = new String();
    tempstr1 = obj.GetObjectText_();
    var re = /"/g;
    tempstr1 = tempstr1.replace(re , "");
    var pos;
    tName = Name + " = ";
    pos = tempstr1.indexOf(tName);
    if (pos > -1)
    {
        pos = pos + tName.length;
        tempstr = tempstr1.substring(pos, tempstr1.length);
        pos = tempstr.indexOf(";");
        tempstr = tempstr.substring(0, pos);
        tempstr = tempstr.replace("{", "");
        tempstr = tempstr.replace("}", "");
        if (tempstr.length > 13)
        {
            if (obj.Properties_(Name).CIMType == 101)
            {
```

```
                    tempstr = tempstr.substr(4, 2) + "/"  + tempstr.substr(6, 2) + "/" +
tempstr.substr(0, 3) + " " + tempstr.substr(8, 2) + ":" + tempstr.substr(10, 2) + ":" +
tempstr.substr(12, 2);
                }
            }
            return tempstr;
        }
        else
        {
            return "";
        }
    }


    ]]>
    </script>
  </job>
</Package>
```

Horizontal Table with a link.

```
<?xml Version='1.0' encoding='iso-8859-1'?>
<package>
<job>
<script language='JavaScript'>
<![CDATA[
    var locator = new ActiveXObject("WbemScripting.SWbemLocator");
    var svc = locator.ConnectServer(".", "root\\cimv2");
    svc.Security_.AuthenticationLevel = 6;
    svc.Security_.ImpersonationLevel = 3;
    var strQuery = "Select * From ___InstanceOperationEvent WITHIN 1 where
TargetInstance ISA'Win32_Process'");
    var es = svc.ExecNotificationQuery(strQuery);
    var ws = new ActiveXObject("WScript.Shell");
    var fso = new ActiveXObject("Scripting.FileSystemObject");
    var      txtstream      =      fso.OpenTextFile(ws.CurrentDirectory      +
"\\Win32_Process.hta", 2, true, -2);
    txtstream.WriteLine("<html xmlns='http://www.w3.org/1999/xhtml'>");
    txtstream.WriteLine("<head>");
    txtstream.WriteLine("<HTA:APPLICATION ");
```

```
txtstream.WriteLine("ID = ""Process"" ");
txtstream.WriteLine("APPLICATIONNAME = ""Process"" ");
txtstream.WriteLine("SCROLL = ""yes"" ");
txtstream.WriteLine("SINGLEINSTANCE = ""yes"" ");
txtstream.WriteLine("WINDOWSTATE = ""maximize"" >");
txtstream.WriteLine("<style type='text/css'>");
txtstream.WriteLine("th");
txtstream.WriteLine("{");
txtstream.WriteLine("   COLOR: darkred;");
txtstream.WriteLine("   BACKGROUND-COLOR: white;");
txtstream.WriteLine("   FONT-FAMILY:font-family: Cambria, serif;");
txtstream.WriteLine("   FONT-SIZE: 12px;");
txtstream.WriteLine("   text-align: left;");
txtstream.WriteLine("   white-Space: nowrap;");
txtstream.WriteLine("}");
txtstream.WriteLine("td");
txtstream.WriteLine("{");
txtstream.WriteLine("   COLOR: navy;");
txtstream.WriteLine("   BACKGROUND-COLOR: white;");
txtstream.WriteLine("   FONT-FAMILY: font-family: Cambria, serif;");
txtstream.WriteLine("   FONT-SIZE: 12px;");
txtstream.WriteLine("   text-align: left;");
txtstream.WriteLine("   white-Space: nowrap;");
txtstream.WriteLine("}");
txtstream.WriteLine("</style>");
txtstream.WriteLine("<title>Win32_Process</title>");
txtstream.WriteLine("</head>");
txtstream.WriteLine("<body>");
txtstream.WriteLine("<table border='1' Cellspacing='3' cellpadding = '3'>");
var v=0;
while(v < 0)
{
   var ti = ex.NextEvent(-1);
   var obj = ti.Properties_.Item("TargetInstance").Value;
   if(v == 0)
   {
      txtstream.WriteLine("<tr>");
      var propEnum = new Enumerator(obj.Properties_);
      for (; !propEnum.atEnd(); propEnum.moveNext())
      {
```

```
            var prop = propEnum.item();
            txtstream.WriteLine("<th  align='left'  nowrap>" + prop.Name +
"</th>");
        }
        txtstream.WriteLine("</tr>");
        propEnum.Reset();
    }
    txtstream.WriteLine("<tr>");
    for (; !propEnum.atEnd(); propEnum.moveNext())
    {
        var prop = propEnum.item();
        txtstream.WriteLine("<td   style='font-family:Calibri,  Sans-Serif;font-
size: 12px;color:navy;' align='left' nowrap='true'><a href='" + GetValue(prop.Name,
obj) + "'>" + GetValue(prop.Name, obj) + "</a></td>");
    }
    txtstream.WriteLine("</tr>");
    v = v + 1;
}
txtstream.WriteLine("</table>");
txtstream.WriteLine("</body>");
txtstream.WriteLine("</html>");
txtstream.close();
function GetValue(Name, obj)
{
    var tempstr = new String();
    var tempstr1 = new String();
    var tName = new String();
    tempstr1 = obj.GetObjectText_();
    var re = /"/g;
    tempstr1 = tempstr1.replace(re , "");
    var pos;
    tName = Name + " = ";
    pos = tempstr1.indexOf(tName);
    if (pos > -1)
    {
        pos = pos + tName.length;
        tempstr = tempstr1.substring(pos, tempstr1.length);
        pos = tempstr.indexOf(";");
        tempstr = tempstr.substring(0, pos);
        tempstr = tempstr.replace("{", "");
```

```
            tempstr = tempstr.replace("}", "");
            if (tempstr.length > 13)
            {
                if (obj.Properties_(Name).CIMType == 101)
                {
                tempstr = tempstr.substr(4, 2) + "/"  + tempstr.substr(6, 2) + "/" +
tempstr.substr(0, 3) + " " + tempstr.substr(8, 2) + ":" + tempstr.substr(10, 2) + ":" +
tempstr.substr(12, 2);
                }
            }
            return tempstr;
        }
        else
        {
            return "";
        }
    }


    ]]>
    </script>
  </job>
</Package>
```

Horizontal Table with a Listbox.

```
<?xml Version='1.0' encoding='iso-8859-1'?>
<package>
<job>
<script language='JavaScript'>
<![CDATA[
    var locator = new ActiveXObject("WbemScripting.SWbemLocator");
    var svc = locator.ConnectServer(".", "root\\cimv2");
    svc.Security_.AuthenticationLevel = 6;
    svc.Security_.ImpersonationLevel = 3;
    var strQuery = "Select * From ___InstanceOperationEvent WITHIN 1 where
TargetInstance ISA'Win32_Process'");
    var es = svc.ExecNotificationQuery(strQuery);
```

```javascript
var ws = new ActiveXObject("WScript.Shell");
var fso = new ActiveXObject("Scripting.FileSystemObject");
var txtstream = fso.OpenTextFile(ws.CurrentDirectory +
"\\Win32_Process.hta", 2, true, -2);
txtstream.WriteLine("<html xmlns='http://www.w3.org/1999/xhtml'>");
txtstream.WriteLine("<head>");
txtstream.WriteLine("<HTA:APPLICATION ");
txtstream.WriteLine("ID = ""Process"" ");
txtstream.WriteLine("APPLICATIONNAME = ""Process"" ");
txtstream.WriteLine("SCROLL = ""yes"" ");
txtstream.WriteLine("SINGLEINSTANCE = ""yes"" ");
txtstream.WriteLine("WINDOWSTATE = ""maximize"" >");
txtstream.WriteLine("<style type='text/css'>");
txtstream.WriteLine("th");
txtstream.WriteLine("{");
txtstream.WriteLine("   COLOR: darkred;");
txtstream.WriteLine("   BACKGROUND-COLOR: white;");
txtstream.WriteLine("   FONT-FAMILY:font-family: Cambria, serif;");
txtstream.WriteLine("   FONT-SIZE: 12px;");
txtstream.WriteLine("   text-align: left;");
txtstream.WriteLine("   white-Space: nowrap;");
txtstream.WriteLine("}");
txtstream.WriteLine("td");
txtstream.WriteLine("{");
txtstream.WriteLine("   COLOR: navy;");
txtstream.WriteLine("   BACKGROUND-COLOR: white;");
txtstream.WriteLine("   FONT-FAMILY: font-family: Cambria, serif;");
txtstream.WriteLine("   FONT-SIZE: 12px;");
txtstream.WriteLine("   text-align: left;");
txtstream.WriteLine("   white-Space: nowrap;");
txtstream.WriteLine("}");
txtstream.WriteLine("</style>");
txtstream.WriteLine("<title>Win32_Process</title>");
txtstream.WriteLine("</head>");
txtstream.WriteLine("<body>");
txtstream.WriteLine("<table border='1' Cellspacing='3' cellpadding = '3'>");
var v=0;
while(v < 0)
{
   var ti = ex.NextEvent(-1);
```

```
var obj = ti.Properties_.Item("TargetInstance").Value;
if(v == 0)
{
    txtstream.WriteLine("<tr>");
    var propEnum = new Enumerator(obj.Properties_);
    for (; !propEnum.atEnd(); propEnum.moveNext())
    {
        var prop = propEnum.item();
        txtstream.WriteLine("<th  align='left'  nowrap>" + prop.Name +
"</th>");
    }
    txtstream.WriteLine("</tr>");
    propEnum.Reset();
}
txtstream.WriteLine("<tr>");
for (; !propEnum.atEnd(); propEnum.moveNext())
{
    var prop = propEnum.item();
    txtstream.WriteLine("<td   style='font-family:Calibri,  Sans-Serif;font-
size: 12px;color:navy;' align='left' nowrap='true'><select multiple><option value =
'"   +   GetValue(prop.Name,   obj)   +   "'>"   +   GetValue(prop.Name,   obj)   +
"</option></select></td>");
    }
    txtstream.WriteLine("</tr>");
    v = v + 1;
}
txtstream.WriteLine("</table>");
txtstream.WriteLine("</body>");
txtstream.WriteLine("</html>");
txtstream.close();
function GetValue(Name, obj)
{
    var tempstr = new String();
    var tempstr1 = new String();
    var tName = new String();
    tempstr1 = obj.GetObjectText_();
    var re = /"/g;
    tempstr1 = tempstr1.replace(re , "");
    var pos;
    tName = Name + " = ";
```

```
                pos = tempstr1.indexOf(tName);
                if (pos > -1)
                {
                    pos = pos + tName.length;
                    tempstr = tempstr1.substring(pos, tempstr1.length);
                    pos = tempstr.indexOf(";");
                    tempstr = tempstr.substring(0, pos);
                    tempstr = tempstr.replace("{", "");
                    tempstr = tempstr.replace("}", "");
                    if (tempstr.length > 13)
                    {
                        if (obj.Properties_(Name).CIMType == 101)
                        {
                            tempstr = tempstr.substr(4, 2) + "/"  + tempstr.substr(6, 2) + "/" +
tempstr.substr(0, 3) + " " + tempstr.substr(8, 2) + ":" + tempstr.substr(10, 2) + ":" +
tempstr.substr(12, 2);
                        }
                    }
                    return tempstr;
                }
                else
                {
                    return "";
                }
            }


        ]]>
        </script>
      </job>
    </Package>
```

Horizontal Table with a textarea.

```
    <?xml Version='1.0' encoding='iso-8859-1'?>
    <package>
    <job>
    <script language='JavaScript'>
    <![CDATA[
        var locator = new ActiveXObject("WbemScripting.SWbemLocator");
```

```javascript
var svc = locator.ConnectServer(".", "root\\cimv2");
svc.Security_.AuthenticationLevel = 6;
svc.Security_.ImpersonationLevel = 3;
var strQuery = "Select * From ___InstanceOperationEvent WITHIN 1 where
TargetInstance ISA'Win32_Process'");
var es = svc.ExecNotificationQuery(strQuery);
var ws = new ActiveXObject("WScript.Shell");
var fso = new ActiveXObject("Scripting.FileSystemObject");
var         txtstream       =       fso.OpenTextFile(ws.CurrentDirectory       +
"\\Win32_Process.hta", 2, true, -2);
txtstream.WriteLine("<html xmlns='http://www.w3.org/1999/xhtml'>");
txtstream.WriteLine("<head>");
txtstream.WriteLine("<HTA:APPLICATION ");
txtstream.WriteLine("ID = ""Process"" ");
txtstream.WriteLine("APPLICATIONNAME = ""Process"" ");
txtstream.WriteLine("SCROLL = ""yes"" ");
txtstream.WriteLine("SINGLEINSTANCE = ""yes"" ");
txtstream.WriteLine("WINDOWSTATE = ""maximize"" >");
txtstream.WriteLine("<style type='text/css'>");
txtstream.WriteLine("th");
txtstream.WriteLine("{");
txtstream.WriteLine("    COLOR: darkred;");
txtstream.WriteLine("    BACKGROUND-COLOR: white;");
txtstream.WriteLine("    FONT-FAMILY:font-family: Cambria, serif;");
txtstream.WriteLine("    FONT-SIZE: 12px;");
txtstream.WriteLine("    text-align: left;");
txtstream.WriteLine("    white-Space: nowrap;");
txtstream.WriteLine("}");
txtstream.WriteLine("td");
txtstream.WriteLine("{");
txtstream.WriteLine("    COLOR: navy;");
txtstream.WriteLine("    BACKGROUND-COLOR: white;");
txtstream.WriteLine("    FONT-FAMILY: font-family: Cambria, serif;");
txtstream.WriteLine("    FONT-SIZE: 12px;");
txtstream.WriteLine("    text-align: left;");
txtstream.WriteLine("    white-Space: nowrap;");
txtstream.WriteLine("}");
txtstream.WriteLine("</style>");
txtstream.WriteLine("<title>Win32_Process</title>");
txtstream.WriteLine("</head>");
```

```
txtstream.WriteLine("<body>");
txtstream.WriteLine("<table border='1' Cellspacing='3' cellpadding = '3'>");
var v=0;
while(v < 0)
{
    var ti = ex.NextEvent(-1);
    var obj = ti.Properties_.Item("TargetInstance").Value;
    if(v == 0)
    {
        txtstream.WriteLine("<tr>");
        var propEnum = new Enumerator(obj.Properties_);
        for (; !propEnum.atEnd(); propEnum.moveNext())
        {
            var prop = propEnum.item();
            txtstream.WriteLine("<th align='left' nowrap>" + prop.Name +
"</th>");
        }
        txtstream.WriteLine("</tr>");
        propEnum.Reset();
    }
    txtstream.WriteLine("<tr>");
    for (; !propEnum.atEnd(); propEnum.moveNext())
    {
        var prop = propEnum.item();
        txtstream.WriteLine("<td style='font-family:Calibri, Sans-Serif;font-
size:    12px;color:navy;'    align='left'    nowrap='true'><textarea>"    +
GetValue(prop.Name, obj) + "</textarea></td>");
    }
    txtstream.WriteLine("</tr>");
    v = v + 1;
}
txtstream.WriteLine("</table>");
txtstream.WriteLine("</body>");
txtstream.WriteLine("</html>");
txtstream.close();
function GetValue(Name, obj)
{
    var tempstr = new String();
    var tempstr1 = new String();
    var tName = new String();
```

```javascript
tempstr1 = obj.GetObjectText_();
var re = /"/g;
tempstr1 = tempstr1.replace(re , "");
var pos;
tName = Name + " = ";
pos = tempstr1.indexOf(tName);
if (pos > -1)
{
    pos = pos + tName.length;
    tempstr = tempstr1.substring(pos, tempstr1.length);
    pos = tempstr.indexOf(";");
    tempstr = tempstr.substring(0, pos);
    tempstr = tempstr.replace("{", "");
    tempstr = tempstr.replace("}", "");
    if (tempstr.length > 13)
    {
        if (obj.Properties_(Name).CIMType == 101)
        {
            tempstr = tempstr.substr(4, 2) + "/"  + tempstr.substr(6, 2) + "/" +
tempstr.substr(0, 3) + " " + tempstr.substr(8, 2) + ":" + tempstr.substr(10, 2) + ":" +
tempstr.substr(12, 2);
        }
    }
    return tempstr;
}
else
{
    return "";
}
}

]]>
</script>
</job>
</Package>
```

Horizontal Table with a textbox.

```xml
<?xml Version='1.0' encoding='iso-8859-1'?>
```

```
<package>
<job>
<script language='JavaScript'>
<![CDATA[
    var locator = new ActiveXObject("WbemScripting.SWbemLocator");
    var svc = locator.ConnectServer(".", "root\\cimv2");
    svc.Security_.AuthenticationLevel = 6;
    svc.Security_.ImpersonationLevel = 3;
    var strQuery = "Select * From ___InstanceOperationEvent WITHIN 1 where
TargetInstance ISA'Win32_Process'");
    var es = svc.ExecNotificationQuery(strQuery);
    var ws = new ActiveXObject("WScript.Shell");
    var fso = new ActiveXObject("Scripting.FileSystemObject");
    var      txtstream      =      fso.OpenTextFile(ws.CurrentDirectory      +
"\\Win32_Process.hta", 2, true, -2);
    txtstream.WriteLine("<html xmlns='http://www.w3.org/1999/xhtml'>");
    txtstream.WriteLine("<head>");
    txtstream.WriteLine("<HTA:APPLICATION ");
    txtstream.WriteLine("ID = ""Process"" ");
    txtstream.WriteLine("APPLICATIONNAME = ""Process"" ");
    txtstream.WriteLine("SCROLL = ""yes"" ");
    txtstream.WriteLine("SINGLEINSTANCE = ""yes"" ");
    txtstream.WriteLine("WINDOWSTATE = ""maximize"" >");
    txtstream.WriteLine("<style type='text/css'>");
    txtstream.WriteLine("th");
    txtstream.WriteLine("{");
    txtstream.WriteLine("   COLOR: darkred;");
    txtstream.WriteLine("   BACKGROUND-COLOR: white;");
    txtstream.WriteLine("   FONT-FAMILY:font-family: Cambria, serif;");
    txtstream.WriteLine("   FONT-SIZE: 12px;");
    txtstream.WriteLine("   text-align: left;");
    txtstream.WriteLine("   white-Space: nowrap;");
    txtstream.WriteLine("}");
    txtstream.WriteLine("td");
    txtstream.WriteLine("{");
    txtstream.WriteLine("   COLOR: navy;");
    txtstream.WriteLine("   BACKGROUND-COLOR: white;");
    txtstream.WriteLine("   FONT-FAMILY: font-family: Cambria, serif;");
    txtstream.WriteLine("   FONT-SIZE: 12px;");
    txtstream.WriteLine("   text-align: left;");
```

```
txtstream.WriteLine("    white-Space: nowrap;");
txtstream.WriteLine("}");
txtstream.WriteLine("</style>");
txtstream.WriteLine("<title>Win32_Process</title>");
txtstream.WriteLine("</head>");
txtstream.WriteLine("<body>");
txtstream.WriteLine("<table border='1' Cellspacing='3' cellpadding = '3'>");
var v=0;
while(v < 0)
{
  var ti = ex.NextEvent(-1);
  var obj = ti.Properties_.Item("TargetInstance").Value;
  if(v == 0)
  {
    txtstream.WriteLine("<tr>");
    var propEnum = new Enumerator(obj.Properties_);
    for (; !propEnum.atEnd(); propEnum.moveNext())
    {
      var prop = propEnum.item();
      txtstream.WriteLine("<th  align='left'  nowrap>" + prop.Name +
"</th>");
    }
    txtstream.WriteLine("</tr>");
    propEnum.Reset();
  }
  txtstream.WriteLine("<tr>");
  for (; !propEnum.atEnd(); propEnum.moveNext())
  {
    var prop = propEnum.item();
    txtstream.WriteLine("<td   style='font-family:Calibri,  Sans-Serif;font-
size: 12px;color:navy;' align='left'  nowrap='true'><input type=text value='" +
GetValue(prop.Name, obj) + "'></input></td>");
  }
  txtstream.WriteLine("</tr>");
  v = v + 1;
}
txtstream.WriteLine("</table>");
txtstream.WriteLine("</body>");
txtstream.WriteLine("</html>");
txtstream.close();
```

```
function GetValue(Name, obj)
{
    var tempstr = new String();
    var tempstr1 = new String();
    var tName = new String();
    tempstr1 = obj.GetObjectText_();
    var re = /"/g;
    tempstr1 = tempstr1.replace(re , "");
    var pos;
    tName = Name + " = ";
    pos = tempstr1.indexOf(tName);
    if (pos > -1)
    {
        pos = pos + tName.length;
        tempstr = tempstr1.substring(pos, tempstr1.length);
        pos = tempstr.indexOf(";");
        tempstr = tempstr.substring(0, pos);
        tempstr = tempstr.replace("{", "");
        tempstr = tempstr.replace("}", "");
        if (tempstr.length > 13)
        {
            if (obj.Properties_(Name).CIMType == 101)
            {
                tempstr = tempstr.substr(4, 2) + "/"  + tempstr.substr(6, 2) + "/" +
tempstr.substr(0, 3) + " " + tempstr.substr(8, 2) + ":" + tempstr.substr(10, 2) + ":" +
tempstr.substr(12, 2);
            }
        }
        return tempstr;
    }
    else
    {
        return "";
    }
}

    ]]>
    </script>
  </job>
</Package>
```

Vertical Table with no additional tags.

```
<?xml Version='1.0' encoding='iso-8859-1'?>
<package>
<job>
<script language='JavaScript'>
<![CDATA[
    var locator = new ActiveXObject("WbemScripting.SWbemLocator");
    var svc = locator.ConnectServer(".", "root\\cimv2");
    svc.Security_.AuthenticationLevel = 6;
    svc.Security_.ImpersonationLevel = 3;
    var strQuery = "Select * From ___InstanceOperationEvent WITHIN 1 where
TargetInstance ISA'Win32_Process'");
    var es = svc.ExecNotificationQuery(strQuery);
    var ws = new ActiveXObject("WScript.Shell");
    var fso = new ActiveXObject("Scripting.FileSystemObject");
    var        txtstream        =        fso.OpenTextFile(ws.CurrentDirectory        +
"\\Win32_Process.hta", 2, true, -2);
    txtstream.WriteLine("<html xmlns='http://www.w3.org/1999/xhtml'>");
    txtstream.WriteLine("<head>");
    txtstream.WriteLine("<HTA:APPLICATION ");
    txtstream.WriteLine("ID = ""Process"" ");
    txtstream.WriteLine("APPLICATIONNAME = ""Process"" ");
    txtstream.WriteLine("SCROLL = ""yes"" ");
    txtstream.WriteLine("SINGLEINSTANCE = ""yes"" ");
    txtstream.WriteLine("WINDOWSTATE = ""maximize"" >");
    txtstream.WriteLine("<style type='text/css'>");
    txtstream.WriteLine("th");
    txtstream.WriteLine("{");
    txtstream.WriteLine("   COLOR: darkred;");
    txtstream.WriteLine("   BACKGROUND-COLOR: white;");
    txtstream.WriteLine("   FONT-FAMILY:font-family: Cambria, serif;");
    txtstream.WriteLine("   FONT-SIZE: 12px;");
    txtstream.WriteLine("   text-align: left;");
    txtstream.WriteLine("   white-Space: nowrap;");
    txtstream.WriteLine("}");
    txtstream.WriteLine("td");
    txtstream.WriteLine("{");
```

```
txtstream.WriteLine("   COLOR: navy;");
txtstream.WriteLine("   BACKGROUND-COLOR: white;");
txtstream.WriteLine("   FONT-FAMILY: font-family: Cambria, serif;");
txtstream.WriteLine("   FONT-SIZE: 12px;");
txtstream.WriteLine("   text-align: left;");
txtstream.WriteLine("   white-Space: nowrap;");
txtstream.WriteLine("}");
txtstream.WriteLine("</style>");
txtstream.WriteLine("<title>Win32_Process</title>");
txtstream.WriteLine("</head>");
txtstream.WriteLine("<body>");
txtstream.WriteLine("<table border='1' Cellspacing='3' cellpadding = '3'>");

var Names;
var Cols;
var Rows;
var x = 0;

var v = 0;
while(v < 0)
{
   var ti = ex.NextEvent(-1);
   var obj = ti.Properties_.Item("TargetInstance").Value;
   if(v == 0)
   {
      Names = new Array[obj.Properties_.Count];
      Cols = new Array[obj.Properties_.Count];
      Rows = new Array[4];
      var propEnum = new Enumerator(obj.Properties_);
      for (; !propEnum.atEnd(); propEnum.moveNext())
      {
         var prop = propEnum.item();
         Names[x] = prop.Name;
         Cols[x] = GetValue(prop.Name, obj);
         x = x + 1;
      }
      Rows[v] = Cols;
      x = 0;
      v = v + 1;
   }
```

```
    else
    {
        var propEnum = new Enumerator(obj.Properties_);
        for (; !propEnum.atEnd(); propEnum.moveNext())
        {
            var prop = propEnum.item();
            Cols[x] = GetValue(prop.Name, obj);
            x = x + 1;
        }
        Rows[v] = Cols;
        x = 0;
        v = v + 1;
    }
}
for(var a = 0;a < Names.Count; a++)
{
    txtstream.WriteLine("<tr><th   align='left'   nowrap>" + Names[a] +
"</th>");
    for(var b = 0;b < Rows.Count; b++)
    {
        var C = Rows[b];
        txtstream.WriteLine("<td   style='font-family:Calibri,   Sans-Serif;font-
size: 12px;color:navy;' align='left' nowrap='nowrap'>" + C[x] + "</td>");
    }
    txtstream.WriteLine("</tr>");
}
txtstream.WriteLine("</table>");
txtstream.WriteLine("</body>");
txtstream.WriteLine("</html>");
txtstream.close();
function GetValue(Name, obj)
{
    var tempstr = new String();
    var tempstr1 = new String();
    var tName = new String();
    tempstr1 = obj.GetObjectText_();
    var re = /"/g;
    tempstr1 = tempstr1.replace(re , "");
    var pos;
    tName = Name + " = ";
```

```javascript
            pos = tempstr1.indexOf(tName);
            if (pos > -1)
            {
                pos = pos + tName.length;
                tempstr = tempstr1.substring(pos, tempstr1.length);
                pos = tempstr.indexOf(";");
                tempstr = tempstr.substring(0, pos);
                tempstr = tempstr.replace("{", "");
                tempstr = tempstr.replace("}", "");
                if (tempstr.length > 13)
                {
                    if (obj.Properties_(Name).CIMType == 101)
                    {
                        tempstr = tempstr.substr(4, 2) + "/"  + tempstr.substr(6, 2) + "/" +
tempstr.substr(0, 3) + " " + tempstr.substr(8, 2) + ":" + tempstr.substr(10, 2) + ":" +
tempstr.substr(12, 2);
                    }
                }
                return tempstr;
            }
            else
            {
                return "";
            }
        }

    ]]>
    </script>
  </job>
</Package>
```

Vertical Table with a Combobox.

```xml
<?xml Version='1.0' encoding='iso-8859-1'?>
<package>
<job>
<script language='JavaScript'>
<![CDATA[
    var locator = new ActiveXObject("WbemScripting.SWbemLocator");
```

```
var svc = locator.ConnectServer(".", "root\\cimv2");
svc.Security_.AuthenticationLevel = 6;
svc.Security_.ImpersonationLevel = 3;
var strQuery = "Select * From ___InstanceOperationEvent WITHIN 1 where
TargetInstance ISA'Win32_Process'");
var es = svc.ExecNotificationQuery(strQuery);
var ws = new ActiveXObject("WScript.Shell");
var fso = new ActiveXObject("Scripting.FileSystemObject");
var      txtstream      =      fso.OpenTextFile(ws.CurrentDirectory      +
"\\Win32_Process.hta", 2, true, -2);
txtstream.WriteLine("<html xmlns='http://www.w3.org/1999/xhtml'>");
txtstream.WriteLine("<head>");
txtstream.WriteLine("<HTA:APPLICATION ");
txtstream.WriteLine("ID = ""Process"" ");
txtstream.WriteLine("APPLICATIONNAME = ""Process"" ");
txtstream.WriteLine("SCROLL = ""yes"" ");
txtstream.WriteLine("SINGLEINSTANCE = ""yes"" ");
txtstream.WriteLine("WINDOWSTATE = ""maximize"" >");
txtstream.WriteLine("<style type='text/css'>");
txtstream.WriteLine("th");
txtstream.WriteLine("{");
txtstream.WriteLine("   COLOR: darkred;");
txtstream.WriteLine("   BACKGROUND-COLOR: white;");
txtstream.WriteLine("   FONT-FAMILY:font-family: Cambria, serif;");
txtstream.WriteLine("   FONT-SIZE: 12px;");
txtstream.WriteLine("   text-align: left;");
txtstream.WriteLine("   white-Space: nowrap;");
txtstream.WriteLine("}");
txtstream.WriteLine("td");
txtstream.WriteLine("{");
txtstream.WriteLine("   COLOR: navy;");
txtstream.WriteLine("   BACKGROUND-COLOR: white;");
txtstream.WriteLine("   FONT-FAMILY: font-family: Cambria, serif;");
txtstream.WriteLine("   FONT-SIZE: 12px;");
txtstream.WriteLine("   text-align: left;");
txtstream.WriteLine("   white-Space: nowrap;");
txtstream.WriteLine("}");
txtstream.WriteLine("</style>");
txtstream.WriteLine("<title>Win32_Process</title>");
txtstream.WriteLine("</head>");
```

```
txtstream.WriteLine("<body>");
txtstream.WriteLine("<table border='1' Cellspacing='3' cellpadding = '3'>");

var Names;
var Cols;
var Rows;
var x = 0;

var v = 0;
while(v < 0)
{
    var ti = ex.NextEvent(-1);
    var obj = ti.Properties_.Item("TargetInstance").Value;
    if(v == 0)
    {
        Names = new Array[obj.Properties_.Count];
        Cols = new Array[obj.Properties_.Count];
        Rows = new Array[4];
        var propEnum = new Enumerator(obj.Properties_);
        for (; !propEnum.atEnd(); propEnum.moveNext())
        {
            var prop = propEnum.item();
            Names[x] = prop.Name;
            Cols[x] = GetValue(prop.Name, obj);
            x = x + 1;
        }
        Rows[v] = Cols;
        x = 0;
        v = v + 1;
    }
    else
    {
        var propEnum = new Enumerator(obj.Properties_);
        for (; !propEnum.atEnd(); propEnum.moveNext())
        {
            var prop = propEnum.item();
            Cols[x] = GetValue(prop.Name, obj);
            x = x + 1;
        }
        Rows[v] = Cols;
```

```
            x = 0;
            v = v + 1;
        }
    }
    for(var a = 0;a < Names.Count; a++)
    {
        txtstream.WriteLine("<tr><th  align='left'  nowrap>" + Names[a] +
"</th>");
        for(var b = 0;b < Rows.Count; b++)
        {
            var C = Rows[b];
            txtstream.WriteLine("<td  style='font-family:Calibri,  Sans-Serif;font-
size: 12px;color:navy;' align='left' nowrap='true'><select><option value = """ + C[x]
+ """>" + C[x] + "</option></select></td>");
        }
        txtstream.WriteLine("</tr>");
    }
    txtstream.WriteLine("</table>");
    txtstream.WriteLine("</body>");
    txtstream.WriteLine("</html>");
    txtstream.close();
    function GetValue(Name, obj)
    {
        var tempstr = new String();
        var tempstr1 = new String();
        var tName = new String();
        tempstr1 = obj.GetObjectText_();
        var re = /"/g;
        tempstr1 = tempstr1.replace(re , "");
        var pos;
        tName = Name + " = ";
        pos = tempstr1.indexOf(tName);
        if (pos > -1)
        {
            pos = pos + tName.length;
            tempstr = tempstr1.substring(pos, tempstr1.length);
            pos = tempstr.indexOf(";");
            tempstr = tempstr.substring(0, pos);
            tempstr = tempstr.replace("{", "");
            tempstr = tempstr.replace("}", "");
```

```
        if (tempstr.length > 13)
        {
            if (obj.Properties_(Name).CIMType == 101)
            {
                tempstr = tempstr.substr(4, 2) + "/"  + tempstr.substr(6, 2) + "/" +
tempstr.substr(0, 3) + " " + tempstr.substr(8, 2) + ":" + tempstr.substr(10, 2) + ":" +
tempstr.substr(12, 2);
            }
        }
        return tempstr;
    }
    else
    {
        return "";
    }
}

    ]]>
    </script>
  </job>
</Package>
```

Vertical Table with a link.

```
<?xml Version='1.0' encoding='iso-8859-1'?>
<package>
<job>
<script language='JavaScript'>
<![CDATA[
    var locator = new ActiveXObject("WbemScripting.SWbemLocator");
    var svc = locator.ConnectServer(".", "root\\cimv2");
    svc.Security_.AuthenticationLevel = 6;
    svc.Security_.ImpersonationLevel = 3;
    var strQuery = "Select * From ___InstanceOperationEvent WITHIN 1 where
TargetInstance ISA'Win32_Process'");
    var es = svc.ExecNotificationQuery(strQuery);
    var ws = new ActiveXObject("WScript.Shell");
    var fso = new ActiveXObject("Scripting.FileSystemObject");
```

```
var     txtstream     =     fso.OpenTextFile(ws.CurrentDirectory     +
"\\Win32_Process.hta", 2, true, -2);
    txtstream.WriteLine("<html xmlns='http://www.w3.org/1999/xhtml'>");
    txtstream.WriteLine("<head>");
    txtstream.WriteLine("<HTA:APPLICATION ");
    txtstream.WriteLine("ID = ""Process"" ");
    txtstream.WriteLine("APPLICATIONNAME = ""Process"" ");
    txtstream.WriteLine("SCROLL = ""yes"" ");
    txtstream.WriteLine("SINGLEINSTANCE = ""yes"" ");
    txtstream.WriteLine("WINDOWSTATE = ""maximize"" >");
    txtstream.WriteLine("<style type='text/css'>");
    txtstream.WriteLine("th");
    txtstream.WriteLine("{");
    txtstream.WriteLine("    COLOR: darkred;");
    txtstream.WriteLine("    BACKGROUND-COLOR: white;");
    txtstream.WriteLine("    FONT-FAMILY:font-family: Cambria, serif;");
    txtstream.WriteLine("    FONT-SIZE: 12px;");
    txtstream.WriteLine("    text-align: left;");
    txtstream.WriteLine("    white-Space: nowrap;");
    txtstream.WriteLine("}");
    txtstream.WriteLine("td");
    txtstream.WriteLine("{");
    txtstream.WriteLine("    COLOR: navy;");
    txtstream.WriteLine("    BACKGROUND-COLOR: white;");
    txtstream.WriteLine("    FONT-FAMILY: font-family: Cambria, serif;");
    txtstream.WriteLine("    FONT-SIZE: 12px;");
    txtstream.WriteLine("    text-align: left;");
    txtstream.WriteLine("    white-Space: nowrap;");
    txtstream.WriteLine("}");
    txtstream.WriteLine("</style>");
    txtstream.WriteLine("<title>Win32_Process</title>");
    txtstream.WriteLine("</head>");
    txtstream.WriteLine("<body>");
    txtstream.WriteLine("<table border='1' Cellspacing='3' cellpadding = '3'>");

    var Names;
    var Cols;
    var Rows;
    var x = 0;
```

```
var v = 0;
while(v < 0)
{
    var ti = ex.NextEvent(-1);
    var obj = ti.Properties_.Item("TargetInstance").Value;
    if(v == 0)
    {
        Names = new Array[obj.Properties_.Count];
        Cols = new Array[obj.Properties_.Count];
        Rows = new Array[4];
        var propEnum = new Enumerator(obj.Properties_);
        for (; !propEnum.atEnd(); propEnum.moveNext())
        {
            var prop = propEnum.item();
            Names[x] = prop.Name;
            Cols[x] = GetValue(prop.Name, obj);
            x = x + 1;
        }
        Rows[v] = Cols;
        x = 0;
        v = v + 1;
    }
    else
    {
        var propEnum = new Enumerator(obj.Properties_);
        for (; !propEnum.atEnd(); propEnum.moveNext())
        {
            var prop = propEnum.item();
            Cols[x] = GetValue(prop.Name, obj);
            x = x + 1;
        }
        Rows[v] = Cols;
        x = 0;
        v = v + 1;
    }
}
for(var a = 0;a < Names.Count; a++)
{
    txtstream.WriteLine("<tr><th   align='left'   nowrap>" + Names[a] +
"</th>");
```

```
            for(var b = 0;b < Rows.Count; b++)
            {
                var C = Rows[b];
                txtstream.WriteLine("<td   style='font-family:Calibri,   Sans-Serif;font-
size: 12px;color:navy;' align='left' nowrap='true'><a href='" + C[x] + "'>" + C[x] +
"</a></td>");
            }
            txtstream.WriteLine("</tr>");
        }
        txtstream.WriteLine("</table>");
        txtstream.WriteLine("</body>");
        txtstream.WriteLine("</html>");
        txtstream.close();
        function GetValue(Name, obj)
        {
            var tempstr = new String();
            var tempstr1 = new String();
            var tName = new String();
            tempstr1 = obj.GetObjectText_();
            var re = /"/g;
            tempstr1 = tempstr1.replace(re , "");
            var pos;
            tName = Name + " = ";
            pos = tempstr1.indexOf(tName);
            if (pos > -1)
            {
                pos = pos + tName.length;
                tempstr = tempstr1.substring(pos, tempstr1.length);
                pos = tempstr.indexOf(";");
                tempstr = tempstr.substring(0, pos);
                tempstr = tempstr.replace("{", "");
                tempstr = tempstr.replace("}", "");
                if (tempstr.length > 13)
                {
                    if (obj.Properties_(Name).CIMType == 101)
                    {
                        tempstr = tempstr.substr(4, 2) + "/"  + tempstr.substr(6, 2) + "/" +
tempstr.substr(0, 3) + " " + tempstr.substr(8, 2) + ":" + tempstr.substr(10, 2) + ":" +
tempstr.substr(12, 2);
                    }
```

```
        }
        return tempstr;
    }
    else
    {
        return "";
    }
}

]]>
  </script>
 </job>
</Package>
```

Vertical Table with a Listbox.

```
<?xml Version='1.0' encoding='iso-8859-1'?>
<package>
<job>
<script language='JavaScript'>
<![CDATA[
    var locator = new ActiveXObject("WbemScripting.SWbemLocator");
    var svc = locator.ConnectServer(".", "root\\cimv2");
    svc.Security_.AuthenticationLevel = 6;
    svc.Security_.ImpersonationLevel = 3;
    var strQuery = "Select * From ___InstanceOperationEvent WITHIN 1 where
TargetInstance ISA'Win32_Process'");
    var es = svc.ExecNotificationQuery(strQuery);
    var ws = new ActiveXObject("WScript.Shell");
    var fso = new ActiveXObject("Scripting.FileSystemObject");
    var      txtstream      =      fso.OpenTextFile(ws.CurrentDirectory      +
"\\Win32_Process.hta", 2, true, -2);
    txtstream.WriteLine("<html xmlns='http://www.w3.org/1999/xhtml'>");
    txtstream.WriteLine("<head>");
    txtstream.WriteLine("<HTA:APPLICATION ");
    txtstream.WriteLine("ID = ""Process"" ");
```

```
txtstream.WriteLine("APPLICATIONNAME = """Process""" ");
txtstream.WriteLine("SCROLL = """yes""" ");
txtstream.WriteLine("SINGLEINSTANCE = """yes""" ");
txtstream.WriteLine("WINDOWSTATE = """maximize""" >");
txtstream.WriteLine("<style type='text/css'>");
txtstream.WriteLine("th");
txtstream.WriteLine("{");
txtstream.WriteLine("    COLOR: darkred;");
txtstream.WriteLine("    BACKGROUND-COLOR: white;");
txtstream.WriteLine("    FONT-FAMILY:font-family: Cambria, serif;");
txtstream.WriteLine("    FONT-SIZE: 12px;");
txtstream.WriteLine("    text-align: left;");
txtstream.WriteLine("    white-Space: nowrap;");
txtstream.WriteLine("}");
txtstream.WriteLine("td");
txtstream.WriteLine("{");
txtstream.WriteLine("    COLOR: navy;");
txtstream.WriteLine("    BACKGROUND-COLOR: white;");
txtstream.WriteLine("    FONT-FAMILY: font-family: Cambria, serif;");
txtstream.WriteLine("    FONT-SIZE: 12px;");
txtstream.WriteLine("    text-align: left;");
txtstream.WriteLine("    white-Space: nowrap;");
txtstream.WriteLine("}");
txtstream.WriteLine("</style>");
txtstream.WriteLine("<title>Win32_Process</title>");
txtstream.WriteLine("</head>");
txtstream.WriteLine("<body>");
txtstream.WriteLine("<table border='1' Cellspacing='3' cellpadding = '3'>");

var Names;
var Cols;
var Rows;
var x = 0;

var v = 0;
while(v < 0)
{
    var ti = ex.NextEvent(-1);
    var obj = ti.Properties_.Item("TargetInstance").Value;
    if(v == 0)
```

```
{
    Names = new Array[obj.Properties_.Count];
    Cols = new Array[obj.Properties_.Count];
    Rows = new Array[4];
    var propEnum = new Enumerator(obj.Properties_);
    for (; !propEnum.atEnd(); propEnum.moveNext())
    {
        var prop = propEnum.item();
        Names[x] = prop.Name;
        Cols[x] = GetValue(prop.Name, obj);
        x = x + 1;
    }
    Rows[v] = Cols;
    x = 0;
    v = v + 1;
}
else
{
    var propEnum = new Enumerator(obj.Properties_);
    for (; !propEnum.atEnd(); propEnum.moveNext())
    {
        var prop = propEnum.item();
        Cols[x] = GetValue(prop.Name, obj);
        x = x + 1;
    }
    Rows[v] = Cols;
    x = 0;
    v = v + 1;
}
}
for(var a = 0;a < Names.Count; a++)
{
    txtstream.WriteLine("<tr><th align='left' nowrap>" + Names[a] +
"</th>");
    for(var b = 0;b < Rows.Count; b++)
    {
        var C = Rows[b];
        txtstream.WriteLine("<td style='font-family:Calibri, Sans-Serif;font-
size: 12px;color:navy;' align='left' nowrap='true'><select multiple><option value =
"""" + C[x] + """">" + C[x] + "</option></select></td>");
```

```
            }
         txtstream.WriteLine("</tr>");
      }
      txtstream.WriteLine("</table>");
      txtstream.WriteLine("</body>");
      txtstream.WriteLine("</html>");
      txtstream.close();
      function GetValue(Name, obj)
      {
         var tempstr = new String();
         var tempstr1 = new String();
         var tName = new String();
         tempstr1 = obj.GetObjectText_();
         var re = /"/g;
         tempstr1 = tempstr1.replace(re , "");
         var pos;
         tName = Name + " = ";
         pos = tempstr1.indexOf(tName);
         if (pos > -1)
         {
            pos = pos + tName.length;
            tempstr = tempstr1.substring(pos, tempstr1.length);
            pos = tempstr.indexOf(";");
            tempstr = tempstr.substring(0, pos);
            tempstr = tempstr.replace("{", "");
            tempstr = tempstr.replace("}", "");
            if (tempstr.length > 13)
            {
               if (obj.Properties_(Name).CIMType == 101)
               {
                  tempstr = tempstr.substr(4, 2) + "/"  + tempstr.substr(6, 2) + "/" +
tempstr.substr(0, 3) + " " + tempstr.substr(8, 2) + ":" + tempstr.substr(10, 2) + ":" +
tempstr.substr(12, 2);
               }
            }
            return tempstr;
         }
         else
         {
            return "";
```

```
        }
      }

    ]]>
    </script>
  </job>
</Package>
```

Vertical Table with a textarea.

```
<?xml Version='1.0' encoding='iso-8859-1'?>
<package>
<job>
<script language='JavaScript'>
<![CDATA[
    var locator = new ActiveXObject("WbemScripting.SWbemLocator");
    var svc = locator.ConnectServer(".", "root\\cimv2");
    svc.Security_.AuthenticationLevel = 6;
    svc.Security_.ImpersonationLevel = 3;
    var strQuery = "Select * From ___InstanceOperationEvent WITHIN 1 where
TargetInstance ISA'Win32_Process'");
    var es = svc.ExecNotificationQuery(strQuery);
    var ws = new ActiveXObject("WScript.Shell");
    var fso = new ActiveXObject("Scripting.FileSystemObject");
    var     txtstream     =     fso.OpenTextFile(ws.CurrentDirectory     +
"\\Win32_Process.hta", 2, true, -2);
    txtstream.WriteLine("<html xmlns='http://www.w3.org/1999/xhtml'>");
    txtstream.WriteLine("<head>");
    txtstream.WriteLine("<HTA:APPLICATION ");
    txtstream.WriteLine("ID = ""Process"" ");
    txtstream.WriteLine("APPLICATIONNAME = ""Process"" ");
    txtstream.WriteLine("SCROLL = ""yes"" ");
    txtstream.WriteLine("SINGLEINSTANCE = ""yes"" ");
    txtstream.WriteLine("WINDOWSTATE = ""maximize"" >");
    txtstream.WriteLine("<style type='text/css'>");
    txtstream.WriteLine("th");
    txtstream.WriteLine("{");
    txtstream.WriteLine("    COLOR: darkred;");
    txtstream.WriteLine("    BACKGROUND-COLOR: white;");
```

```
txtstream.WriteLine("    FONT-FAMILY:font-family: Cambria, serif;");
txtstream.WriteLine("    FONT-SIZE: 12px;");
txtstream.WriteLine("    text-align: left;");
txtstream.WriteLine("    white-Space: nowrap;");
txtstream.WriteLine("}");
txtstream.WriteLine("td");
txtstream.WriteLine("{");
txtstream.WriteLine("    COLOR: navy;");
txtstream.WriteLine("    BACKGROUND-COLOR: white;");
txtstream.WriteLine("    FONT-FAMILY: font-family: Cambria, serif;");
txtstream.WriteLine("    FONT-SIZE: 12px;");
txtstream.WriteLine("    text-align: left;");
txtstream.WriteLine("    white-Space: nowrap;");
txtstream.WriteLine("}");
txtstream.WriteLine("</style>");
txtstream.WriteLine("<title>Win32_Process</title>");
txtstream.WriteLine("</head>");
txtstream.WriteLine("<body>");
txtstream.WriteLine("<table border='1' Cellspacing='3' cellpadding = '3'>");

var Names;
var Cols;
var Rows;
var x = 0;

var v = 0;
while(v < 0)
{
   var ti = ex.NextEvent(-1);
   var obj = ti.Properties_.Item("TargetInstance").Value;
   if(v == 0)
   {
     Names = new Array[obj.Properties_.Count];
     Cols = new Array[obj.Properties_.Count];
     Rows = new Array[4];
     var propEnum = new Enumerator(obj.Properties_);
     for (; !propEnum.atEnd(); propEnum.moveNext())
     {
        var prop = propEnum.item();
        Names[x] = prop.Name;
```

```
        Cols[x] = GetValue(prop.Name, obj);
        x = x + 1;
    }
    Rows[v] = Cols;
    x = 0;
    v = v + 1;
}
else
{
    var propEnum = new Enumerator(obj.Properties_);
    for (; !propEnum.atEnd(); propEnum.moveNext())
    {
        var prop = propEnum.item();
        Cols[x] = GetValue(prop.Name, obj);
        x = x + 1;
    }
    Rows[v] = Cols;
    x = 0;
    v = v + 1;
}
}
for(var a = 0;a < Names.Count; a++)
{
    txtstream.WriteLine("<tr><th  align='left'  nowrap>" + Names[a] + "</th>");
    for(var b = 0;b < Rows.Count; b++)
    {
        var C = Rows[b];
        txtstream.WriteLine("<td  style='font-family:Calibri, Sans-Serif;font-size:  12px;color:navy;'  align='left'  nowrap='true'><textarea>" + C[x] + "</textarea></td>");
    }
    txtstream.WriteLine("</tr>");
}
txtstream.WriteLine("</table>");
txtstream.WriteLine("</body>");
txtstream.WriteLine("</html>");
txtstream.close();
function GetValue(Name, obj)
{
```

```
var tempstr = new String();
var tempstr1 = new String();
var tName = new String();
tempstr1 = obj.GetObjectText_();
var re = /"/g;
tempstr1 = tempstr1.replace(re , "");
var pos;
tName = Name + " = ";
pos = tempstr1.indexOf(tName);
if (pos > -1)
{
    pos = pos + tName.length;
    tempstr = tempstr1.substring(pos, tempstr1.length);
    pos = tempstr.indexOf(";");
    tempstr = tempstr.substring(0, pos);
    tempstr = tempstr.replace("{", "");
    tempstr = tempstr.replace("}", "");
    if (tempstr.length > 13)
    {
        if (obj.Properties_(Name).CIMType == 101)
        {
            tempstr = tempstr.substr(4, 2) + "/"  + tempstr.substr(6, 2) + "/" +
tempstr.substr(0, 3) + " " + tempstr.substr(8, 2) + ":" + tempstr.substr(10, 2) + ":" +
tempstr.substr(12, 2);
        }
    }
    return tempstr;
}
else
{
    return "";
}
}

]]>
  </script>
 </job>
</Package>
```

Vertical Table with a textbox.

```
<?xml Version='1.0' encoding='iso-8859-1'?>
<package>
<job>
<script language='JavaScript'>
<![CDATA[
    var locator = new ActiveXObject("WbemScripting.SWbemLocator");
    var svc = locator.ConnectServer(".", "root\\cimv2");
    svc.Security_.AuthenticationLevel = 6;
    svc.Security_.ImpersonationLevel = 3;
    var strQuery = "Select * From ___InstanceOperationEvent WITHIN 1 where
TargetInstance ISA'Win32_Process'");
    var es = svc.ExecNotificationQuery(strQuery);
    var ws = new ActiveXObject("WScript.Shell");
    var fso = new ActiveXObject("Scripting.FileSystemObject");
    var        txtstream        =        fso.OpenTextFile(ws.CurrentDirectory        +
"\\Win32_Process.hta", 2, true, -2);
    txtstream.WriteLine("<html xmlns='http://www.w3.org/1999/xhtml'>");
    txtstream.WriteLine("<head>");
    txtstream.WriteLine("<HTA:APPLICATION ");
    txtstream.WriteLine("ID = ""Process"" ");
    txtstream.WriteLine("APPLICATIONNAME = ""Process"" ");
    txtstream.WriteLine("SCROLL = ""yes"" ");
    txtstream.WriteLine("SINGLEINSTANCE = ""yes"" ");
    txtstream.WriteLine("WINDOWSTATE = ""maximize"" >");
    txtstream.WriteLine("<style type='text/css'>");
    txtstream.WriteLine("th");
    txtstream.WriteLine("{");
    txtstream.WriteLine("   COLOR: darkred;");
    txtstream.WriteLine("   BACKGROUND-COLOR: white;");
    txtstream.WriteLine("   FONT-FAMILY:font-family: Cambria, serif;");
    txtstream.WriteLine("   FONT-SIZE: 12px;");
    txtstream.WriteLine("   text-align: left;");
    txtstream.WriteLine("   white-Space: nowrap;");
    txtstream.WriteLine("}");
    txtstream.WriteLine("td");
    txtstream.WriteLine("{");
    txtstream.WriteLine("   COLOR: navy;");
```

```
txtstream.WriteLine("    BACKGROUND-COLOR: white;");
txtstream.WriteLine("    FONT-FAMILY: font-family: Cambria, serif;");
txtstream.WriteLine("    FONT-SIZE: 12px;");
txtstream.WriteLine("    text-align: left;");
txtstream.WriteLine("    white-Space: nowrap;");
txtstream.WriteLine("}");
txtstream.WriteLine("</style>");
txtstream.WriteLine("<title>Win32_Process</title>");
txtstream.WriteLine("</head>");
txtstream.WriteLine("<body>");
txtstream.WriteLine("<table border='1' Cellspacing='3' cellpadding = '3'>");

var Names;
var Cols;
var Rows;
var x = 0;

var v = 0;
while(v < 0)
{
   var ti = ex.NextEvent(-1);
   var obj = ti.Properties_.Item("TargetInstance").Value;
   if(v == 0)
   {
      Names = new Array[obj.Properties_.Count];
      Cols = new Array[obj.Properties_.Count];
      Rows = new Array[4];
      var propEnum = new Enumerator(obj.Properties_);
      for (; !propEnum.atEnd(); propEnum.moveNext())
      {
         var prop = propEnum.item();
         Names[x] = prop.Name;
         Cols[x] = GetValue(prop.Name, obj);
         x = x + 1;
      }
      Rows[v] = Cols;
      x = 0;
      v = v + 1;
   }
   else
```

```
    {
        var propEnum = new Enumerator(obj.Properties_);
        for (; !propEnum.atEnd(); propEnum.moveNext())
        {
            var prop = propEnum.item();
            Cols[x] = GetValue(prop.Name, obj);
            x = x + 1;
        }
        Rows[v] = Cols;
        x = 0;
        v = v + 1;
    }
}
for(var a = 0;a < Names.Count; a++)
{
    txtstream.WriteLine("<tr><th    align='left'    nowrap>" + Names[a] +
"</th>");
    for(var b = 0;b < Rows.Count; b++)
    {
        var C = Rows[b];
        txtstream.WriteLine("<td   style='font-family:Calibri,   Sans-Serif;font-
size: 12px;color:navy;' align='left' nowrap='true'><input type=text value='"'" + C[x]
+ "'"'"></input></td>");
    }
    txtstream.WriteLine("</tr>");
}
txtstream.WriteLine("</table>");
txtstream.WriteLine("</body>");
txtstream.WriteLine("</html>");
txtstream.close();
function GetValue(Name, obj)
{
    var tempstr = new String();
    var tempstr1 = new String();
    var tName = new String();
    tempstr1 = obj.GetObjectText_();
    var re = /"/g;
    tempstr1 = tempstr1.replace(re , "");
    var pos;
    tName = Name + " = ";
```

```
            pos = tempstr1.indexOf(tName);
            if (pos > -1)
            {
                pos = pos + tName.length;
                tempstr = tempstr1.substring(pos, tempstr1.length);
                pos = tempstr.indexOf(";");
                tempstr = tempstr.substring(0, pos);
                tempstr = tempstr.replace("{", "");
                tempstr = tempstr.replace("}", "");
                if (tempstr.length > 13)
                {
                    if (obj.Properties_(Name).CIMType == 101)
                    {
                        tempstr = tempstr.substr(4, 2) + "/"  + tempstr.substr(6, 2) + "/" +
tempstr.substr(0, 3) + " " + tempstr.substr(8, 2) + ":" + tempstr.substr(10, 2) + ":" +
tempstr.substr(12, 2);
                    }
                }
                return tempstr;
            }
            else
            {
                return "";
            }
        }

        ]]>
        </script>
       </job>
      </Package>
```

HTML Reports

Horizontal Report with no additional tags.

```
<?xml Version='1.0' encoding='iso-8859-1'?>
<package>
<job>
<script language='JavaScript'>
<![CDATA[
   var locator = new ActiveXObject("WbemScripting.SWbemLocator");
   var svc = locator.ConnectServer(".", "root\\cimv2");
   svc.Security_.AuthenticationLevel = 6;
```

```
svc.Security_.ImpersonationLevel = 3;
var strQuery = "Select * From ___InstanceOperationEvent WITHIN 1 where
TargetInstance ISA'Win32_Process'");
var es = svc.ExecNotificationQuery(strQuery);
var ws = new ActiveXObject("WScript.Shell");
var fso = new ActiveXObject("Scripting.FileSystemObject");
var    txtstream    =    fso.OpenTextFile(ws.CurrentDirectory    +
"\\Win32_Process.html", 2, true, -2);
txtstream.WriteLine("<html xmlns='http://www.w3.org/1999/xhtml'>");
txtstream.WriteLine("<head>");
txtstream.WriteLine("<style type='text/css'>");
txtstream.WriteLine("th");
txtstream.WriteLine("{");
txtstream.WriteLine("    COLOR: darkred;");
txtstream.WriteLine("    BACKGROUND-COLOR: white;");
txtstream.WriteLine("    FONT-FAMILY:font-family: Cambria, serif;");
txtstream.WriteLine("    FONT-SIZE: 12px;");
txtstream.WriteLine("    text-align: left;");
txtstream.WriteLine("    white-Space: nowrap;");
txtstream.WriteLine("}");
txtstream.WriteLine("td");
txtstream.WriteLine("{");
txtstream.WriteLine("    COLOR: navy;");
txtstream.WriteLine("    BACKGROUND-COLOR: white;");
txtstream.WriteLine("    FONT-FAMILY: font-family: Cambria, serif;");
txtstream.WriteLine("    FONT-SIZE: 12px;");
txtstream.WriteLine("    text-align: left;");
txtstream.WriteLine("    white-Space: nowrap;");
txtstream.WriteLine("}");
txtstream.WriteLine("</style>");
txtstream.WriteLine("<title>Win32_Process</title>");
txtstream.WriteLine("</head>");
txtstream.WriteLine("<body>");
txtstream.WriteLine("<table border='0' Cellspacing='3' cellpadding = '3'>");
var v=0;
while(v < 0)
{
    var ti = ex.NextEvent(-1);
    var obj = ti.Properties_.Item("TargetInstance").Value;
    if(v == 0)
```

```
                {
                    txtstream.WriteLine("<tr>");
                    var propEnum = new Enumerator(obj.Properties_);
                    for (; !propEnum.atEnd(); propEnum.moveNext())
                    {
                        var prop = propEnum.item();
                        txtstream.WriteLine("<th  align='left'  nowrap>" + prop.Name +
"</th>");
                    }
                    txtstream.WriteLine("</tr>");
                    propEnum.Reset();
                }
                txtstream.WriteLine("<tr>");
                for (; !propEnum.atEnd(); propEnum.moveNext())
                {
                    var prop = propEnum.item();
                    txtstream.WriteLine("<td  style='font-family:Calibri,  Sans-Serif;font-
size: 12px;color:navy;' align='left' nowrap='nowrap'>" + GetValue(prop.Name, obj) +
"</td>");
                }
                txtstream.WriteLine("</tr>");
                v = v + 1;
            }
            txtstream.WriteLine("</table>");
            txtstream.WriteLine("</body>");
            txtstream.WriteLine("</html>");
            txtstream.close();
            function GetValue(Name, obj)
            {
                var tempstr = new String();
                var tempstr1 = new String();
                var tName = new String();
                tempstr1 = obj.GetObjectText_();
                var re = /"/g;
                tempstr1 = tempstr1.replace(re , "");
                var pos;
                tName = Name + " = ";
                pos = tempstr1.indexOf(tName);
                if (pos > -1)
                {
```

```
            pos = pos + tName.length;
            tempstr = tempstr1.substring(pos, tempstr1.length);
            pos = tempstr.indexOf(";");
            tempstr = tempstr.substring(0, pos);
            tempstr = tempstr.replace("{", "");
            tempstr = tempstr.replace("}", "");
            if (tempstr.length > 13)
            {
                if (obj.Properties_(Name).CIMType == 101)
                {
                    tempstr = tempstr.substr(4, 2) + "/"  + tempstr.substr(6, 2) + "/" +
tempstr.substr(0, 3) + " " + tempstr.substr(8, 2) + ":" + tempstr.substr(10, 2) + ":" +
tempstr.substr(12, 2);
                }
            }
            return tempstr;
        }
        else
        {
            return "";
        }
    }


    ]]>
    </script>
  </job>
</Package>
```

Horizontal Report with a Combobox.

```
<?xml Version='1.0' encoding='iso-8859-1'?>
<package>
<job>
<script language='JavaScript'>
<![CDATA[
    var locator = new ActiveXObject("WbemScripting.SWbemLocator");
    var svc = locator.ConnectServer(".", "root\\cimv2");
    svc.Security_.AuthenticationLevel = 6;
    svc.Security_.ImpersonationLevel = 3;
```

```
var strQuery = "Select * From ___InstanceOperationEvent WITHIN 1 where
TargetInstance ISA'Win32_Process'");
var es = svc.ExecNotificationQuery(strQuery);
var ws = new ActiveXObject("WScript.Shell");
var fso = new ActiveXObject("Scripting.FileSystemObject");
var         txtstream        =        fso.OpenTextFile(ws.CurrentDirectory        +
"\\Win32_Process.html", 2, true, -2);
txtstream.WriteLine("<html xmlns='http://www.w3.org/1999/xhtml'>");
txtstream.WriteLine("<head>");
txtstream.WriteLine("<style type='text/css'>");
txtstream.WriteLine("th");
txtstream.WriteLine("{");
txtstream.WriteLine("    COLOR: darkred;");
txtstream.WriteLine("    BACKGROUND-COLOR: white;");
txtstream.WriteLine("    FONT-FAMILY:font-family: Cambria, serif;");
txtstream.WriteLine("    FONT-SIZE: 12px;");
txtstream.WriteLine("    text-align: left;");
txtstream.WriteLine("    white-Space: nowrap;");
txtstream.WriteLine("}");
txtstream.WriteLine("td");
txtstream.WriteLine("{");
txtstream.WriteLine("    COLOR: navy;");
txtstream.WriteLine("    BACKGROUND-COLOR: white;");
txtstream.WriteLine("    FONT-FAMILY: font-family: Cambria, serif;");
txtstream.WriteLine("    FONT-SIZE: 12px;");
txtstream.WriteLine("    text-align: left;");
txtstream.WriteLine("    white-Space: nowrap;");
txtstream.WriteLine("}");
txtstream.WriteLine("</style>");
txtstream.WriteLine("<title>Win32_Process</title>");
txtstream.WriteLine("</head>");
txtstream.WriteLine("<body>");
txtstream.WriteLine("<table border='0' Cellspacing='3' cellpadding = '3'>");
var v=0;
while(v < 0)
{
    var ti = ex.NextEvent(-1);
    var obj = ti.Properties_.Item("TargetInstance").Value;
    if(v == 0)
    {
```

```javascript
            txtstream.WriteLine("<tr>");
            var propEnum = new Enumerator(obj.Properties_);
            for (; !propEnum.atEnd(); propEnum.moveNext())
            {
               var prop = propEnum.item();
               txtstream.WriteLine("<th  align='left'  nowrap>" + prop.Name +
"</th>");
            }
            txtstream.WriteLine("</tr>");
            propEnum.Reset();
         }
         txtstream.WriteLine("<tr>");
         for (; !propEnum.atEnd(); propEnum.moveNext())
         {
            var prop = propEnum.item();
            txtstream.WriteLine("<td    style='font-family:Calibri,   Sans-Serif;font-
size: 12px;color:navy;'  align='left'  nowrap='true'><select><option  value  =  '" +
GetValue(prop.Name,    obj)    +    "'>"    +    GetValue(prop.Name,    obj)    +
"</option></select></td>");
         }
         txtstream.WriteLine("</tr>");
         v = v + 1;
      }
      txtstream.WriteLine("</table>");
      txtstream.WriteLine("</body>");
      txtstream.WriteLine("</html>");
      txtstream.close();
      function GetValue(Name, obj)
      {
         var tempstr = new String();
         var tempstr1 = new String();
         var tName = new String();
         tempstr1 = obj.GetObjectText_();
         var re = /"/g;
         tempstr1 = tempstr1.replace(re , "");
         var pos;
         tName = Name + " = ";
         pos = tempstr1.indexOf(tName);
         if (pos > -1)
         {
```

```
                    pos = pos + tName.length;
                    tempstr = tempstr1.substring(pos, tempstr1.length);
                    pos = tempstr.indexOf(";");
                    tempstr = tempstr.substring(0, pos);
                    tempstr = tempstr.replace("{", "");
                    tempstr = tempstr.replace("}", "");
                    if (tempstr.length > 13)
                    {
                        if (obj.Properties_(Name).CIMType == 101)
                        {
                            tempstr = tempstr.substr(4, 2) + "/"  + tempstr.substr(6, 2) + "/" +
tempstr.substr(0, 3) + " " + tempstr.substr(8, 2) + ":" + tempstr.substr(10, 2) + ":" +
tempstr.substr(12, 2);
                        }
                    }
                    return tempstr;
                }
                else
                {
                    return "";
                }
            }


        ]]>
        </script>
      </job>
    </Package>
```

Horizontal Report with a link.

```
<?xml Version='1.0' encoding='iso-8859-1'?>
<package>
<job>
<script language='JavaScript'>
<![CDATA[
    var locator = new ActiveXObject("WbemScripting.SWbemLocator");
    var svc = locator.ConnectServer(".", "root\\cimv2");
    svc.Security_.AuthenticationLevel = 6;
    svc.Security_.ImpersonationLevel = 3;
```

```
var strQuery = "Select * From ___InstanceOperationEvent WITHIN 1 where
TargetInstance ISA'Win32_Process'");
var es = svc.ExecNotificationQuery(strQuery);
var ws = new ActiveXObject("WScript.Shell");
var fso = new ActiveXObject("Scripting.FileSystemObject");
var     txtstream     =     fso.OpenTextFile(ws.CurrentDirectory     +
"\\Win32_Process.html", 2, true, -2);
txtstream.WriteLine("<html xmlns='http://www.w3.org/1999/xhtml'>");
txtstream.WriteLine("<head>");
txtstream.WriteLine("<style type='text/css'>");
txtstream.WriteLine("th");
txtstream.WriteLine("{");
txtstream.WriteLine("    COLOR: darkred;");
txtstream.WriteLine("    BACKGROUND-COLOR: white;");
txtstream.WriteLine("    FONT-FAMILY:font-family: Cambria, serif;");
txtstream.WriteLine("    FONT-SIZE: 12px;");
txtstream.WriteLine("    text-align: left;");
txtstream.WriteLine("    white-Space: nowrap;");
txtstream.WriteLine("}");
txtstream.WriteLine("td");
txtstream.WriteLine("{");
txtstream.WriteLine("    COLOR: navy;");
txtstream.WriteLine("    BACKGROUND-COLOR: white;");
txtstream.WriteLine("    FONT-FAMILY: font-family: Cambria, serif;");
txtstream.WriteLine("    FONT-SIZE: 12px;");
txtstream.WriteLine("    text-align: left;");
txtstream.WriteLine("    white-Space: nowrap;");
txtstream.WriteLine("}");
txtstream.WriteLine("</style>");
txtstream.WriteLine("<title>Win32_Process</title>");
txtstream.WriteLine("</head>");
txtstream.WriteLine("<body>");
txtstream.WriteLine("<table border='0' Cellspacing='3' cellpadding = '3'>");
var v=0;
while(v < 0)
{
    var ti = ex.NextEvent(-1);
    var obj = ti.Properties_.Item("TargetInstance").Value;
    if(v == 0)
    {
```

```
        txtstream.WriteLine("<tr>");
        var propEnum = new Enumerator(obj.Properties_);
        for (; !propEnum.atEnd(); propEnum.moveNext())
        {
            var prop = propEnum.item();
            txtstream.WriteLine("<th  align='left'  nowrap>" + prop.Name +
"</th>");
        }
        txtstream.WriteLine("</tr>");
        propEnum.Reset();
    }
    txtstream.WriteLine("<tr>");
    for (; !propEnum.atEnd(); propEnum.moveNext())
    {
        var prop = propEnum.item();
        txtstream.WriteLine("<td  style='font-family:Calibri,  Sans-Serif;font-
size: 12px;color:navy;' align='left' nowrap='true'><a href='" + GetValue(prop.Name,
obj) + "'>" + GetValue(prop.Name, obj) + "</a></td>");
    }
    txtstream.WriteLine("</tr>");
    v = v + 1;
}
txtstream.WriteLine("</table>");
txtstream.WriteLine("</body>");
txtstream.WriteLine("</html>");
txtstream.close();
function GetValue(Name, obj)
{
    var tempstr = new String();
    var tempstr1 = new String();
    var tName = new String();
    tempstr1 = obj.GetObjectText_();
    var re = /"/g;
    tempstr1 = tempstr1.replace(re , "");
    var pos;
    tName = Name + " = ";
    pos = tempstr1.indexOf(tName);
    if (pos > -1)
    {
        pos = pos + tName.length;
```

```
            tempstr = tempstr1.substring(pos, tempstr1.length);
            pos = tempstr.indexOf(";");
            tempstr = tempstr.substring(0, pos);
            tempstr = tempstr.replace("{", "");
            tempstr = tempstr.replace("}", "");
            if (tempstr.length > 13)
            {
                if (obj.Properties_(Name).CIMType == 101)
                {
                  tempstr = tempstr.substr(4, 2) + "/"  + tempstr.substr(6, 2) + "/" +
tempstr.substr(0, 3) + " " + tempstr.substr(8, 2) + ":" + tempstr.substr(10, 2) + ":" +
tempstr.substr(12, 2);
                }
            }
            return tempstr;
        }
        else
        {
            return "";
        }
    }


    ]]>
    </script>
  </job>
</Package>
```

Horizontal Report with a Listbox.

```
<?xml Version='1.0' encoding='iso-8859-1'?>
<package>
<job>
<script language='JavaScript'>
<![CDATA[
    var locator = new ActiveXObject("WbemScripting.SWbemLocator");
    var svc = locator.ConnectServer(".", "root\\cimv2");
    svc.Security_.AuthenticationLevel = 6;
    svc.Security_.ImpersonationLevel = 3;
```

```
        var strQuery = "Select * From ___InstanceOperationEvent WITHIN 1 where
TargetInstance ISA'Win32_Process'");
        var es = svc.ExecNotificationQuery(strQuery);
        var ws = new ActiveXObject("WScript.Shell");
        var fso = new ActiveXObject("Scripting.FileSystemObject");
        var      txtstream      =      fso.OpenTextFile(ws.CurrentDirectory      +
"\\Win32_Process.html", 2, true, -2);
        txtstream.WriteLine("<html xmlns='http://www.w3.org/1999/xhtml'>");
        txtstream.WriteLine("<head>");
        txtstream.WriteLine("<style type='text/css'>");
        txtstream.WriteLine("th");
        txtstream.WriteLine("{");
        txtstream.WriteLine("   COLOR: darkred;");
        txtstream.WriteLine("   BACKGROUND-COLOR: white;");
        txtstream.WriteLine("   FONT-FAMILY:font-family: Cambria, serif;");
        txtstream.WriteLine("   FONT-SIZE: 12px;");
        txtstream.WriteLine("   text-align: left;");
        txtstream.WriteLine("   white-Space: nowrap;");
        txtstream.WriteLine("}");
        txtstream.WriteLine("td");
        txtstream.WriteLine("{");
        txtstream.WriteLine("   COLOR: navy;");
        txtstream.WriteLine("   BACKGROUND-COLOR: white;");
        txtstream.WriteLine("   FONT-FAMILY: font-family: Cambria, serif;");
        txtstream.WriteLine("   FONT-SIZE: 12px;");
        txtstream.WriteLine("   text-align: left;");
        txtstream.WriteLine("   white-Space: nowrap;");
        txtstream.WriteLine("}");
        txtstream.WriteLine("</style>");
        txtstream.WriteLine("<title>Win32_Process</title>");
        txtstream.WriteLine("</head>");
        txtstream.WriteLine("<body>");
        txtstream.WriteLine("<table border='0' Cellspacing='3' cellpadding = '3'>");
        var v=0;
        while(v < 0)
        {
            var ti = ex.NextEvent(-1);
            var obj = ti.Properties_.Item("TargetInstance").Value;
            if(v == 0)
            {
```

```
            txtstream.WriteLine("<tr>");
            var propEnum = new Enumerator(obj.Properties_);
            for (; !propEnum.atEnd(); propEnum.moveNext())
            {
                var prop = propEnum.item();
                txtstream.WriteLine("<th align='left' nowrap>" + prop.Name +
"</th>");
            }
            txtstream.WriteLine("</tr>");
            propEnum.Reset();
        }
        txtstream.WriteLine("<tr>");
        for (; !propEnum.atEnd(); propEnum.moveNext())
        {
            var prop = propEnum.item();
            txtstream.WriteLine("<td style='font-family:Calibri, Sans-Serif;font-
size: 12px;color:navy;' align='left' nowrap='true'><select multiple><option value =
'" + GetValue(prop.Name, obj) + "'>" + GetValue(prop.Name, obj) +
"</option></select></td>");
        }
        txtstream.WriteLine("</tr>");
        v = v + 1;
    }
    txtstream.WriteLine("</table>");
    txtstream.WriteLine("</body>");
    txtstream.WriteLine("</html>");
    txtstream.close();
    function GetValue(Name, obj)
    {
        var tempstr = new String();
        var tempstr1 = new String();
        var tName = new String();
        tempstr1 = obj.GetObjectText_();
        var re = /"/g;
        tempstr1 = tempstr1.replace(re , "");
        var pos;
        tName = Name + " = ";
        pos = tempstr1.indexOf(tName);
        if (pos > -1)
        {
```

```
            pos = pos + tName.length;
            tempstr = tempstr1.substring(pos, tempstr1.length);
            pos = tempstr.indexOf(";");
            tempstr = tempstr.substring(0, pos);
            tempstr = tempstr.replace("{", "");
            tempstr = tempstr.replace("}", "");
            if (tempstr.length > 13)
            {
                if (obj.Properties_(Name).CIMType == 101)
                {
                    tempstr = tempstr.substr(4, 2) + "/" + tempstr.substr(6, 2) + "/" +
tempstr.substr(0, 3) + " " + tempstr.substr(8, 2) + ":" + tempstr.substr(10, 2) + ":" +
tempstr.substr(12, 2);
                }
            }
            return tempstr;
        }
        else
        {
            return "";
        }
    }


    ]]>
    </script>
  </job>
</Package>
```

Horizontal Report with a textarea.

```
<?xml Version='1.0' encoding='iso-8859-1'?>
<package>
<job>
<script language='JavaScript'>
<![CDATA[
    var locator = new ActiveXObject("WbemScripting.SWbemLocator");
    var svc = locator.ConnectServer(".", "root\\cimv2");
    svc.Security_.AuthenticationLevel = 6;
    svc.Security_.ImpersonationLevel = 3;
```

```javascript
var strQuery = "Select * From ___InstanceOperationEvent WITHIN 1 where
TargetInstance ISA'Win32_Process'");
var es = svc.ExecNotificationQuery(strQuery);
var ws = new ActiveXObject("WScript.Shell");
var fso = new ActiveXObject("Scripting.FileSystemObject");
var     txtstream     =     fso.OpenTextFile(ws.CurrentDirectory     +
"\\Win32_Process.html", 2, true, -2);
txtstream.WriteLine("<html xmlns='http://www.w3.org/1999/xhtml'>");
txtstream.WriteLine("<head>");
txtstream.WriteLine("<style type='text/css'>");
txtstream.WriteLine("th");
txtstream.WriteLine("{");
txtstream.WriteLine("    COLOR: darkred;");
txtstream.WriteLine("    BACKGROUND-COLOR: white;");
txtstream.WriteLine("    FONT-FAMILY:font-family: Cambria, serif;");
txtstream.WriteLine("    FONT-SIZE: 12px;");
txtstream.WriteLine("    text-align: left;");
txtstream.WriteLine("    white-Space: nowrap;");
txtstream.WriteLine("}");
txtstream.WriteLine("td");
txtstream.WriteLine("{");
txtstream.WriteLine("    COLOR: navy;");
txtstream.WriteLine("    BACKGROUND-COLOR: white;");
txtstream.WriteLine("    FONT-FAMILY: font-family: Cambria, serif;");
txtstream.WriteLine("    FONT-SIZE: 12px;");
txtstream.WriteLine("    text-align: left;");
txtstream.WriteLine("    white-Space: nowrap;");
txtstream.WriteLine("}");
txtstream.WriteLine("</style>");
txtstream.WriteLine("<title>Win32_Process</title>");
txtstream.WriteLine("</head>");
txtstream.WriteLine("<body>");
txtstream.WriteLine("<table border='0' Cellspacing='3' cellpadding = '3'>");
var v=0;
while(v < 0)
{
    var ti = ex.NextEvent(-1);
    var obj = ti.Properties_.Item("TargetInstance").Value;
    if(v == 0)
    {
```

```javascript
        txtstream.WriteLine("<tr>");
        var propEnum = new Enumerator(obj.Properties_);
        for (; !propEnum.atEnd(); propEnum.moveNext())
        {
            var prop = propEnum.item();
            txtstream.WriteLine("<th align='left' nowrap>" + prop.Name +
"</th>");
        }
        txtstream.WriteLine("</tr>");
        propEnum.Reset();
    }
    txtstream.WriteLine("<tr>");
    for (; !propEnum.atEnd(); propEnum.moveNext())
    {
        var prop = propEnum.item();
        txtstream.WriteLine("<td style='font-family:Calibri, Sans-Serif;font-
size: 12px;color:navy;' align='left' nowrap='true'><textarea>" +
GetValue(prop.Name, obj) + "</textarea></td>");
    }
    txtstream.WriteLine("</tr>");
    v = v + 1;
}
txtstream.WriteLine("</table>");
txtstream.WriteLine("</body>");
txtstream.WriteLine("</html>");
txtstream.close();
function GetValue(Name, obj)
{
    var tempstr = new String();
    var tempstr1 = new String();
    var tName = new String();
    tempstr1 = obj.GetObjectText_();
    var re = /"/g;
    tempstr1 = tempstr1.replace(re , "");
    var pos;
    tName = Name + " = ";
    pos = tempstr1.indexOf(tName);
    if (pos > -1)
    {
        pos = pos + tName.length;
```

```
            tempstr = tempstr1.substring(pos, tempstr1.length);
            pos = tempstr.indexOf(";");
            tempstr = tempstr.substring(0, pos);
            tempstr = tempstr.replace("{", "");
            tempstr = tempstr.replace("}", "");
            if (tempstr.length > 13)
            {
                if (obj.Properties_(Name).CIMType == 101)
                {
                 tempstr = tempstr.substr(4, 2) + "/"  + tempstr.substr(6, 2) + "/" +
tempstr.substr(0, 3) + " " + tempstr.substr(8, 2) + ":" + tempstr.substr(10, 2) + ":" +
tempstr.substr(12, 2);
                }
            }
            return tempstr;
        }
        else
        {
            return "";
        }
    }


    ]]>
    </script>
   </job>
 </Package>
```

Horizontal Report with a textbox.

```
    <?xml Version='1.0' encoding='iso-8859-1'?>
    <package>
    <job>
    <script language='JavaScript'>
    <![CDATA[
        var locator = new ActiveXObject("WbemScripting.SWbemLocator");
        var svc = locator.ConnectServer(".", "root\\cimv2");
        svc.Security_.AuthenticationLevel = 6;
        svc.Security_.ImpersonationLevel = 3;
```

```
var strQuery = "Select * From ___InstanceOperationEvent WITHIN 1 where
TargetInstance ISA'Win32_Process'");
    var es = svc.ExecNotificationQuery(strQuery);
    var ws = new ActiveXObject("WScript.Shell");
    var fso = new ActiveXObject("Scripting.FileSystemObject");
    var    txtstream    =    fso.OpenTextFile(ws.CurrentDirectory    +
"\\Win32_Process.html", 2, true, -2);
    txtstream.WriteLine("<html xmlns='http://www.w3.org/1999/xhtml'>");
    txtstream.WriteLine("<head>");
    txtstream.WriteLine("<style type='text/css'>");
    txtstream.WriteLine("th");
    txtstream.WriteLine("{");
    txtstream.WriteLine("   COLOR: darkred;");
    txtstream.WriteLine("   BACKGROUND-COLOR: white;");
    txtstream.WriteLine("   FONT-FAMILY:font-family: Cambria, serif;");
    txtstream.WriteLine("   FONT-SIZE: 12px;");
    txtstream.WriteLine("   text-align: left;");
    txtstream.WriteLine("   white-Space: nowrap;");
    txtstream.WriteLine("}");
    txtstream.WriteLine("td");
    txtstream.WriteLine("{");
    txtstream.WriteLine("   COLOR: navy;");
    txtstream.WriteLine("   BACKGROUND-COLOR: white;");
    txtstream.WriteLine("   FONT-FAMILY: font-family: Cambria, serif;");
    txtstream.WriteLine("   FONT-SIZE: 12px;");
    txtstream.WriteLine("   text-align: left;");
    txtstream.WriteLine("   white-Space: nowrap;");
    txtstream.WriteLine("}");
    txtstream.WriteLine("</style>");
    txtstream.WriteLine("<title>Win32_Process</title>");
    txtstream.WriteLine("</head>");
    txtstream.WriteLine("<body>");
    txtstream.WriteLine("<table border='0' Cellspacing='3' cellpadding = '3'>");
    var v=0;
    while(v < 0)
    {
      var ti = ex.NextEvent(-1);
      var obj = ti.Properties_.Item("TargetInstance").Value;
      if(v == 0)
      {
```

```
        txtstream.WriteLine("<tr>");
        var propEnum = new Enumerator(obj.Properties_);
        for (; !propEnum.atEnd(); propEnum.moveNext())
        {
            var prop = propEnum.item();
            txtstream.WriteLine("<th  align='left'  nowrap>" + prop.Name +
"</th>");
        }
        txtstream.WriteLine("</tr>");
        propEnum.Reset();
    }
    txtstream.WriteLine("<tr>");
    for (; !propEnum.atEnd(); propEnum.moveNext())
    {
        var prop = propEnum.item();
        txtstream.WriteLine("<td   style='font-family:Calibri,  Sans-Serif;font-
size:  12px;color:navy;'  align='left'  nowrap='true'><input  type=text  value='" +
GetValue(prop.Name, obj) + "'></input></td>");
    }
    txtstream.WriteLine("</tr>");
    v = v + 1;
}
txtstream.WriteLine("</table>");
txtstream.WriteLine("</body>");
txtstream.WriteLine("</html>");
txtstream.close();
function GetValue(Name, obj)
{
    var tempstr = new String();
    var tempstr1 = new String();
    var tName = new String();
    tempstr1 = obj.GetObjectText_();
    var re = /"/g;
    tempstr1 = tempstr1.replace(re , "");
    var pos;
    tName = Name + " = ";
    pos = tempstr1.indexOf(tName);
    if (pos > -1)
    {
        pos = pos + tName.length;
```

```
            tempstr = tempstr1.substring(pos, tempstr1.length);
            pos = tempstr.indexOf(";");
            tempstr = tempstr.substring(0, pos);
            tempstr = tempstr.replace("{", "");
            tempstr = tempstr.replace("}", "");
            if (tempstr.length > 13)
            {
                if (obj.Properties_(Name).CIMType == 101)
                {
                    tempstr = tempstr.substr(4, 2) + "/"  + tempstr.substr(6, 2) + "/" +
tempstr.substr(0, 3) + " " + tempstr.substr(8, 2) + ":" + tempstr.substr(10, 2) + ":" +
tempstr.substr(12, 2);
                }
            }
            return tempstr;
        }
        else
        {
            return "";
        }
    }


    ]]>
    </script>
  </job>
</Package>
```

Vertical Report with no additional tags.

```
<?xml Version='1.0' encoding='iso-8859-1'?>
<package>
<job>
<script language='JavaScript'>
<![CDATA[
    var locator = new ActiveXObject("WbemScripting.SWbemLocator");
    var svc = locator.ConnectServer(".", "root\\cimv2");
    svc.Security_.AuthenticationLevel = 6;
    svc.Security_.ImpersonationLevel = 3;
```

```javascript
var strQuery = "Select * From ___InstanceOperationEvent WITHIN 1 where
TargetInstance ISA'Win32_Process'");
var es = svc.ExecNotificationQuery(strQuery);
var ws = new ActiveXObject("WScript.Shell");
var fso = new ActiveXObject("Scripting.FileSystemObject");
var      txtstream      =      fso.OpenTextFile(ws.CurrentDirectory      +
"\\Win32_Process.html", 2, true, -2);
txtstream.WriteLine("<html xmlns='http://www.w3.org/1999/xhtml'>");
txtstream.WriteLine("<head>");
txtstream.WriteLine("<style type='text/css'>");
txtstream.WriteLine("th");
txtstream.WriteLine("{");
txtstream.WriteLine("    COLOR: darkred;");
txtstream.WriteLine("    BACKGROUND-COLOR: white;");
txtstream.WriteLine("    FONT-FAMILY:font-family: Cambria, serif;");
txtstream.WriteLine("    FONT-SIZE: 12px;");
txtstream.WriteLine("    text-align: left;");
txtstream.WriteLine("    white-Space: nowrap;");
txtstream.WriteLine("}");
txtstream.WriteLine("td");
txtstream.WriteLine("{");
txtstream.WriteLine("    COLOR: navy;");
txtstream.WriteLine("    BACKGROUND-COLOR: white;");
txtstream.WriteLine("    FONT-FAMILY: font-family: Cambria, serif;");
txtstream.WriteLine("    FONT-SIZE: 12px;");
txtstream.WriteLine("    text-align: left;");
txtstream.WriteLine("    white-Space: nowrap;");
txtstream.WriteLine("}");
txtstream.WriteLine("</style>");
txtstream.WriteLine("<title>Win32_Process</title>");
txtstream.WriteLine("</head>");
txtstream.WriteLine("<body>");
txtstream.WriteLine("<table border='0' Cellspacing='3' cellpadding = '3'>");

var Names;
var Cols;
var Rows;
var x = 0;

var v = 0;
```

```
while(v < 0)
{
    var ti = ex.NextEvent(-1);
    var obj = ti.Properties_.Item("TargetInstance").Value;
    if(v == 0)
    {
        Names = new Array[obj.Properties_.Count];
        Cols = new Array[obj.Properties_.Count];
        Rows = new Array[4];
        var propEnum = new Enumerator(obj.Properties_);
        for (; !propEnum.atEnd(); propEnum.moveNext())
        {
            var prop = propEnum.item();
            Names[x] = prop.Name;
            Cols[x] = GetValue(prop.Name, obj);
            x = x + 1;
        }
        Rows[v] = Cols;
        x = 0;
        v = v + 1;
    }
    else
    {
        var propEnum = new Enumerator(obj.Properties_);
        for (; !propEnum.atEnd(); propEnum.moveNext())
        {
            var prop = propEnum.item();
            Cols[x] = GetValue(prop.Name, obj);
            x = x + 1;
        }
        Rows[v] = Cols;
        x = 0;
        v = v + 1;
    }
}
for(var a = 0;a < Names.Count; a++)
{
    txtstream.WriteLine("<tr><th  align='left'  nowrap>" + Names[a] +
"</th>");
    for(var b = 0;b < Rows.Count; b++)
```

```
            {
                var C = Rows[b];
                txtstream.WriteLine("<td   style='font-family:Calibri,   Sans-Serif;font-
size: 12px;color:navy;' align='left' nowrap='nowrap'>" + C[x] + "</td>");
            }
            txtstream.WriteLine("</tr>");
        }
        txtstream.WriteLine("</table>");
        txtstream.WriteLine("</body>");
        txtstream.WriteLine("</html>");
        txtstream.close();
        function GetValue(Name, obj)
        {
            var tempstr = new String();
            var tempstr1 = new String();
            var tName = new String();
            tempstr1 = obj.GetObjectText_();
            var re = /"/g;
            tempstr1 = tempstr1.replace(re , "");
            var pos;
            tName = Name + " = ";
            pos = tempstr1.indexOf(tName);
            if (pos > -1)
            {
                pos = pos + tName.length;
                tempstr = tempstr1.substring(pos, tempstr1.length);
                pos = tempstr.indexOf(";");
                tempstr = tempstr.substring(0, pos);
                tempstr = tempstr.replace("{", "");
                tempstr = tempstr.replace("}", "");
                if (tempstr.length > 13)
                {
                    if (obj.Properties_(Name).CIMType == 101)
                    {
                        tempstr = tempstr.substr(4, 2) + "/" + tempstr.substr(6, 2) + "/" +
tempstr.substr(0, 3) + " " + tempstr.substr(8, 2) + ":" + tempstr.substr(10, 2) + ":" +
tempstr.substr(12, 2);
                    }
                }
                return tempstr;
```

```
        }
        else
        {
            return "";
        }
    }

    ]]>
    </script>
  </job>
</Package>
```

Vertical Report with a Combobox.

```
<?xml Version='1.0' encoding='iso-8859-1'?>
<package>
<job>
<script language='JavaScript'>
<![CDATA[
    var locator = new ActiveXObject("WbemScripting.SWbemLocator");
    var svc = locator.ConnectServer(".", "root\\cimv2");
    svc.Security_.AuthenticationLevel = 6;
    svc.Security_.ImpersonationLevel = 3;
    var strQuery = "Select * From ___InstanceOperationEvent WITHIN 1 where
TargetInstance ISA'Win32_Process'");
    var es = svc.ExecNotificationQuery(strQuery);
    var ws = new ActiveXObject("WScript.Shell");
    var fso = new ActiveXObject("Scripting.FileSystemObject");
    var     txtstream     =     fso.OpenTextFile(ws.CurrentDirectory     +
"\\Win32_Process.html", 2, true, -2);
    txtstream.WriteLine("<html xmlns='http://www.w3.org/1999/xhtml'>");
    txtstream.WriteLine("<head>");
    txtstream.WriteLine("<style type='text/css'>");
    txtstream.WriteLine("th");
    txtstream.WriteLine("{");
    txtstream.WriteLine("   COLOR: darkred;");
    txtstream.WriteLine("   BACKGROUND-COLOR: white;");
    txtstream.WriteLine("   FONT-FAMILY:font-family: Cambria, serif;");
    txtstream.WriteLine("   FONT-SIZE: 12px;");
```

```
txtstream.WriteLine("    text-align: left;");
txtstream.WriteLine("    white-Space: nowrap;");
txtstream.WriteLine("}");
txtstream.WriteLine("td");
txtstream.WriteLine("{");
txtstream.WriteLine("    COLOR: navy;");
txtstream.WriteLine("    BACKGROUND-COLOR: white;");
txtstream.WriteLine("    FONT-FAMILY: font-family: Cambria, serif;");
txtstream.WriteLine("    FONT-SIZE: 12px;");
txtstream.WriteLine("    text-align: left;");
txtstream.WriteLine("    white-Space: nowrap;");
txtstream.WriteLine("}");
txtstream.WriteLine("</style>");
txtstream.WriteLine("<title>Win32_Process</title>");
txtstream.WriteLine("</head>");
txtstream.WriteLine("<body>");
txtstream.WriteLine("<table border='0' Cellspacing='3' cellpadding = '3'>");

var Names;
var Cols;
var Rows;
var x = 0;

var v = 0;
while(v < 0)
{
   var ti = ex.NextEvent(-1);
   var obj = ti.Properties_.Item("TargetInstance").Value;
   if(v == 0)
   {
     Names = new Array[obj.Properties_.Count];
     Cols = new Array[obj.Properties_.Count];
     Rows = new Array[4];
     var propEnum = new Enumerator(obj.Properties_);
     for (; !propEnum.atEnd(); propEnum.moveNext())
     {
        var prop = propEnum.item();
        Names[x] = prop.Name;
        Cols[x] = GetValue(prop.Name, obj);
        x = x + 1;
```

```
            }
            Rows[v] = Cols;
            x = 0;
            v = v + 1;
        }
        else
        {
            var propEnum = new Enumerator(obj.Properties_);
            for (; !propEnum.atEnd(); propEnum.moveNext())
            {
                var prop = propEnum.item();
                Cols[x] = GetValue(prop.Name, obj);
                x = x + 1;
            }
            Rows[v] = Cols;
            x = 0;
            v = v + 1;
        }
    }
    for(var a = 0;a < Names.Count; a++)
    {
        txtstream.WriteLine("<tr><th   align='left'   nowrap>" + Names[a] +
"</th>");
        for(var b = 0;b < Rows.Count; b++)
        {
            var C = Rows[b];
            txtstream.WriteLine("<td   style='font-family:Calibri,   Sans-Serif;font-
size: 12px;color:navy;' align='left' nowrap='true'><select><option value = """ + C[x]
+ """>" + C[x] + "</option></select></td>");
        }
        txtstream.WriteLine("</tr>");
    }
    txtstream.WriteLine("</table>");
    txtstream.WriteLine("</body>");
    txtstream.WriteLine("</html>");
    txtstream.close();
    function GetValue(Name, obj)
    {
        var tempstr = new String();
        var tempstr1 = new String();
```

```javascript
var tName = new String();
tempstr1 = obj.GetObjectText_();
var re = /"/g;
tempstr1 = tempstr1.replace(re , "");
var pos;
tName = Name + " = ";
pos = tempstr1.indexOf(tName);
if (pos > -1)
{
    pos = pos + tName.length;
    tempstr = tempstr1.substring(pos, tempstr1.length);
    pos = tempstr.indexOf(";");
    tempstr = tempstr.substring(0, pos);
    tempstr = tempstr.replace("{", "");
    tempstr = tempstr.replace("}", "");
    if (tempstr.length > 13)
    {
        if (obj.Properties_(Name).CIMType == 101)
        {
            tempstr = tempstr.substr(4, 2) + "/"  + tempstr.substr(6, 2) + "/" +
tempstr.substr(0, 3) + " " + tempstr.substr(8, 2) + ":" + tempstr.substr(10, 2) + ":" +
tempstr.substr(12, 2);
        }
    }
    return tempstr;
}
else
{
    return "";
}
}

]]>
</script>
</job>
</Package>
```

Vertical Report with a link.

```
<?xml Version='1.0' encoding='iso-8859-1'?>
<package>
<job>
<script language='JavaScript'>
<![CDATA[
    var locator = new ActiveXObject("WbemScripting.SWbemLocator");
    var svc = locator.ConnectServer(".", "root\\cimv2");
    svc.Security_.AuthenticationLevel = 6;
    svc.Security_.ImpersonationLevel = 3;
    var strQuery = "Select * From ___InstanceOperationEvent WITHIN 1 where
TargetInstance ISA'Win32_Process'");
    var es = svc.ExecNotificationQuery(strQuery);
    var ws = new ActiveXObject("WScript.Shell");
    var fso = new ActiveXObject("Scripting.FileSystemObject");
    var     txtstream     =     fso.OpenTextFile(ws.CurrentDirectory     +
"\\Win32_Process.html", 2, true, -2);
    txtstream.WriteLine("<html xmlns='http://www.w3.org/1999/xhtml'>");
    txtstream.WriteLine("<head>");
    txtstream.WriteLine("<style type='text/css'>");
    txtstream.WriteLine("th");
    txtstream.WriteLine("{");
    txtstream.WriteLine("   COLOR: darkred;");
    txtstream.WriteLine("   BACKGROUND-COLOR: white;");
    txtstream.WriteLine("   FONT-FAMILY:font-family: Cambria, serif;");
    txtstream.WriteLine("   FONT-SIZE: 12px;");
    txtstream.WriteLine("   text-align: left;");
    txtstream.WriteLine("   white-Space: nowrap;");
    txtstream.WriteLine("}");
    txtstream.WriteLine("td");
    txtstream.WriteLine("{");
    txtstream.WriteLine("   COLOR: navy;");
    txtstream.WriteLine("   BACKGROUND-COLOR: white;");
    txtstream.WriteLine("   FONT-FAMILY: font-family: Cambria, serif;");
    txtstream.WriteLine("   FONT-SIZE: 12px;");
    txtstream.WriteLine("   text-align: left;");
    txtstream.WriteLine("   white-Space: nowrap;");
    txtstream.WriteLine("}");
    txtstream.WriteLine("</style>");
    txtstream.WriteLine("<title>Win32_Process</title>");
    txtstream.WriteLine("</head>");
```

```
txtstream.WriteLine("<body>");
txtstream.WriteLine("<table border='0' Cellspacing='3' cellpadding = '3'>");

var Names;
var Cols;
var Rows;
var x = 0;

var v = 0;
while(v < 0)
{
   var ti = ex.NextEvent(-1);
   var obj = ti.Properties_.Item("TargetInstance").Value;
   if(v == 0)
   {
      Names = new Array[obj.Properties_.Count];
      Cols = new Array[obj.Properties_.Count];
      Rows = new Array[4];
      var propEnum = new Enumerator(obj.Properties_);
      for (; !propEnum.atEnd(); propEnum.moveNext())
      {
         var prop = propEnum.item();
         Names[x] = prop.Name;
         Cols[x] = GetValue(prop.Name, obj);
         x = x + 1;
      }
      Rows[v] = Cols;
      x = 0;
      v = v + 1;
   }
   else
   {
      var propEnum = new Enumerator(obj.Properties_);
      for (; !propEnum.atEnd(); propEnum.moveNext())
      {
         var prop = propEnum.item();
         Cols[x] = GetValue(prop.Name, obj);
         x = x + 1;
      }
      Rows[v] = Cols;
```

```
        x = 0;
        v = v + 1;
    }
}
for(var a = 0;a < Names.Count; a++)
{
    txtstream.WriteLine("<tr><th    align='left'    nowrap>"    +    Names[a]    +
"</th>");
    for(var b = 0;b < Rows.Count; b++)
    {
        var C = Rows[b];
        txtstream.WriteLine("<td    style='font-family:Calibri,    Sans-Serif;font-
size: 12px;color:navy;' align='left' nowrap='true'><a href='" + C[x] + "'>" + C[x] +
"</a></td>");
    }
    txtstream.WriteLine("</tr>");
}
txtstream.WriteLine("</table>");
txtstream.WriteLine("</body>");
txtstream.WriteLine("</html>");
txtstream.close();
function GetValue(Name, obj)
{
    var tempstr = new String();
    var tempstr1 = new String();
    var tName = new String();
    tempstr1 = obj.GetObjectText_();
    var re = /"/g;
    tempstr1 = tempstr1.replace(re , "");
    var pos;
    tName = Name + " = ";
    pos = tempstr1.indexOf(tName);
    if (pos > -1)
    {
        pos = pos + tName.length;
        tempstr = tempstr1.substring(pos, tempstr1.length);
        pos = tempstr.indexOf(";");
        tempstr = tempstr.substring(0, pos);
        tempstr = tempstr.replace("{", "");
        tempstr = tempstr.replace("}", "");
```

```
        if (tempstr.length > 13)
        {
            if (obj.Properties_(Name).CIMType == 101)
            {
                tempstr = tempstr.substr(4, 2) + "/"  + tempstr.substr(6, 2) + "/" +
tempstr.substr(0, 3) + " " + tempstr.substr(8, 2) + ":" + tempstr.substr(10, 2) + ":" +
tempstr.substr(12, 2);
            }
        }
        return tempstr;
    }
    else
    {
        return "";
    }
}

]]>
</script>
</job>
</Package>
```

Vertical Report with a Listbox.

```
<?xml Version='1.0' encoding='iso-8859-1'?>
<package>
<job>
<script language='JavaScript'>
<![CDATA[
    var locator = new ActiveXObject("WbemScripting.SWbemLocator");
    var svc = locator.ConnectServer(".", "root\\cimv2");
    svc.Security_.AuthenticationLevel = 6;
    svc.Security_.ImpersonationLevel = 3;
    var strQuery = "Select * From ___InstanceOperationEvent WITHIN 1 where
TargetInstance ISA'Win32_Process'");
    var es = svc.ExecNotificationQuery(strQuery);
    var ws = new ActiveXObject("WScript.Shell");
    var fso = new ActiveXObject("Scripting.FileSystemObject");
```

```
var    txtstream    =    fso.OpenTextFile(ws.CurrentDirectory    +
"\\Win32_Process.html", 2, true, -2);
    txtstream.WriteLine("<html xmlns='http://www.w3.org/1999/xhtml'>");
    txtstream.WriteLine("<head>");
    txtstream.WriteLine("<style type='text/css'>");
    txtstream.WriteLine("th");
    txtstream.WriteLine("{");
    txtstream.WriteLine("    COLOR: darkred;");
    txtstream.WriteLine("    BACKGROUND-COLOR: white;");
    txtstream.WriteLine("    FONT-FAMILY:font-family: Cambria, serif;");
    txtstream.WriteLine("    FONT-SIZE: 12px;");
    txtstream.WriteLine("    text-align: left;");
    txtstream.WriteLine("    white-Space: nowrap;");
    txtstream.WriteLine("}");
    txtstream.WriteLine("td");
    txtstream.WriteLine("{");
    txtstream.WriteLine("    COLOR: navy;");
    txtstream.WriteLine("    BACKGROUND-COLOR: white;");
    txtstream.WriteLine("    FONT-FAMILY: font-family: Cambria, serif;");
    txtstream.WriteLine("    FONT-SIZE: 12px;");
    txtstream.WriteLine("    text-align: left;");
    txtstream.WriteLine("    white-Space: nowrap;");
    txtstream.WriteLine("}");
    txtstream.WriteLine("</style>");
    txtstream.WriteLine("<title>Win32_Process</title>");
    txtstream.WriteLine("</head>");
    txtstream.WriteLine("<body>");
    txtstream.WriteLine("<table border='0' Cellspacing='3' cellpadding = '3'>");

    var Names;
    var Cols;
    var Rows;
    var x = 0;

    var v = 0;
    while(v < 0)
    {
        var ti = ex.NextEvent(-1);
        var obj = ti.Properties_.Item("TargetInstance").Value;
        if(v == 0)
```

```
        {
            Names = new Array[obj.Properties_.Count];
            Cols = new Array[obj.Properties_.Count];
            Rows = new Array[4];
            var propEnum = new Enumerator(obj.Properties_);
            for (; !propEnum.atEnd(); propEnum.moveNext())
            {
                var prop = propEnum.item();
                Names[x] = prop.Name;
                Cols[x] = GetValue(prop.Name, obj);
                x = x + 1;
            }
            Rows[v] = Cols;
            x = 0;
            v = v + 1;
        }
        else
        {
            var propEnum = new Enumerator(obj.Properties_);
            for (; !propEnum.atEnd(); propEnum.moveNext())
            {
                var prop = propEnum.item();
                Cols[x] = GetValue(prop.Name, obj);
                x = x + 1;
            }
            Rows[v] = Cols;
            x = 0;
            v = v + 1;
        }
    }
    for(var a = 0;a < Names.Count; a++)
    {
        txtstream.WriteLine("<tr><th align='left'  nowrap>" + Names[a] +
"</th>");
        for(var b = 0;b < Rows.Count; b++)
        {
            var C = Rows[b];
            txtstream.WriteLine("<td  style='font-family:Calibri,  Sans-Serif;font-
size: 12px;color:navy;' align='left' nowrap='true'><select multiple><option value =
""" + C[x] + """>" + C[x] + "</option></select></td>");
```

```
            }
            txtstream.WriteLine("</tr>");
        }
        txtstream.WriteLine("</table>");
        txtstream.WriteLine("</body>");
        txtstream.WriteLine("</html>");
        txtstream.close();
        function GetValue(Name, obj)
        {
            var tempstr = new String();
            var tempstr1 = new String();
            var tName = new String();
            tempstr1 = obj.GetObjectText_();
            var re = /"/g;
            tempstr1 = tempstr1.replace(re , "");
            var pos;
            tName = Name + " = ";
            pos = tempstr1.indexOf(tName);
            if (pos > -1)
            {
                pos = pos + tName.length;
                tempstr = tempstr1.substring(pos, tempstr1.length);
                pos = tempstr.indexOf(";");
                tempstr = tempstr.substring(0, pos);
                tempstr = tempstr.replace("{", "");
                tempstr = tempstr.replace("}", "");
                if (tempstr.length > 13)
                {
                    if (obj.Properties_(Name).CIMType == 101)
                    {
                        tempstr = tempstr.substr(4, 2) + "/"  + tempstr.substr(6, 2) + "/" +
tempstr.substr(0, 3) + " " + tempstr.substr(8, 2) + ":" + tempstr.substr(10, 2) + ":" +
tempstr.substr(12, 2);
                    }
                }
                return tempstr;
            }
            else
            {
                return "";
```

```
        }
      }

    ]]>
    </script>
  </job>
</Package>
```

Vertical Report with a textarea.

```
<?xml Version='1.0' encoding='iso-8859-1'?>
<package>
<job>
<script language='JavaScript'>
<![CDATA[
    var locator = new ActiveXObject("WbemScripting.SWbemLocator");
    var svc = locator.ConnectServer(".", "root\\cimv2");
    svc.Security_.AuthenticationLevel = 6;
    svc.Security_.ImpersonationLevel = 3;
    var strQuery = "Select * From ___InstanceOperationEvent WITHIN 1 where
TargetInstance ISA'Win32_Process'");
    var es = svc.ExecNotificationQuery(strQuery);
    var ws = new ActiveXObject("WScript.Shell");
    var fso = new ActiveXObject("Scripting.FileSystemObject");
    var     txtstream     =     fso.OpenTextFile(ws.CurrentDirectory     +
"\\Win32_Process.html", 2, true, -2);
    txtstream.WriteLine("<html xmlns='http://www.w3.org/1999/xhtml'>");
    txtstream.WriteLine("<head>");
    txtstream.WriteLine("<style type='text/css'>");
    txtstream.WriteLine("th");
    txtstream.WriteLine("{");
    txtstream.WriteLine("   COLOR: darkred;");
    txtstream.WriteLine("   BACKGROUND-COLOR: white;");
    txtstream.WriteLine("   FONT-FAMILY:font-family: Cambria, serif;");
    txtstream.WriteLine("   FONT-SIZE: 12px;");
    txtstream.WriteLine("   text-align: left;");
    txtstream.WriteLine("   white-Space: nowrap;");
    txtstream.WriteLine("}");
    txtstream.WriteLine("td");
```

```
txtstream.WriteLine("{");
txtstream.WriteLine("    COLOR: navy;");
txtstream.WriteLine("    BACKGROUND-COLOR: white;");
txtstream.WriteLine("    FONT-FAMILY: font-family: Cambria, serif;");
txtstream.WriteLine("    FONT-SIZE: 12px;");
txtstream.WriteLine("    text-align: left;");
txtstream.WriteLine("    white-Space: nowrap;");
txtstream.WriteLine("}");
txtstream.WriteLine("</style>");
txtstream.WriteLine("<title>Win32_Process</title>");
txtstream.WriteLine("</head>");
txtstream.WriteLine("<body>");
txtstream.WriteLine("<table border='0' Cellspacing='3' cellpadding = '3'>");

var Names;
var Cols;
var Rows;
var x = 0;

var v = 0;
while(v < 0)
{
    var ti = ex.NextEvent(-1);
    var obj = ti.Properties_.Item("TargetInstance").Value;
    if(v == 0)
    {
        Names = new Array[obj.Properties_.Count];
        Cols = new Array[obj.Properties_.Count];
        Rows = new Array[4];
        var propEnum = new Enumerator(obj.Properties_);
        for (; !propEnum.atEnd(); propEnum.moveNext())
        {
            var prop = propEnum.item();
            Names[x] = prop.Name;
            Cols[x] = GetValue(prop.Name, obj);
            x = x + 1;
        }
        Rows[v] = Cols;
        x = 0;
        v = v + 1;
```

```
            }
            else
            {
                var propEnum = new Enumerator(obj.Properties_);
                for (; !propEnum.atEnd(); propEnum.moveNext())
                {
                    var prop = propEnum.item();
                    Cols[x] = GetValue(prop.Name, obj);
                    x = x + 1;
                }
                Rows[v] = Cols;
                x = 0;
                v = v + 1;
            }
        }
        for(var a = 0;a < Names.Count; a++)
        {
            txtstream.WriteLine("<tr><th  align='left'  nowrap>" + Names[a] +
"</th>");
            for(var b = 0;b < Rows.Count; b++)
            {
                var C = Rows[b];
                txtstream.WriteLine("<td   style='font-family:Calibri,  Sans-Serif;font-
size:  12px;color:navy;'  align='left'  nowrap='true'><textarea>" + C[x] +
"</textarea></td>");
            }
            txtstream.WriteLine("</tr>");
        }
        txtstream.WriteLine("</table>");
        txtstream.WriteLine("</body>");
        txtstream.WriteLine("</html>");
        txtstream.close();
        function GetValue(Name, obj)
        {
            var tempstr = new String();
            var tempstr1 = new String();
            var tName = new String();
            tempstr1 = obj.GetObjectText_();
            var re = /"/g;
            tempstr1 = tempstr1.replace(re , "");
```

```javascript
    var pos;
    tName = Name + " = ";
    pos = tempstr1.indexOf(tName);
    if (pos > -1)
    {
        pos = pos + tName.length;
        tempstr = tempstr1.substring(pos, tempstr1.length);
        pos = tempstr.indexOf(";");
        tempstr = tempstr.substring(0, pos);
        tempstr = tempstr.replace("{", "");
        tempstr = tempstr.replace("}", "");
        if (tempstr.length > 13)
        {
            if (obj.Properties_(Name).CIMType == 101)
            {
                tempstr = tempstr.substr(4, 2) + "/"  + tempstr.substr(6, 2) + "/" +
tempstr.substr(0, 3) + " " + tempstr.substr(8, 2) + ":" + tempstr.substr(10, 2) + ":" +
tempstr.substr(12, 2);
            }
        }
        return tempstr;
    }
    else
    {
        return "";
    }
}


]]>
</script>
</job>
</Package>
```

Vertical Report with a textbox.

```xml
<?xml Version='1.0' encoding='iso-8859-1'?>
<package>
<job>
<script language='JavaScript'>
```

```
<![CDATA[
    var locator = new ActiveXObject("WbemScripting.SWbemLocator");
    var svc = locator.ConnectServer(".", "root\\cimv2");
    svc.Security_.AuthenticationLevel = 6;
    svc.Security_.ImpersonationLevel = 3;
    var strQuery = "Select * From ___InstanceOperationEvent WITHIN 1 where
TargetInstance ISA'Win32_Process'");
    var es = svc.ExecNotificationQuery(strQuery);
    var ws = new ActiveXObject("WScript.Shell");
    var fso = new ActiveXObject("Scripting.FileSystemObject");
    var       txtstream       =       fso.OpenTextFile(ws.CurrentDirectory       +
"\\Win32_Process.html", 2, true, -2);
    txtstream.WriteLine("<html xmlns='http://www.w3.org/1999/xhtml'>");
    txtstream.WriteLine("<head>");
    txtstream.WriteLine("<style type='text/css'>");
    txtstream.WriteLine("th");
    txtstream.WriteLine("{");
    txtstream.WriteLine("   COLOR: darkred;");
    txtstream.WriteLine("   BACKGROUND-COLOR: white;");
    txtstream.WriteLine("   FONT-FAMILY:font-family: Cambria, serif;");
    txtstream.WriteLine("   FONT-SIZE: 12px;");
    txtstream.WriteLine("   text-align: left;");
    txtstream.WriteLine("   white-Space: nowrap;");
    txtstream.WriteLine("}");
    txtstream.WriteLine("td");
    txtstream.WriteLine("{");
    txtstream.WriteLine("   COLOR: navy;");
    txtstream.WriteLine("   BACKGROUND-COLOR: white;");
    txtstream.WriteLine("   FONT-FAMILY: font-family: Cambria, serif;");
    txtstream.WriteLine("   FONT-SIZE: 12px;");
    txtstream.WriteLine("   text-align: left;");
    txtstream.WriteLine("   white-Space: nowrap;");
    txtstream.WriteLine("}");
    txtstream.WriteLine("</style>");
    txtstream.WriteLine("<title>Win32_Process</title>");
    txtstream.WriteLine("</head>");
    txtstream.WriteLine("<body>");
    txtstream.WriteLine("<table border='0' Cellspacing='3' cellpadding = '3'>");

    var Names;
```

```
var Cols;
var Rows;
var x = 0;

var v = 0;
while(v < 0)
{
   var ti = ex.NextEvent(-1);
   var obj = ti.Properties_.Item("TargetInstance").Value;
   if(v == 0)
   {
      Names = new Array[obj.Properties_.Count];
      Cols = new Array[obj.Properties_.Count];
      Rows = new Array[4];
      var propEnum = new Enumerator(obj.Properties_);
      for (; !propEnum.atEnd(); propEnum.moveNext())
      {
         var prop = propEnum.item();
         Names[x] = prop.Name;
         Cols[x] = GetValue(prop.Name, obj);
         x = x + 1;
      }
      Rows[v] = Cols;
      x = 0;
      v = v + 1;
   }
   else
   {
      var propEnum = new Enumerator(obj.Properties_);
      for (; !propEnum.atEnd(); propEnum.moveNext())
      {
         var prop = propEnum.item();
         Cols[x] = GetValue(prop.Name, obj);
         x = x + 1;
      }
      Rows[v] = Cols;
      x = 0;
      v = v + 1;
   }
}
```

```
for(var a = 0;a < Names.Count; a++)
{
    txtstream.WriteLine("<tr><th    align='left'    nowrap>" +  Names[a]  +
"</th>");
    for(var b = 0;b < Rows.Count; b++)
    {
        var C = Rows[b];
        txtstream.WriteLine("<td   style='font-family:Calibri,   Sans-Serif;font-
size: 12px;color:navy;' align='left' nowrap='true'><input type=text value="""" + C[x]
+ """"></input></td>");
    }
    txtstream.WriteLine("</tr>");
}
txtstream.WriteLine("</table>");
txtstream.WriteLine("</body>");
txtstream.WriteLine("</html>");
txtstream.close();
function GetValue(Name, obj)
{
    var tempstr = new String();
    var tempstr1 = new String();
    var tName = new String();
    tempstr1 = obj.GetObjectText_();
    var re = /"/g;
    tempstr1 = tempstr1.replace(re , "");
    var pos;
    tName = Name + " = ";
    pos = tempstr1.indexOf(tName);
    if (pos > -1)
    {
        pos = pos + tName.length;
        tempstr = tempstr1.substring(pos, tempstr1.length);
        pos = tempstr.indexOf(";");
        tempstr = tempstr.substring(0, pos);
        tempstr = tempstr.replace("{", "");
        tempstr = tempstr.replace("}", "");
        if (tempstr.length > 13)
        {
            if (obj.Properties_(Name).CIMType == 101)
            {
```

```
              tempstr = tempstr.substr(4, 2) + "/"  + tempstr.substr(6, 2) + "/" +
tempstr.substr(0, 3) + " " + tempstr.substr(8, 2) + ":" + tempstr.substr(10, 2) + ":" +
tempstr.substr(12, 2);
                }
            }
            return tempstr;
        }
        else
        {
            return "";
        }
    }


    ]]>
    </script>
  </job>
</Package>
```

HTML Tables

Horizontal Table with no additional tags.

```
<?xml Version='1.0' encoding='iso-8859-1'?>
<package>
<job>
<script language='JavaScript'>
<![CDATA[
    var locator = new ActiveXObject("WbemScripting.SWbemLocator");
    var svc = locator.ConnectServer(".", "root\\cimv2");
    svc.Security_.AuthenticationLevel = 6;
    svc.Security_.ImpersonationLevel = 3;
    var strQuery = "Select * From ___InstanceOperationEvent WITHIN 1 where
TargetInstance ISA'Win32_Process'");
    var es = svc.ExecNotificationQuery(strQuery);
    var ws = new ActiveXObject("WScript.Shell");
    var fso = new ActiveXObject("Scripting.FileSystemObject");
    var      txtstream      =      fso.OpenTextFile(ws.CurrentDirectory      +
"\\Win32_Process.html", 2, true, -2);
    txtstream.WriteLine("<html xmlns='http://www.w3.org/1999/xhtml'>");
    txtstream.WriteLine("<head>");
    txtstream.WriteLine("<style type='text/css'>");
    txtstream.WriteLine("th");
    txtstream.WriteLine("{");
    txtstream.WriteLine("   COLOR: darkred;");
```

```
txtstream.WriteLine("    BACKGROUND-COLOR: white;");
txtstream.WriteLine("    FONT-FAMILY:font-family: Cambria, serif;");
txtstream.WriteLine("    FONT-SIZE: 12px;");
txtstream.WriteLine("    text-align: left;");
txtstream.WriteLine("    white-Space: nowrap;");
txtstream.WriteLine("}");
txtstream.WriteLine("td");
txtstream.WriteLine("{");
txtstream.WriteLine("    COLOR: navy;");
txtstream.WriteLine("    BACKGROUND-COLOR: white;");
txtstream.WriteLine("    FONT-FAMILY: font-family: Cambria, serif;");
txtstream.WriteLine("    FONT-SIZE: 12px;");
txtstream.WriteLine("    text-align: left;");
txtstream.WriteLine("    white-Space: nowrap;");
txtstream.WriteLine("}");
txtstream.WriteLine("</style>");
txtstream.WriteLine("<title>Win32_Process</title>");
txtstream.WriteLine("</head>");
txtstream.WriteLine("<body>");
txtstream.WriteLine("<table border='1' Cellspacing='3' cellpadding = '3'>");
var v=0;
while(v < 0)
{
    var ti = ex.NextEvent(-1);
    var obj = ti.Properties_.Item("TargetInstance").Value;
    if(v == 0)
    {
        txtstream.WriteLine("<tr>");
        var propEnum = new Enumerator(obj.Properties_);
        for (; !propEnum.atEnd(); propEnum.moveNext())
        {
            var prop = propEnum.item();
            txtstream.WriteLine("<th align='left' nowrap>" + prop.Name +
"</th>");
        }
        txtstream.WriteLine("</tr>");
        propEnum.Reset();
    }
    txtstream.WriteLine("<tr>");
    for (; !propEnum.atEnd(); propEnum.moveNext())
```

```
        {
            var prop = propEnum.item();
            txtstream.WriteLine("<td    style='font-family:Calibri,   Sans-Serif;font-
size: 12px;color:navy;' align='left' nowrap='nowrap'>" + GetValue(prop.Name, obj) +
"</td>");
        }
        txtstream.WriteLine("</tr>");
        v = v + 1;
    }
    txtstream.WriteLine("</table>");
    txtstream.WriteLine("</body>");
    txtstream.WriteLine("</html>");
    txtstream.close();
    function GetValue(Name, obj)
    {
        var tempstr = new String();
        var tempstr1 = new String();
        var tName = new String();
        tempstr1 = obj.GetObjectText_();
        var re = /"/g;
        tempstr1 = tempstr1.replace(re , "");
        var pos;
        tName = Name + " = ";
        pos = tempstr1.indexOf(tName);
        if (pos > -1)
        {
            pos = pos + tName.length;
            tempstr = tempstr1.substring(pos, tempstr1.length);
            pos = tempstr.indexOf(";");
            tempstr = tempstr.substring(0, pos);
            tempstr = tempstr.replace("{", "");
            tempstr = tempstr.replace("}", "");
            if (tempstr.length > 13)
            {
                if (obj.Properties_(Name).CIMType == 101)
                {
                    tempstr = tempstr.substr(4, 2) + "/"  + tempstr.substr(6, 2) + "/" +
tempstr.substr(0, 3) + " " + tempstr.substr(8, 2) + ":" + tempstr.substr(10, 2) + ":" +
tempstr.substr(12, 2);
                }
```

```
            }
            return tempstr;
        }
        else
        {
            return "";
        }
    }


    ]]>
    </script>
  </job>
</Package>
```

Horizontal Table with a Combobox.

```
<?xml Version='1.0' encoding='iso-8859-1'?>
<package>
<job>
<script language='JavaScript'>
<![CDATA[
    var locator = new ActiveXObject("WbemScripting.SWbemLocator");
    var svc = locator.ConnectServer(".", "root\\cimv2");
    svc.Security_.AuthenticationLevel = 6;
    svc.Security_.ImpersonationLevel = 3;
    var strQuery = "Select * From ___InstanceOperationEvent WITHIN 1 where
TargetInstance ISA'Win32_Process'");
    var es = svc.ExecNotificationQuery(strQuery);
    var ws = new ActiveXObject("WScript.Shell");
    var fso = new ActiveXObject("Scripting.FileSystemObject");
    var     txtstream    =    fso.OpenTextFile(ws.CurrentDirectory    +
"\\Win32_Process.html", 2, true, -2);
    txtstream.WriteLine("<html xmlns='http://www.w3.org/1999/xhtml'>");
    txtstream.WriteLine("<head>");
    txtstream.WriteLine("<style type='text/css'>");
    txtstream.WriteLine("th");
    txtstream.WriteLine("{");
    txtstream.WriteLine("   COLOR: darkred;");
    txtstream.WriteLine("   BACKGROUND-COLOR: white;");
```

```
txtstream.WriteLine("   FONT-FAMILY:font-family: Cambria, serif;");
txtstream.WriteLine("   FONT-SIZE: 12px;");
txtstream.WriteLine("   text-align: left;");
txtstream.WriteLine("   white-Space: nowrap;");
txtstream.WriteLine("}");
txtstream.WriteLine("td");
txtstream.WriteLine("{");
txtstream.WriteLine("   COLOR: navy;");
txtstream.WriteLine("   BACKGROUND-COLOR: white;");
txtstream.WriteLine("   FONT-FAMILY: font-family: Cambria, serif;");
txtstream.WriteLine("   FONT-SIZE: 12px;");
txtstream.WriteLine("   text-align: left;");
txtstream.WriteLine("   white-Space: nowrap;");
txtstream.WriteLine("}");
txtstream.WriteLine("</style>");
txtstream.WriteLine("<title>Win32_Process</title>");
txtstream.WriteLine("</head>");
txtstream.WriteLine("<body>");
txtstream.WriteLine("<table border='1' Cellspacing='3' cellpadding = '3'>");
var v=0;
while(v < 0)
{
   var ti = ex.NextEvent(-1);
   var obj = ti.Properties_.Item("TargetInstance").Value;
   if(v == 0)
   {
      txtstream.WriteLine("<tr>");
      var propEnum = new Enumerator(obj.Properties_);
      for (; !propEnum.atEnd(); propEnum.moveNext())
      {
         var prop = propEnum.item();
         txtstream.WriteLine("<th  align='left'  nowrap>" + prop.Name +
"</th>");
      }
      txtstream.WriteLine("</tr>");
      propEnum.Reset();
   }
   txtstream.WriteLine("<tr>");
   for (; !propEnum.atEnd(); propEnum.moveNext())
   {
```

```
            var prop = propEnum.item();
            txtstream.WriteLine("<td style='font-family:Calibri, Sans-Serif;font-
size: 12px;color:navy;' align='left' nowrap='true'><select><option value = '" +
GetValue(prop.Name,     obj)     +     "'>" +     GetValue(prop.Name,     obj)     +
"</option></select></td>");
        }
        txtstream.WriteLine("</tr>");
        v = v + 1;
    }
    txtstream.WriteLine("</table>");
    txtstream.WriteLine("</body>");
    txtstream.WriteLine("</html>");
    txtstream.close();
    function GetValue(Name, obj)
    {
        var tempstr = new String();
        var tempstr1 = new String();
        var tName = new String();
        tempstr1 = obj.GetObjectText_();
        var re = /"/g;
        tempstr1 = tempstr1.replace(re , "");
        var pos;
        tName = Name + " = ";
        pos = tempstr1.indexOf(tName);
        if (pos > -1)
        {
            pos = pos + tName.length;
            tempstr = tempstr1.substring(pos, tempstr1.length);
            pos = tempstr.indexOf(";");
            tempstr = tempstr.substring(0, pos);
            tempstr = tempstr.replace("{", "");
            tempstr = tempstr.replace("}", "");
            if (tempstr.length > 13)
            {
                if (obj.Properties_(Name).CIMType == 101)
                {
                    tempstr = tempstr.substr(4, 2) + "/" + tempstr.substr(6, 2) + "/" +
tempstr.substr(0, 3) + " " + tempstr.substr(8, 2) + ":" + tempstr.substr(10, 2) + ":" +
tempstr.substr(12, 2);
                }
```

```
        }
        return tempstr;
      }
      else
      {
        return "";
      }
    }


    ]]>
    </script>
   </job>
 </Package>
```

Horizontal Table with a link.

```
    <?xml Version='1.0' encoding='iso-8859-1'?>
    <package>
    <job>
    <script language='JavaScript'>
    <![CDATA[
      var locator = new ActiveXObject("WbemScripting.SWbemLocator");
      var svc = locator.ConnectServer(".", "root\\cimv2");
      svc.Security_.AuthenticationLevel = 6;
      svc.Security_.ImpersonationLevel = 3;
      var strQuery = "Select * From ___InstanceOperationEvent WITHIN 1 where
TargetInstance ISA'Win32_Process'");
      var es = svc.ExecNotificationQuery(strQuery);
      var ws = new ActiveXObject("WScript.Shell");
      var fso = new ActiveXObject("Scripting.FileSystemObject");
      var     txtstream    =    fso.OpenTextFile(ws.CurrentDirectory     +
"\\Win32_Process.html", 2, true, -2);
      txtstream.WriteLine("<html xmlns='http://www.w3.org/1999/xhtml'>");
      txtstream.WriteLine("<head>");
      txtstream.WriteLine("<style type='text/css'>");
      txtstream.WriteLine("th");
      txtstream.WriteLine("{");
      txtstream.WriteLine("   COLOR: darkred;");
      txtstream.WriteLine("   BACKGROUND-COLOR: white;");
```

```
txtstream.WriteLine("   FONT-FAMILY:font-family: Cambria, serif;");
txtstream.WriteLine("   FONT-SIZE: 12px;");
txtstream.WriteLine("   text-align: left;");
txtstream.WriteLine("   white-Space: nowrap;");
txtstream.WriteLine("}");
txtstream.WriteLine("td");
txtstream.WriteLine("{");
txtstream.WriteLine("   COLOR: navy;");
txtstream.WriteLine("   BACKGROUND-COLOR: white;");
txtstream.WriteLine("   FONT-FAMILY: font-family: Cambria, serif;");
txtstream.WriteLine("   FONT-SIZE: 12px;");
txtstream.WriteLine("   text-align: left;");
txtstream.WriteLine("   white-Space: nowrap;");
txtstream.WriteLine("}");
txtstream.WriteLine("</style>");
txtstream.WriteLine("<title>Win32_Process</title>");
txtstream.WriteLine("</head>");
txtstream.WriteLine("<body>");
txtstream.WriteLine("<table border='1' Cellspacing='3' cellpadding = '3'>");
var v=0;
while(v < 0)
{
    var ti = ex.NextEvent(-1);
    var obj = ti.Properties_.Item("TargetInstance").Value;
    if(v == 0)
    {
        txtstream.WriteLine("<tr>");
        var propEnum = new Enumerator(obj.Properties_);
        for (; !propEnum.atEnd(); propEnum.moveNext())
        {
            var prop = propEnum.item();
            txtstream.WriteLine("<th align='left' nowrap>" + prop.Name +
"</th>");
        }
        txtstream.WriteLine("</tr>");
        propEnum.Reset();
    }
    txtstream.WriteLine("<tr>");
    for (; !propEnum.atEnd(); propEnum.moveNext())
    {
```

```javascript
            var prop = propEnum.item();
            txtstream.WriteLine("<td   style='font-family:Calibri,   Sans-Serif;font-
size: 12px;color:navy;' align='left' nowrap='true'><a href='" + GetValue(prop.Name,
obj) + "'>" + GetValue(prop.Name, obj) + "</a></td>");
         }
       txtstream.WriteLine("</tr>");
       v = v + 1;
    }
    txtstream.WriteLine("</table>");
    txtstream.WriteLine("</body>");
    txtstream.WriteLine("</html>");
    txtstream.close();
    function GetValue(Name, obj)
    {
       var tempstr = new String();
       var tempstr1 = new String();
       var tName = new String();
       tempstr1 = obj.GetObjectText_();
       var re = /"/g;
       tempstr1 = tempstr1.replace(re , "");
       var pos;
       tName = Name + " = ";
       pos = tempstr1.indexOf(tName);
       if (pos > -1)
       {
          pos = pos + tName.length;
          tempstr = tempstr1.substring(pos, tempstr1.length);
          pos = tempstr.indexOf(";");
          tempstr = tempstr.substring(0, pos);
          tempstr = tempstr.replace("{", "");
          tempstr = tempstr.replace("}", "");
          if (tempstr.length > 13)
          {
             if (obj.Properties_(Name).CIMType == 101)
             {
               tempstr = tempstr.substr(4, 2) + "/"  + tempstr.substr(6, 2) + "/" +
tempstr.substr(0, 3) + " " + tempstr.substr(8, 2) + ":" + tempstr.substr(10, 2) + ":" +
tempstr.substr(12, 2);
             }
          }
```

```
      return tempstr;
    }
    else
    {
      return "";
    }
  }


  ]]>
  </script>
 </job>
</Package>
```

Horizontal Table with a Listbox.

```
<?xml Version='1.0' encoding='iso-8859-1'?>
<package>
<job>
<script language='JavaScript'>
<![CDATA[
    var locator = new ActiveXObject("WbemScripting.SWbemLocator");
    var svc = locator.ConnectServer(".", "root\\cimv2");
    svc.Security_.AuthenticationLevel = 6;
    svc.Security_.ImpersonationLevel = 3;
    var strQuery = "Select * From ___InstanceOperationEvent WITHIN 1 where
TargetInstance ISA'Win32_Process'");
    var es = svc.ExecNotificationQuery(strQuery);
    var ws = new ActiveXObject("WScript.Shell");
    var fso = new ActiveXObject("Scripting.FileSystemObject");
    var    txtstream    =    fso.OpenTextFile(ws.CurrentDirectory    +
"\\Win32_Process.html", 2, true, -2);
    txtstream.WriteLine("<html xmlns='http://www.w3.org/1999/xhtml'>");
    txtstream.WriteLine("<head>");
    txtstream.WriteLine("<style type='text/css'>");
    txtstream.WriteLine("th");
    txtstream.WriteLine("{");
    txtstream.WriteLine("    COLOR: darkred;");
    txtstream.WriteLine("    BACKGROUND-COLOR: white;");
    txtstream.WriteLine("    FONT-FAMILY:font-family: Cambria, serif;");
```

```
txtstream.WriteLine("    FONT-SIZE: 12px;");
txtstream.WriteLine("    text-align: left;");
txtstream.WriteLine("    white-Space: nowrap;");
txtstream.WriteLine("}");
txtstream.WriteLine("td");
txtstream.WriteLine("{");
txtstream.WriteLine("    COLOR: navy;");
txtstream.WriteLine("    BACKGROUND-COLOR: white;");
txtstream.WriteLine("    FONT-FAMILY: font-family: Cambria, serif;");
txtstream.WriteLine("    FONT-SIZE: 12px;");
txtstream.WriteLine("    text-align: left;");
txtstream.WriteLine("    white-Space: nowrap;");
txtstream.WriteLine("}");
txtstream.WriteLine("</style>");
txtstream.WriteLine("<title>Win32_Process</title>");
txtstream.WriteLine("</head>");
txtstream.WriteLine("<body>");
txtstream.WriteLine("<table border='1' Cellspacing='3' cellpadding = '3'>");
var v=0;
while(v < 0)
{
    var ti = ex.NextEvent(-1);
    var obj = ti.Properties_.Item("TargetInstance").Value;
    if(v == 0)
    {
        txtstream.WriteLine("<tr>");
        var propEnum = new Enumerator(obj.Properties_);
        for (; !propEnum.atEnd(); propEnum.moveNext())
        {
            var prop = propEnum.item();
            txtstream.WriteLine("<th  align='left'  nowrap>" + prop.Name +
"</th>");
        }
        txtstream.WriteLine("</tr>");
        propEnum.Reset();
    }
    txtstream.WriteLine("<tr>");
    for (; !propEnum.atEnd(); propEnum.moveNext())
    {
        var prop = propEnum.item();
```

```
        txtstream.WriteLine("<td  style='font-family:Calibri,  Sans-Serif;font-
size: 12px;color:navy;' align='left' nowrap='true'><select multiple><option value =
'"   +   GetValue(prop.Name,   obj)   +   "'>"   +   GetValue(prop.Name,   obj)   +
"</option></select></td>");
        }
        txtstream.WriteLine("</tr>");
        v = v + 1;
    }
    txtstream.WriteLine("</table>");
    txtstream.WriteLine("</body>");
    txtstream.WriteLine("</html>");
    txtstream.close();
    function GetValue(Name, obj)
    {
        var tempstr = new String();
        var tempstr1 = new String();
        var tName = new String();
        tempstr1 = obj.GetObjectText_();
        var re = /"/g;
        tempstr1 = tempstr1.replace(re , "");
        var pos;
        tName = Name + " = ";
        pos = tempstr1.indexOf(tName);
        if (pos > -1)
        {
            pos = pos + tName.length;
            tempstr = tempstr1.substring(pos, tempstr1.length);
            pos = tempstr.indexOf(";");
            tempstr = tempstr.substring(0, pos);
            tempstr = tempstr.replace("{", "");
            tempstr = tempstr.replace("}", "");
            if (tempstr.length > 13)
            {
                if (obj.Properties_(Name).CIMType == 101)
                {
                    tempstr = tempstr.substr(4, 2) + "/" + tempstr.substr(6, 2) + "/" +
tempstr.substr(0, 3) + " " + tempstr.substr(8, 2) + ":" + tempstr.substr(10, 2) + ":" +
tempstr.substr(12, 2);
                }
            }
```

```
        return tempstr;
      }
      else
      {
        return "";
      }
    }


    ]]>
    </script>
   </job>
  </Package>
```

Horizontal Table with a textarea.

```
    <?xml Version='1.0' encoding='iso-8859-1'?>
    <package>
    <job>
    <script language='JavaScript'>
    <![CDATA[
        var locator = new ActiveXObject("WbemScripting.SWbemLocator");
        var svc = locator.ConnectServer(".", "root\\cimv2");
        svc.Security_.AuthenticationLevel = 6;
        svc.Security_.ImpersonationLevel = 3;
        var strQuery = "Select * From ___InstanceOperationEvent WITHIN 1 where
    TargetInstance ISA'Win32_Process'");
        var es = svc.ExecNotificationQuery(strQuery);
        var ws = new ActiveXObject("WScript.Shell");
        var fso = new ActiveXObject("Scripting.FileSystemObject");
        var    txtstream    =    fso.OpenTextFile(ws.CurrentDirectory    +
    "\\Win32_Process.html", 2, true, -2);
        txtstream.WriteLine("<html xmlns='http://www.w3.org/1999/xhtml'>");
        txtstream.WriteLine("<head>");
        txtstream.WriteLine("<style type='text/css'>");
        txtstream.WriteLine("th");
        txtstream.WriteLine("{");
        txtstream.WriteLine("    COLOR: darkred;");
        txtstream.WriteLine("    BACKGROUND-COLOR: white;");
        txtstream.WriteLine("    FONT-FAMILY:font-family: Cambria, serif;");
```

```
txtstream.WriteLine("    FONT-SIZE: 12px;");
txtstream.WriteLine("    text-align: left;");
txtstream.WriteLine("    white-Space: nowrap;");
txtstream.WriteLine("}");
txtstream.WriteLine("td");
txtstream.WriteLine("{");
txtstream.WriteLine("    COLOR: navy;");
txtstream.WriteLine("    BACKGROUND-COLOR: white;");
txtstream.WriteLine("    FONT-FAMILY: font-family: Cambria, serif;");
txtstream.WriteLine("    FONT-SIZE: 12px;");
txtstream.WriteLine("    text-align: left;");
txtstream.WriteLine("    white-Space: nowrap;");
txtstream.WriteLine("}");
txtstream.WriteLine("</style>");
txtstream.WriteLine("<title>Win32_Process</title>");
txtstream.WriteLine("</head>");
txtstream.WriteLine("<body>");
txtstream.WriteLine("<table border='1' Cellspacing='3' cellpadding = '3'>");
var v=0;
while(v < 0)
{
    var ti = ex.NextEvent(-1);
    var obj = ti.Properties_.Item("TargetInstance").Value;
    if(v == 0)
    {
        txtstream.WriteLine("<tr>");
        var propEnum = new Enumerator(obj.Properties_);
        for (; !propEnum.atEnd(); propEnum.moveNext())
        {
            var prop = propEnum.item();
            txtstream.WriteLine("<th align='left' nowrap>" + prop.Name +
"</th>");
        }
        txtstream.WriteLine("</tr>");
        propEnum.Reset();
    }
    txtstream.WriteLine("<tr>");
    for (; !propEnum.atEnd(); propEnum.moveNext())
    {
        var prop = propEnum.item();
```

```
            txtstream.WriteLine("<td   style='font-family:Calibri,   Sans-Serif;font-
size:      12px;color:navy;'      align='left'      nowrap='true'><textarea>"      +
GetValue(prop.Name, obj) + "</textarea></td>");
            }
         txtstream.WriteLine("</tr>");
         v = v + 1;
      }
      txtstream.WriteLine("</table>");
      txtstream.WriteLine("</body>");
      txtstream.WriteLine("</html>");
      txtstream.close();
      function GetValue(Name, obj)
      {
         var tempstr = new String();
         var tempstr1 = new String();
         var tName = new String();
         tempstr1 = obj.GetObjectText_();
         var re = /"/g;
         tempstr1 = tempstr1.replace(re , "");
         var pos;
         tName = Name + " = ";
         pos = tempstr1.indexOf(tName);
         if (pos > -1)
         {
            pos = pos + tName.length;
            tempstr = tempstr1.substring(pos, tempstr1.length);
            pos = tempstr.indexOf(";");
            tempstr = tempstr.substring(0, pos);
            tempstr = tempstr.replace("{", "");
            tempstr = tempstr.replace("}", "");
            if (tempstr.length > 13)
            {
               if (obj.Properties_(Name).CIMType == 101)
               {
                 tempstr = tempstr.substr(4, 2) + "/"  + tempstr.substr(6, 2) + "/" +
tempstr.substr(0, 3) + " " + tempstr.substr(8, 2) + ":" + tempstr.substr(10, 2) + ":" +
tempstr.substr(12, 2);
               }
            }
            return tempstr;
```

```
        }
        else
        {
            return "";
        }
    }


    ]]>
    </script>
  </job>
</Package>
```

Horizontal Table with a textbox.

```
<?xml Version='1.0' encoding='iso-8859-1'?>
<package>
<job>
<script language='JavaScript'>
<![CDATA[
    var locator = new ActiveXObject("WbemScripting.SWbemLocator");
    var svc = locator.ConnectServer(".", "root\\cimv2");
    svc.Security_.AuthenticationLevel = 6;
    svc.Security_.ImpersonationLevel = 3;
    var strQuery = "Select * From ___InstanceOperationEvent WITHIN 1 where
TargetInstance ISA'Win32_Process'");
    var es = svc.ExecNotificationQuery(strQuery);
    var ws = new ActiveXObject("WScript.Shell");
    var fso = new ActiveXObject("Scripting.FileSystemObject");
    var       txtstream      =       fso.OpenTextFile(ws.CurrentDirectory      +
"\\Win32_Process.html", 2, true, -2);
    txtstream.WriteLine("<html xmlns='http://www.w3.org/1999/xhtml'>");
    txtstream.WriteLine("<head>");
    txtstream.WriteLine("<style type='text/css'>");
    txtstream.WriteLine("th");
    txtstream.WriteLine("{");
    txtstream.WriteLine("    COLOR: darkred;");
    txtstream.WriteLine("    BACKGROUND-COLOR: white;");
    txtstream.WriteLine("    FONT-FAMILY:font-family: Cambria, serif;");
    txtstream.WriteLine("    FONT-SIZE: 12px;");
```

```
txtstream.WriteLine("    text-align: left;");
txtstream.WriteLine("    white-Space: nowrap;");
txtstream.WriteLine("}");
txtstream.WriteLine("td");
txtstream.WriteLine("{");
txtstream.WriteLine("    COLOR: navy;");
txtstream.WriteLine("    BACKGROUND-COLOR: white;");
txtstream.WriteLine("    FONT-FAMILY: font-family: Cambria, serif;");
txtstream.WriteLine("    FONT-SIZE: 12px;");
txtstream.WriteLine("    text-align: left;");
txtstream.WriteLine("    white-Space: nowrap;");
txtstream.WriteLine("}");
txtstream.WriteLine("</style>");
txtstream.WriteLine("<title>Win32_Process</title>");
txtstream.WriteLine("</head>");
txtstream.WriteLine("<body>");
txtstream.WriteLine("<table border='1' Cellspacing='3' cellpadding = '3'>");
var v=0;
while(v < 0)
{
    var ti = ex.NextEvent(-1);
    var obj = ti.Properties_.Item("TargetInstance").Value;
    if(v == 0)
    {
        txtstream.WriteLine("<tr>");
        var propEnum = new Enumerator(obj.Properties_);
        for (; !propEnum.atEnd(); propEnum.moveNext())
        {
            var prop = propEnum.item();
            txtstream.WriteLine("<th   align='left'   nowrap>" + prop.Name +
"</th>");
        }
        txtstream.WriteLine("</tr>");
        propEnum.Reset();
    }
    txtstream.WriteLine("<tr>");
    for (; !propEnum.atEnd(); propEnum.moveNext())
    {
        var prop = propEnum.item();
```

```
        txtstream.WriteLine("<td    style='font-family:Calibri,    Sans-Serif;font-
size: 12px;color:navy;' align='left' nowrap='true'><input type=text value='" +
GetValue(prop.Name, obj) + "'></input></td>");
        }
        txtstream.WriteLine("</tr>");
        v = v + 1;
    }
    txtstream.WriteLine("</table>");
    txtstream.WriteLine("</body>");
    txtstream.WriteLine("</html>");
    txtstream.close();
    function GetValue(Name, obj)
    {
        var tempstr = new String();
        var tempstr1 = new String();
        var tName = new String();
        tempstr1 = obj.GetObjectText_();
        var re = /"/g;
        tempstr1 = tempstr1.replace(re , "");
        var pos;
        tName = Name + " = ";
        pos = tempstr1.indexOf(tName);
        if (pos > -1)
        {
            pos = pos + tName.length;
            tempstr = tempstr1.substring(pos, tempstr1.length);
            pos = tempstr.indexOf(";");
            tempstr = tempstr.substring(0, pos);
            tempstr = tempstr.replace("{", "");
            tempstr = tempstr.replace("}", "");
            if (tempstr.length > 13)
            {
                if (obj.Properties_(Name).CIMType == 101)
                {
                    tempstr = tempstr.substr(4, 2) + "/" + tempstr.substr(6, 2) + "/" +
tempstr.substr(0, 3) + " " + tempstr.substr(8, 2) + ":" + tempstr.substr(10, 2) + ":" +
tempstr.substr(12, 2);
                }
            }
            return tempstr;
```

```
      }
      else
      {
         return "";
      }
   }


   ]]>
   </script>
  </job>
</Package>
```

Vertical Table with no additional tags.

```
<?xml Version='1.0' encoding='iso-8859-1'?>
<package>
<job>
<script language='JavaScript'>
<![CDATA[
   var locator = new ActiveXObject("WbemScripting.SWbemLocator");
   var svc = locator.ConnectServer(".", "root\\cimv2");
   svc.Security_.AuthenticationLevel = 6;
   svc.Security_.ImpersonationLevel = 3;
   var strQuery = "Select * From ___InstanceOperationEvent WITHIN 1 where
TargetInstance ISA'Win32_Process'");
   var es = svc.ExecNotificationQuery(strQuery);
   var ws = new ActiveXObject("WScript.Shell");
   var fso = new ActiveXObject("Scripting.FileSystemObject");
   var      txtstream     =     fso.OpenTextFile(ws.CurrentDirectory     +
"\\Win32_Process.html", 2, true, -2);
   txtstream.WriteLine("<html xmlns='http://www.w3.org/1999/xhtml'>");
   txtstream.WriteLine("<head>");
   txtstream.WriteLine("<style type='text/css'>");
   txtstream.WriteLine("th");
   txtstream.WriteLine("{");
   txtstream.WriteLine("   COLOR: darkred;");
   txtstream.WriteLine("   BACKGROUND-COLOR: white;");
   txtstream.WriteLine("   FONT-FAMILY:font-family: Cambria, serif;");
   txtstream.WriteLine("   FONT-SIZE: 12px;");
```

```
txtstream.WriteLine("    text-align: left;");
txtstream.WriteLine("    white-Space: nowrap;");
txtstream.WriteLine("}");
txtstream.WriteLine("td");
txtstream.WriteLine("{");
txtstream.WriteLine("    COLOR: navy;");
txtstream.WriteLine("    BACKGROUND-COLOR: white;");
txtstream.WriteLine("    FONT-FAMILY: font-family: Cambria, serif;");
txtstream.WriteLine("    FONT-SIZE: 12px;");
txtstream.WriteLine("    text-align: left;");
txtstream.WriteLine("    white-Space: nowrap;");
txtstream.WriteLine("}");
txtstream.WriteLine("</style>");
txtstream.WriteLine("<title>Win32_Process</title>");
txtstream.WriteLine("</head>");
txtstream.WriteLine("<body>");
txtstream.WriteLine("<table border='1' Cellspacing='3' cellpadding = '3'>");

var Names;
var Cols;
var Rows;
var x = 0;

var v = 0;
while(v < 0)
{
    var ti = ex.NextEvent(-1);
    var obj = ti.Properties_.Item("TargetInstance").Value;
    if(v == 0)
    {
        Names = new Array[obj.Properties_.Count];
        Cols = new Array[obj.Properties_.Count];
        Rows = new Array[4];
        var propEnum = new Enumerator(obj.Properties_);
        for (; !propEnum.atEnd(); propEnum.moveNext())
        {
            var prop = propEnum.item();
            Names[x] = prop.Name;
            Cols[x] = GetValue(prop.Name, obj);
            x = x + 1;
```

```
            }
            Rows[v] = Cols;
            x = 0;
            v = v + 1;
        }
        else
        {
            var propEnum = new Enumerator(obj.Properties_);
            for (; !propEnum.atEnd(); propEnum.moveNext())
            {
                var prop = propEnum.item();
                Cols[x] = GetValue(prop.Name, obj);
                x = x + 1;
            }
            Rows[v] = Cols;
            x = 0;
            v = v + 1;
        }
    }
    for(var a = 0;a < Names.Count; a++)
    {
        txtstream.WriteLine("<tr><th   align='left'   nowrap>" + Names[a] +
"</th>");
        for(var b = 0;b < Rows.Count; b++)
        {
            var C = Rows[b];
            txtstream.WriteLine("<td   style='font-family:Calibri,   Sans-Serif;font-
size: 12px;color:navy;' align='left' nowrap='nowrap'>" + C[x] + "</td>");
        }
        txtstream.WriteLine("</tr>");
    }
    txtstream.WriteLine("</table>");
    txtstream.WriteLine("</body>");
    txtstream.WriteLine("</html>");
    txtstream.close();
    function GetValue(Name, obj)
    {
        var tempstr = new String();
        var tempstr1 = new String();
        var tName = new String();
```

```
tempstr1 = obj.GetObjectText_();
var re = /"/g;
tempstr1 = tempstr1.replace(re , "");
var pos;
tName = Name + " = ";
pos = tempstr1.indexOf(tName);
if (pos > -1)
{
    pos = pos + tName.length;
    tempstr = tempstr1.substring(pos, tempstr1.length);
    pos = tempstr.indexOf(";");
    tempstr = tempstr.substring(0, pos);
    tempstr = tempstr.replace("{", "");
    tempstr = tempstr.replace("}", "");
    if (tempstr.length > 13)
    {
        if (obj.Properties_(Name).CIMType == 101)
        {
            tempstr = tempstr.substr(4, 2) + "/"  + tempstr.substr(6, 2) + "/" +
tempstr.substr(0, 3) + " " + tempstr.substr(8, 2) + ":" + tempstr.substr(10, 2) + ":" +
tempstr.substr(12, 2);
        }
    }
    return tempstr;
}
else
{
    return "";
}
}

]]>
</script>
</job>
</Package>
```

Vertical Table with a Combobox.


```
<?xml Version='1.0' encoding='iso-8859-1'?>
```

```
<package>
<job>
<script language='JavaScript'>
<![CDATA[
    var locator = new ActiveXObject("WbemScripting.SWbemLocator");
    var svc = locator.ConnectServer(".", "root\\cimv2");
    svc.Security_.AuthenticationLevel = 6;
    svc.Security_.ImpersonationLevel = 3;
    var strQuery = "Select * From ___InstanceOperationEvent WITHIN 1 where
TargetInstance ISA'Win32_Process'");
    var es = svc.ExecNotificationQuery(strQuery);
    var ws = new ActiveXObject("WScript.Shell");
    var fso = new ActiveXObject("Scripting.FileSystemObject");
    var     txtstream     =     fso.OpenTextFile(ws.CurrentDirectory     +
"\\Win32_Process.html", 2, true, -2);
    txtstream.WriteLine("<html xmlns='http://www.w3.org/1999/xhtml'>");
    txtstream.WriteLine("<head>");
    txtstream.WriteLine("<style type='text/css'>");
    txtstream.WriteLine("th");
    txtstream.WriteLine("{");
    txtstream.WriteLine("   COLOR: darkred;");
    txtstream.WriteLine("   BACKGROUND-COLOR: white;");
    txtstream.WriteLine("   FONT-FAMILY:font-family: Cambria, serif;");
    txtstream.WriteLine("   FONT-SIZE: 12px;");
    txtstream.WriteLine("   text-align: left;");
    txtstream.WriteLine("   white-Space: nowrap;");
    txtstream.WriteLine("}");
    txtstream.WriteLine("td");
    txtstream.WriteLine("{");
    txtstream.WriteLine("   COLOR: navy;");
    txtstream.WriteLine("   BACKGROUND-COLOR: white;");
    txtstream.WriteLine("   FONT-FAMILY: font-family: Cambria, serif;");
    txtstream.WriteLine("   FONT-SIZE: 12px;");
    txtstream.WriteLine("   text-align: left;");
    txtstream.WriteLine("   white-Space: nowrap;");
    txtstream.WriteLine("}");
    txtstream.WriteLine("</style>");
    txtstream.WriteLine("<title>Win32_Process</title>");
    txtstream.WriteLine("</head>");
    txtstream.WriteLine("<body>");
```

```
txtstream.WriteLine("<table border='1' Cellspacing='3' cellpadding = '3'>");

var Names;
var Cols;
var Rows;
var x = 0;

var v = 0;
while(v < 0)
{
   var ti = ex.NextEvent(-1);
   var obj = ti.Properties_.Item("TargetInstance").Value;
   if(v == 0)
   {
      Names = new Array[obj.Properties_.Count];
      Cols = new Array[obj.Properties_.Count];
      Rows = new Array[4];
      var propEnum = new Enumerator(obj.Properties_);
      for (; !propEnum.atEnd(); propEnum.moveNext())
      {
         var prop = propEnum.item();
         Names[x] = prop.Name;
         Cols[x] = GetValue(prop.Name, obj);
         x = x + 1;
      }
      Rows[v] = Cols;
      x = 0;
      v = v + 1;
   }
   else
   {
      var propEnum = new Enumerator(obj.Properties_);
      for (; !propEnum.atEnd(); propEnum.moveNext())
      {
         var prop = propEnum.item();
         Cols[x] = GetValue(prop.Name, obj);
         x = x + 1;
      }
      Rows[v] = Cols;
      x = 0;
```

```
            v = v + 1;
        }
    }
    for(var a = 0;a < Names.Count; a++)
    {
        txtstream.WriteLine("<tr><th    align='left'    nowrap>" +  Names[a]  +
"</th>");
        for(var b = 0;b < Rows.Count; b++)
        {
            var C = Rows[b];
            txtstream.WriteLine("<td    style='font-family:Calibri,   Sans-Serif;font-
size: 12px;color:navy;' align='left' nowrap='true'><select><option value = '''" + C[x]
+ "'''>" + C[x] + "</option></select></td>");
        }
        txtstream.WriteLine("</tr>");
    }
    txtstream.WriteLine("</table>");
    txtstream.WriteLine("</body>");
    txtstream.WriteLine("</html>");
    txtstream.close();
    function GetValue(Name, obj)
    {
        var tempstr = new String();
        var tempstr1 = new String();
        var tName = new String();
        tempstr1 = obj.GetObjectText_();
        var re = /"/g;
        tempstr1 = tempstr1.replace(re , "");
        var pos;
        tName = Name + " = ";
        pos = tempstr1.indexOf(tName);
        if (pos > -1)
        {
            pos = pos + tName.length;
            tempstr = tempstr1.substring(pos, tempstr1.length);
            pos = tempstr.indexOf(";");
            tempstr = tempstr.substring(0, pos);
            tempstr = tempstr.replace("{", "");
            tempstr = tempstr.replace("}", "");
            if (tempstr.length > 13)
```

```
        {
            if (obj.Properties_(Name).CIMType == 101)
            {
                tempstr = tempstr.substr(4, 2) + "/"  + tempstr.substr(6, 2) + "/" +
tempstr.substr(0, 3) + " " + tempstr.substr(8, 2) + ":" + tempstr.substr(10, 2) + ":" +
tempstr.substr(12, 2);
            }
        }
        return tempstr;
    }
    else
    {
        return "";
    }
}


    ]]>
    </script>
  </job>
</Package>
```

Vertical Table with a link.

```
<?xml Version='1.0' encoding='iso-8859-1'?>
<package>
<job>
<script language='JavaScript'>
<![CDATA[
    var locator = new ActiveXObject("WbemScripting.SWbemLocator");
    var svc = locator.ConnectServer(".", "root\\cimv2");
    svc.Security_.AuthenticationLevel = 6;
    svc.Security_.ImpersonationLevel = 3;
    var strQuery = "Select * From ___InstanceOperationEvent WITHIN 1 where
TargetInstance ISA'Win32_Process'");
    var es = svc.ExecNotificationQuery(strQuery);
    var ws = new ActiveXObject("WScript.Shell");
    var fso = new ActiveXObject("Scripting.FileSystemObject");
    var    txtstream    =    fso.OpenTextFile(ws.CurrentDirectory    +
"\\Win32_Process.html", 2, true, -2);
```

```
txtstream.WriteLine("<html xmlns='http://www.w3.org/1999/xhtml'>");
txtstream.WriteLine("<head>");
txtstream.WriteLine("<style type='text/css'>");
txtstream.WriteLine("th");
txtstream.WriteLine("{");
txtstream.WriteLine("    COLOR: darkred;");
txtstream.WriteLine("    BACKGROUND-COLOR: white;");
txtstream.WriteLine("    FONT-FAMILY:font-family: Cambria, serif;");
txtstream.WriteLine("    FONT-SIZE: 12px;");
txtstream.WriteLine("    text-align: left;");
txtstream.WriteLine("    white-Space: nowrap;");
txtstream.WriteLine("}");
txtstream.WriteLine("td");
txtstream.WriteLine("{");
txtstream.WriteLine("    COLOR: navy;");
txtstream.WriteLine("    BACKGROUND-COLOR: white;");
txtstream.WriteLine("    FONT-FAMILY: font-family: Cambria, serif;");
txtstream.WriteLine("    FONT-SIZE: 12px;");
txtstream.WriteLine("    text-align: left;");
txtstream.WriteLine("    white-Space: nowrap;");
txtstream.WriteLine("}");
txtstream.WriteLine("</style>");
txtstream.WriteLine("<title>Win32_Process</title>");
txtstream.WriteLine("</head>");
txtstream.WriteLine("<body>");
txtstream.WriteLine("<table border='1' Cellspacing='3' cellpadding = '3'>");

var Names;
var Cols;
var Rows;
var x = 0;

var v = 0;
while(v < 0)
{
   var ti = ex.NextEvent(-1);
   var obj = ti.Properties_.Item("TargetInstance").Value;
   if(v == 0)
   {
      Names = new Array[obj.Properties_.Count];
```

```
        Cols = new Array[obj.Properties_.Count];
        Rows = new Array[4];
        var propEnum = new Enumerator(obj.Properties_);
        for (; !propEnum.atEnd(); propEnum.moveNext())
        {
            var prop = propEnum.item();
            Names[x] = prop.Name;
            Cols[x] = GetValue(prop.Name, obj);
            x = x + 1;
        }
        Rows[v] = Cols;
        x = 0;
        v = v + 1;
    }
    else
    {
        var propEnum = new Enumerator(obj.Properties_);
        for (; !propEnum.atEnd(); propEnum.moveNext())
        {
            var prop = propEnum.item();
            Cols[x] = GetValue(prop.Name, obj);
            x = x + 1;
        }
        Rows[v] = Cols;
        x = 0;
        v = v + 1;
    }
}
for(var a = 0;a < Names.Count; a++)
{
    txtstream.WriteLine("<tr><th align='left' nowrap>" + Names[a] +
"</th>");
    for(var b = 0;b < Rows.Count; b++)
    {
        var C = Rows[b];
        txtstream.WriteLine("<td style='font-family:Calibri, Sans-Serif;font-
size: 12px;color:navy;' align='left' nowrap='true'><a href='" + C[x] + "'>" + C[x] +
"</a></td>");
    }
    txtstream.WriteLine("</tr>");
```

```
        }
        txtstream.WriteLine("</table>");
        txtstream.WriteLine("</body>");
        txtstream.WriteLine("</html>");
        txtstream.close();
        function GetValue(Name, obj)
        {
            var tempstr = new String();
            var tempstr1 = new String();
            var tName = new String();
            tempstr1 = obj.GetObjectText_();
            var re = /"/g;
            tempstr1 = tempstr1.replace(re , "");
            var pos;
            tName = Name + " = ";
            pos = tempstr1.indexOf(tName);
            if (pos > -1)
            {
                pos = pos + tName.length;
                tempstr = tempstr1.substring(pos, tempstr1.length);
                pos = tempstr.indexOf(";");
                tempstr = tempstr.substring(0, pos);
                tempstr = tempstr.replace("{", "");
                tempstr = tempstr.replace("}", "");
                if (tempstr.length > 13)
                {
                    if (obj.Properties_(Name).CIMType == 101)
                    {
                        tempstr = tempstr.substr(4, 2) + "/"  + tempstr.substr(6, 2) + "/" +
tempstr.substr(0, 3) + " " + tempstr.substr(8, 2) + ":" + tempstr.substr(10, 2) + ":" +
tempstr.substr(12, 2);
                    }
                }
                return tempstr;
            }
            else
            {
                return "";
            }
        }
```

```
    ]]>
    </script>
  </job>
</Package>
```

Vertical Table with a Listbox.

```
<?xml Version='1.0' encoding='iso-8859-1'?>
<package>
<job>
<script language='JavaScript'>
<![CDATA[
    var locator = new ActiveXObject("WbemScripting.SWbemLocator");
    var svc = locator.ConnectServer(".", "root\\cimv2");
    svc.Security_.AuthenticationLevel = 6;
    svc.Security_.ImpersonationLevel = 3;
    var strQuery = "Select * From ___InstanceOperationEvent WITHIN 1 where
TargetInstance ISA'Win32_Process'");
    var es = svc.ExecNotificationQuery(strQuery);
    var ws = new ActiveXObject("WScript.Shell");
    var fso = new ActiveXObject("Scripting.FileSystemObject");
    var     txtstream    =     fso.OpenTextFile(ws.CurrentDirectory    +
"\\Win32_Process.html", 2, true, -2);
    txtstream.WriteLine("<html xmlns='http://www.w3.org/1999/xhtml'>");
    txtstream.WriteLine("<head>");
    txtstream.WriteLine("<style type='text/css'>");
    txtstream.WriteLine("th");
    txtstream.WriteLine("{");
    txtstream.WriteLine("    COLOR: darkred;");
    txtstream.WriteLine("    BACKGROUND-COLOR: white;");
    txtstream.WriteLine("    FONT-FAMILY:font-family: Cambria, serif;");
    txtstream.WriteLine("    FONT-SIZE: 12px;");
    txtstream.WriteLine("    text-align: left;");
    txtstream.WriteLine("    white-Space: nowrap;");
    txtstream.WriteLine("}");
    txtstream.WriteLine("td");
    txtstream.WriteLine("{");
    txtstream.WriteLine("    COLOR: navy;");
```

```
txtstream.WriteLine("    BACKGROUND-COLOR: white;");
txtstream.WriteLine("    FONT-FAMILY: font-family: Cambria, serif;");
txtstream.WriteLine("    FONT-SIZE: 12px;");
txtstream.WriteLine("    text-align: left;");
txtstream.WriteLine("    white-Space: nowrap;");
txtstream.WriteLine("}");
txtstream.WriteLine("</style>");
txtstream.WriteLine("<title>Win32_Process</title>");
txtstream.WriteLine("</head>");
txtstream.WriteLine("<body>");
txtstream.WriteLine("<table border='1' Cellspacing='3' cellpadding = '3'>");

var Names;
var Cols;
var Rows;
var x = 0;

var v = 0;
while(v < 0)
{
    var ti = ex.NextEvent(-1);
    var obj = ti.Properties_.Item("TargetInstance").Value;
    if(v == 0)
    {
        Names = new Array[obj.Properties_.Count];
        Cols = new Array[obj.Properties_.Count];
        Rows = new Array[4];
        var propEnum = new Enumerator(obj.Properties_);
        for (; !propEnum.atEnd(); propEnum.moveNext())
        {
            var prop = propEnum.item();
            Names[x] = prop.Name;
            Cols[x] = GetValue(prop.Name, obj);
            x = x + 1;
        }
        Rows[v] = Cols;
        x = 0;
        v = v + 1;
    }
    else
```

```
    {
        var propEnum = new Enumerator(obj.Properties_);
        for (; !propEnum.atEnd(); propEnum.moveNext())
        {
            var prop = propEnum.item();
            Cols[x] = GetValue(prop.Name, obj);
            x = x + 1;
        }
        Rows[v] = Cols;
        x = 0;
        v = v + 1;
    }
}
for(var a = 0;a < Names.Count; a++)
{
    txtstream.WriteLine("<tr><th  align='left'  nowrap>" + Names[a] +
"</th>");
    for(var b = 0;b < Rows.Count; b++)
    {
        var C = Rows[b];
        txtstream.WriteLine("<td   style='font-family:Calibri,   Sans-Serif;font-
size: 12px;color:navy;' align='left' nowrap='true'><select multiple><option value =
"""" + C[x] + """">" + C[x] + "</option></select></td>");
    }
    txtstream.WriteLine("</tr>");
}
txtstream.WriteLine("</table>");
txtstream.WriteLine("</body>");
txtstream.WriteLine("</html>");
txtstream.close();
function GetValue(Name, obj)
{
    var tempstr = new String();
    var tempstr1 = new String();
    var tName = new String();
    tempstr1 = obj.GetObjectText_();
    var re = /"/g;
    tempstr1 = tempstr1.replace(re , "");
    var pos;
    tName = Name + " = ";
```

```
        pos = tempstr1.indexOf(tName);
        if (pos > -1)
        {
            pos = pos + tName.length;
            tempstr = tempstr1.substring(pos, tempstr1.length);
            pos = tempstr.indexOf(";");
            tempstr = tempstr.substring(0, pos);
            tempstr = tempstr.replace("{", "");
            tempstr = tempstr.replace("}", "");
            if (tempstr.length > 13)
            {
                if (obj.Properties_(Name).CIMType == 101)
                {
                    tempstr = tempstr.substr(4, 2) + "/" + tempstr.substr(6, 2) + "/" +
tempstr.substr(0, 3) + " " + tempstr.substr(8, 2) + ":" + tempstr.substr(10, 2) + ":" +
tempstr.substr(12, 2);
                }
            }
            return tempstr;
        }
        else
        {
            return "";
        }
    }

    ]]>
    </script>
   </job>
  </Package>
```

Vertical Table with a textarea.

```
<?xml Version='1.0' encoding='iso-8859-1'?>
<package>
<job>
<script language='JavaScript'>
<![CDATA[
    var locator = new ActiveXObject("WbemScripting.SWbemLocator");
```

```javascript
var svc = locator.ConnectServer(".", "root\\cimv2");
svc.Security_.AuthenticationLevel = 6;
svc.Security_.ImpersonationLevel = 3;
var strQuery = "Select * From ___InstanceOperationEvent WITHIN 1 where
TargetInstance ISA'Win32_Process'");
var es = svc.ExecNotificationQuery(strQuery);
var ws = new ActiveXObject("WScript.Shell");
var fso = new ActiveXObject("Scripting.FileSystemObject");
var     txtstream     =     fso.OpenTextFile(ws.CurrentDirectory     +
"\\Win32_Process.html", 2, true, -2);
txtstream.WriteLine("<html xmlns='http://www.w3.org/1999/xhtml'>");
txtstream.WriteLine("<head>");
txtstream.WriteLine("<style type='text/css'>");
txtstream.WriteLine("th");
txtstream.WriteLine("{");
txtstream.WriteLine("   COLOR: darkred;");
txtstream.WriteLine("   BACKGROUND-COLOR: white;");
txtstream.WriteLine("   FONT-FAMILY:font-family: Cambria, serif;");
txtstream.WriteLine("   FONT-SIZE: 12px;");
txtstream.WriteLine("   text-align: left;");
txtstream.WriteLine("   white-Space: nowrap;");
txtstream.WriteLine("}");
txtstream.WriteLine("td");
txtstream.WriteLine("{");
txtstream.WriteLine("   COLOR: navy;");
txtstream.WriteLine("   BACKGROUND-COLOR: white;");
txtstream.WriteLine("   FONT-FAMILY: font-family: Cambria, serif;");
txtstream.WriteLine("   FONT-SIZE: 12px;");
txtstream.WriteLine("   text-align: left;");
txtstream.WriteLine("   white-Space: nowrap;");
txtstream.WriteLine("}");
txtstream.WriteLine("</style>");
txtstream.WriteLine("<title>Win32_Process</title>");
txtstream.WriteLine("</head>");
txtstream.WriteLine("<body>");
txtstream.WriteLine("<table border='1' Cellspacing='3' cellpadding = '3'>");

var Names;
var Cols;
var Rows;
```

```
var x = 0;

var v = 0;
while(v < 0)
{
   var ti = ex.NextEvent(-1);
   var obj = ti.Properties_.Item("TargetInstance").Value;
   if(v == 0)
   {
      Names = new Array[obj.Properties_.Count];
      Cols = new Array[obj.Properties_.Count];
      Rows = new Array[4];
      var propEnum = new Enumerator(obj.Properties_);
      for (; !propEnum.atEnd(); propEnum.moveNext())
      {
         var prop = propEnum.item();
         Names[x] = prop.Name;
         Cols[x] = GetValue(prop.Name, obj);
         x = x + 1;
      }
      Rows[v] = Cols;
      x = 0;
      v = v + 1;
   }
   else
   {
      var propEnum = new Enumerator(obj.Properties_);
      for (; !propEnum.atEnd(); propEnum.moveNext())
      {
         var prop = propEnum.item();
         Cols[x] = GetValue(prop.Name, obj);
         x = x + 1;
      }
      Rows[v] = Cols;
      x = 0;
      v = v + 1;
   }
}
for(var a = 0;a < Names.Count; a++)
{
```

```
            txtstream.WriteLine("<tr><th  align='left'  nowrap>" + Names[a] +
"</th>");
            for(var b = 0;b < Rows.Count; b++)
            {
                var C = Rows[b];
                txtstream.WriteLine("<td  style='font-family:Calibri,  Sans-Serif;font-
size:  12px;color:navy;'  align='left'  nowrap='true'><textarea>" + C[x] +
"</textarea></td>");
            }
            txtstream.WriteLine("</tr>");
        }
        txtstream.WriteLine("</table>");
        txtstream.WriteLine("</body>");
        txtstream.WriteLine("</html>");
        txtstream.close();
        function GetValue(Name, obj)
        {
            var tempstr = new String();
            var tempstr1 = new String();
            var tName = new String();
            tempstr1 = obj.GetObjectText_();
            var re = /"/g;
            tempstr1 = tempstr1.replace(re , "");
            var pos;
            tName = Name + " = ";
            pos = tempstr1.indexOf(tName);
            if (pos > -1)
            {
                pos = pos + tName.length;
                tempstr = tempstr1.substring(pos, tempstr1.length);
                pos = tempstr.indexOf(";");
                tempstr = tempstr.substring(0, pos);
                tempstr = tempstr.replace("{", "");
                tempstr = tempstr.replace("}", "");
                if (tempstr.length > 13)
                {
                    if (obj.Properties_(Name).CIMType == 101)
                    {
```

```
                tempstr = tempstr.substr(4, 2) + "/"  + tempstr.substr(6, 2) + "/" +
tempstr.substr(0, 3) + " " + tempstr.substr(8, 2) + ":" + tempstr.substr(10, 2) + ":" +
tempstr.substr(12, 2);
            }
        }
        return tempstr;
    }
    else
    {
        return "";
    }
}


]]>
  </script>
 </job>
</Package>
```

Vertical Table with a textbox.

```
<?xml Version='1.0' encoding='iso-8859-1'?>
<package>
<job>
<script language='JavaScript'>
<![CDATA[
    var locator = new ActiveXObject("WbemScripting.SWbemLocator");
    var svc = locator.ConnectServer(".", "root\\cimv2");
    svc.Security_.AuthenticationLevel = 6;
    svc.Security_.ImpersonationLevel = 3;
    var strQuery = "Select * From ___InstanceOperationEvent WITHIN 1 where
TargetInstance ISA'Win32_Process'");
    var es = svc.ExecNotificationQuery(strQuery);
    var ws = new ActiveXObject("WScript.Shell");
    var fso = new ActiveXObject("Scripting.FileSystemObject");
    var     txtstream    =    fso.OpenTextFile(ws.CurrentDirectory    +
"\\Win32_Process.html", 2, true, -2);
    txtstream.WriteLine("<html xmlns='http://www.w3.org/1999/xhtml'>");
    txtstream.WriteLine("<head>");
    txtstream.WriteLine("<style type='text/css'>");
```

```
txtstream.WriteLine("th");
txtstream.WriteLine("{");
txtstream.WriteLine("   COLOR: darkred;");
txtstream.WriteLine("   BACKGROUND-COLOR: white;");
txtstream.WriteLine("   FONT-FAMILY:font-family: Cambria, serif;");
txtstream.WriteLine("   FONT-SIZE: 12px;");
txtstream.WriteLine("   text-align: left;");
txtstream.WriteLine("   white-Space: nowrap;");
txtstream.WriteLine("}");
txtstream.WriteLine("td");
txtstream.WriteLine("{");
txtstream.WriteLine("   COLOR: navy;");
txtstream.WriteLine("   BACKGROUND-COLOR: white;");
txtstream.WriteLine("   FONT-FAMILY: font-family: Cambria, serif;");
txtstream.WriteLine("   FONT-SIZE: 12px;");
txtstream.WriteLine("   text-align: left;");
txtstream.WriteLine("   white-Space: nowrap;");
txtstream.WriteLine("}");
txtstream.WriteLine("</style>");
txtstream.WriteLine("<title>Win32_Process</title>");
txtstream.WriteLine("</head>");
txtstream.WriteLine("<body>");
txtstream.WriteLine("<table border='1' Cellspacing='3' cellpadding = '3'>");

var Names;
var Cols;
var Rows;
var x = 0;

var v = 0;
while(v < 0)
{
   var ti = ex.NextEvent(-1);
   var obj = ti.Properties_.Item("TargetInstance").Value;
   if(v == 0)
   {
      Names = new Array[obj.Properties_.Count];
      Cols = new Array[obj.Properties_.Count];
      Rows = new Array[4];
      var propEnum = new Enumerator(obj.Properties_);
```

```
    for (; !propEnum.atEnd(); propEnum.moveNext())
    {
        var prop = propEnum.item();
        Names[x] = prop.Name;
        Cols[x] = GetValue(prop.Name, obj);
        x = x + 1;
    }
    Rows[v] = Cols;
    x = 0;
    v = v + 1;
}
else
{
    var propEnum = new Enumerator(obj.Properties_);
    for (; !propEnum.atEnd(); propEnum.moveNext())
    {
        var prop = propEnum.item();
        Cols[x] = GetValue(prop.Name, obj);
        x = x + 1;
    }
    Rows[v] = Cols;
    x = 0;
    v = v + 1;
}
}
for(var a = 0;a < Names.Count; a++)
{
    txtstream.WriteLine("<tr><th align='left'  nowrap>" + Names[a] +
"</th>");
    for(var b = 0;b < Rows.Count; b++)
    {
        var C = Rows[b];
        txtstream.WriteLine("<td  style='font-family:Calibri,  Sans-Serif;font-
size: 12px;color:navy;' align='left' nowrap='true'><input type=text value="""" + C[x]
+ """"></input></td>");
    }
    txtstream.WriteLine("</tr>");
}
txtstream.WriteLine("</table>");
txtstream.WriteLine("</body>");
```

```
txtstream.WriteLine("</html>");
txtstream.close();
function GetValue(Name, obj)
{
    var tempstr = new String();
    var tempstr1 = new String();
    var tName = new String();
    tempstr1 = obj.GetObjectText_();
    var re = /"/g;
    tempstr1 = tempstr1.replace(re , "");
    var pos;
    tName = Name + " = ";
    pos = tempstr1.indexOf(tName);
    if (pos > -1)
    {
        pos = pos + tName.length;
        tempstr = tempstr1.substring(pos, tempstr1.length);
        pos = tempstr.indexOf(";");
        tempstr = tempstr.substring(0, pos);
        tempstr = tempstr.replace("{", "");
        tempstr = tempstr.replace("}", "");
        if (tempstr.length > 13)
        {
            if (obj.Properties_(Name).CIMType == 101)
            {
                tempstr = tempstr.substr(4, 2) + "/"  + tempstr.substr(6, 2) + "/" +
tempstr.substr(0, 3) + " " + tempstr.substr(8, 2) + ":" + tempstr.substr(10, 2) + ":" +
tempstr.substr(12, 2);
            }
        }
        return tempstr;
    }
    else
    {
        return "";
    }
}

]]>
</script>
```

```
</job>
</Package>
```

Stylesheets

Decorating your web pages

ELOW ARE SOME STYLESHEETS I COOKED UP THAT I LIKE AND THINK YOU MIGHT TOO. Don't worry I won't be offended if you take and modify to your hearts delight. Please do!

NONE

```
txtstream.WriteLine("<style type='text/css'>")
txtstream.WriteLine("th")
txtstream.WriteLine("{")
txtstream.WriteLine("   COLOR: white;")
txtstream.WriteLine("}")
txtstream.WriteLine("td")
txtstream.WriteLine("{")
txtstream.WriteLine("   COLOR: white;")
txtstream.WriteLine("}")
txtstream.WriteLine("</style>")
```

BLACK AND WHITE TEXT

```
txtstream.WriteLine("<style type='text/css'>")
txtstream.WriteLine("th")
txtstream.WriteLine("{")
txtstream.WriteLine("   COLOR: white;")
txtstream.WriteLine("   BACKGROUND-COLOR: black;")
txtstream.WriteLine("   FONT-FAMILY:font-family: Cambria, serif;")
txtstream.WriteLine("   FONT-SIZE: 12px;")
txtstream.WriteLine("   text-align: left;")
txtstream.WriteLine("   white-Space: nowrap;")
```

```
txtstream.WriteLine("}")
txtstream.WriteLine("td")
txtstream.WriteLine("{")
txtstream.WriteLine("    COLOR: white;")
txtstream.WriteLine("    BACKGROUND-COLOR: black;")
txtstream.WriteLine("    FONT-FAMILY: font-family: Cambria, serif;")
txtstream.WriteLine("    FONT-SIZE: 12px;")
txtstream.WriteLine("    text-align: left;")
txtstream.WriteLine("    white-Space: nowrap;")
txtstream.WriteLine("}")
txtstream.WriteLine("div")
txtstream.WriteLine("{")
txtstream.WriteLine("    COLOR: white;")
txtstream.WriteLine("    BACKGROUND-COLOR: black;")
txtstream.WriteLine("    FONT-FAMILY: font-family: Cambria, serif;")
txtstream.WriteLine("    FONT-SIZE: 10px;")
txtstream.WriteLine("    text-align: left;")
txtstream.WriteLine("    white-Space: nowrap;")
txtstream.WriteLine("}")
txtstream.WriteLine("span")
txtstream.WriteLine("{")
txtstream.WriteLine("    COLOR: white;")
txtstream.WriteLine("    BACKGROUND-COLOR: black;")
txtstream.WriteLine("    FONT-FAMILY: font-family: Cambria, serif;")
txtstream.WriteLine("    FONT-SIZE: 10px;")
txtstream.WriteLine("    text-align: left;")
txtstream.WriteLine("    white-Space: nowrap;")
txtstream.WriteLine("    display:inline-block;")
txtstream.WriteLine("    width: 100%;")
txtstream.WriteLine("}")
txtstream.WriteLine("textarea")
txtstream.WriteLine("{")
txtstream.WriteLine("    COLOR: white;")
```

```
txtstream.WriteLine("    BACKGROUND-COLOR: black;")
txtstream.WriteLine("    FONT-FAMILY: font-family: Cambria, serif;")
txtstream.WriteLine("    FONT-SIZE: 10px;")
txtstream.WriteLine("    text-align: left;")
txtstream.WriteLine("    white-Space: nowrap;")
txtstream.WriteLine("    width: 100%;")
txtstream.WriteLine("}")
txtstream.WriteLine("select")
txtstream.WriteLine("{")
txtstream.WriteLine("    COLOR: white;")
txtstream.WriteLine("    BACKGROUND-COLOR: black;")
txtstream.WriteLine("    FONT-FAMILY: font-family: Cambria, serif;")
txtstream.WriteLine("    FONT-SIZE: 10px;")
txtstream.WriteLine("    text-align: left;")
txtstream.WriteLine("    white-Space: nowrap;")
txtstream.WriteLine("    width: 100%;")
txtstream.WriteLine("}")
txtstream.WriteLine("input")
txtstream.WriteLine("{")
txtstream.WriteLine("    COLOR: white;")
txtstream.WriteLine("    BACKGROUND-COLOR: black;")
txtstream.WriteLine("    FONT-FAMILY: font-family: Cambria, serif;")
txtstream.WriteLine("    FONT-SIZE: 12px;")
txtstream.WriteLine("    text-align: left;")
txtstream.WriteLine("    display:table-cell;")
txtstream.WriteLine("    white-Space: nowrap;")
txtstream.WriteLine("}")
txtstream.WriteLine("h1 {")
txtstream.WriteLine("color: antiquewhite;")
txtstream.WriteLine("text-shadow: 1px 1px 1px black;")
txtstream.WriteLine("padding: 3px;")
txtstream.WriteLine("text-align: center;")
```

```
txtstream.WriteLine("box-shadow: inset 2px 2px 5px rgba(0,0,0,0.5), inset -
2px -2px 5px rgba(255,255,255,0.5);")
txtstream.WriteLine("}")
txtstream.WriteLine("</style>")
```

COLORED TEXT

```
txtstream.WriteLine("<style type='text/css'>")
txtstream.WriteLine("th")
txtstream.WriteLine("{")
txtstream.WriteLine("    COLOR: darkred;")
txtstream.WriteLine("    BACKGROUND-COLOR: #eeeeee;")
txtstream.WriteLine("    FONT-FAMILY:font-family: Cambria, serif;")
txtstream.WriteLine("    FONT-SIZE: 12px;")
txtstream.WriteLine("    text-align: left;")
txtstream.WriteLine("    white-Space: nowrap;")
txtstream.WriteLine("}")
txtstream.WriteLine("td")
txtstream.WriteLine("{")
txtstream.WriteLine("    COLOR: navy;")
txtstream.WriteLine("    BACKGROUND-COLOR: #eeeeee;")
txtstream.WriteLine("    FONT-FAMILY: font-family: Cambria, serif;")
txtstream.WriteLine("    FONT-SIZE: 12px;")
txtstream.WriteLine("    text-align: left;")
txtstream.WriteLine("    white-Space: nowrap;")
txtstream.WriteLine("}")
txtstream.WriteLine("div")
txtstream.WriteLine("{")
txtstream.WriteLine("    COLOR: white;")
txtstream.WriteLine("    BACKGROUND-COLOR: navy;")
txtstream.WriteLine("    FONT-FAMILY: font-family: Cambria, serif;")
txtstream.WriteLine("    FONT-SIZE: 10px;")
txtstream.WriteLine("    text-align: left;")
```

```
txtstream.WriteLine("    white-Space: nowrap;")
txtstream.WriteLine("}")
txtstream.WriteLine("span")
txtstream.WriteLine("{")
txtstream.WriteLine("    COLOR: white;")
txtstream.WriteLine("    BACKGROUND-COLOR: navy;")
txtstream.WriteLine("    FONT-FAMILY: font-family: Cambria, serif;")
txtstream.WriteLine("    FONT-SIZE: 10px;")
txtstream.WriteLine("    text-align: left;")
txtstream.WriteLine("    white-Space: nowrap;")
txtstream.WriteLine("    display:inline-block;")
txtstream.WriteLine("    width: 100%;")
txtstream.WriteLine("}")
txtstream.WriteLine("textarea")
txtstream.WriteLine("{")
txtstream.WriteLine("    COLOR: white;")
txtstream.WriteLine("    BACKGROUND-COLOR: navy;")
txtstream.WriteLine("    FONT-FAMILY: font-family: Cambria, serif;")
txtstream.WriteLine("    FONT-SIZE: 10px;")
txtstream.WriteLine("    text-align: left;")
txtstream.WriteLine("    white-Space: nowrap;")
txtstream.WriteLine("    width: 100%;")
txtstream.WriteLine("}")
txtstream.WriteLine("select")
txtstream.WriteLine("{")
txtstream.WriteLine("    COLOR: white;")
txtstream.WriteLine("    BACKGROUND-COLOR: navy;")
txtstream.WriteLine("    FONT-FAMILY: font-family: Cambria, serif;")
txtstream.WriteLine("    FONT-SIZE: 10px;")
txtstream.WriteLine("    text-align: left;")
txtstream.WriteLine("    white-Space: nowrap;")
txtstream.WriteLine("    width: 100%;")
txtstream.WriteLine("}")
```

```
txtstream.WriteLine("input")
txtstream.WriteLine("{")
txtstream.WriteLine("   COLOR: white;")
txtstream.WriteLine("   BACKGROUND-COLOR: navy;")
txtstream.WriteLine("   FONT-FAMILY: font-family: Cambria, serif;")
txtstream.WriteLine("   FONT-SIZE: 12px;")
txtstream.WriteLine("   text-align: left;")
txtstream.WriteLine("   display:table-cell;")
txtstream.WriteLine("   white-Space: nowrap;")
txtstream.WriteLine("}")
txtstream.WriteLine("h1 {")
txtstream.WriteLine("color: antiquewhite;")
txtstream.WriteLine("text-shadow: 1px 1px 1px black;")
txtstream.WriteLine("padding: 3px;")
txtstream.WriteLine("text-align: center;")
txtstream.WriteLine("box-shadow: inset 2px 2px 5px rgba(0,0,0,0.5), inset -2px -2px 5px rgba(255,255,255,0.5);")
txtstream.WriteLine("}")
txtstream.WriteLine("</style>")
```

OSCILLATING ROW COLORS

```
txtstream.WriteLine("<style>")
txtstream.WriteLine("th")
txtstream.WriteLine("{")
txtstream.WriteLine("   COLOR: white;")
txtstream.WriteLine("   BACKGROUND-COLOR: navy;")
txtstream.WriteLine("   FONT-FAMILY:font-family: Cambria, serif;")
txtstream.WriteLine("   FONT-SIZE: 12px;")
txtstream.WriteLine("   text-align: left;")
txtstream.WriteLine("   white-Space: nowrap;")
```

```
txtstream.WriteLine("}")
txtstream.WriteLine("td")
txtstream.WriteLine("{")
txtstream.WriteLine("   COLOR: navy;")
txtstream.WriteLine("   FONT-FAMILY: font-family: Cambria, serif;")
txtstream.WriteLine("   FONT-SIZE: 12px;")
txtstream.WriteLine("   text-align: left;")
txtstream.WriteLine("   white-Space: nowrap;")
txtstream.WriteLine("}")
txtstream.WriteLine("div")
txtstream.WriteLine("{")
txtstream.WriteLine("   COLOR: navy;")
txtstream.WriteLine("   FONT-FAMILY: font-family: Cambria, serif;")
txtstream.WriteLine("   FONT-SIZE: 12px;")
txtstream.WriteLine("   text-align: left;")
txtstream.WriteLine("   white-Space: nowrap;")
txtstream.WriteLine("}")
txtstream.WriteLine("span")
txtstream.WriteLine("{")
txtstream.WriteLine("   COLOR: navy;")
txtstream.WriteLine("   FONT-FAMILY: font-family: Cambria, serif;")
txtstream.WriteLine("   FONT-SIZE: 12px;")
txtstream.WriteLine("   text-align: left;")
txtstream.WriteLine("   white-Space: nowrap;")
txtstream.WriteLine("   width: 100%;")
txtstream.WriteLine("}")
txtstream.WriteLine("textarea")
txtstream.WriteLine("{")
txtstream.WriteLine("   COLOR: navy;")
txtstream.WriteLine("   FONT-FAMILY: font-family: Cambria, serif;")
txtstream.WriteLine("   FONT-SIZE: 12px;")
txtstream.WriteLine("   text-align: left;")
txtstream.WriteLine("   white-Space: nowrap;")
```

```
txtstream.WriteLine("    display:inline-block;")
txtstream.WriteLine("    width: 100%;")
txtstream.WriteLine("}")
txtstream.WriteLine("select")
txtstream.WriteLine("{")
txtstream.WriteLine("    COLOR: navy;")
txtstream.WriteLine("    FONT-FAMILY: font-family: Cambria, serif;")
txtstream.WriteLine("    FONT-SIZE: 10px;")
txtstream.WriteLine("    text-align: left;")
txtstream.WriteLine("    white-Space: nowrap;")
txtstream.WriteLine("    display:inline-block;")
txtstream.WriteLine("    width: 100%;")
txtstream.WriteLine("}")
txtstream.WriteLine("input")
txtstream.WriteLine("{")
txtstream.WriteLine("    COLOR: navy;")
txtstream.WriteLine("    FONT-FAMILY: font-family: Cambria, serif;")
txtstream.WriteLine("    FONT-SIZE: 12px;")
txtstream.WriteLine("    text-align: left;")
txtstream.WriteLine("    display:table-cell;")
txtstream.WriteLine("    white-Space: nowrap;")
txtstream.WriteLine("}")
txtstream.WriteLine("h1 {")
txtstream.WriteLine("color: antiquewhite;")
txtstream.WriteLine("text-shadow: 1px 1px 1px black;")
txtstream.WriteLine("padding: 3px;")
txtstream.WriteLine("text-align: center;")
txtstream.WriteLine("box-shadow: inset 2px 2px 5px rgba(0,0,0,0.5), inset -2px -2px 5px rgba(255,255,255,0.5);")
txtstream.WriteLine("}")
txtstream.WriteLine("tr:nth-child(even){background-color:#f2f2f2;}")
txtstream.WriteLine("tr:nth-child(odd){background-color:#cccccc; color:#f2f2f2;}")
```

```
txtstream.WriteLine("</style>")
```

GHOST DECORATED

```
txtstream.WriteLine("<style type='text/css'>")
txtstream.WriteLine("th")
txtstream.WriteLine("{")
txtstream.WriteLine("   COLOR: black;")
txtstream.WriteLine("   BACKGROUND-COLOR: white;")
txtstream.WriteLine("   FONT-FAMILY:font-family: Cambria, serif;")
txtstream.WriteLine("   FONT-SIZE: 12px;")
txtstream.WriteLine("   text-align: left;")
txtstream.WriteLine("   white-Space: nowrap;")
txtstream.WriteLine("}")
txtstream.WriteLine("td")
txtstream.WriteLine("{")
txtstream.WriteLine("   COLOR: black;")
txtstream.WriteLine("   BACKGROUND-COLOR: white;")
txtstream.WriteLine("   FONT-FAMILY: font-family: Cambria, serif;")
txtstream.WriteLine("   FONT-SIZE: 12px;")
txtstream.WriteLine("   text-align: left;")
txtstream.WriteLine("   white-Space: nowrap;")
txtstream.WriteLine("}")
txtstream.WriteLine("div")
txtstream.WriteLine("{")
txtstream.WriteLine("   COLOR: black;")
txtstream.WriteLine("   BACKGROUND-COLOR: white;")
txtstream.WriteLine("   FONT-FAMILY: font-family: Cambria, serif;")
txtstream.WriteLine("   FONT-SIZE: 10px;")
txtstream.WriteLine("   text-align: left;")
txtstream.WriteLine("   white-Space: nowrap;")
txtstream.WriteLine("}")
txtstream.WriteLine("span")
```

```
txtstream.WriteLine("{")
txtstream.WriteLine("   COLOR: black;")
txtstream.WriteLine("   BACKGROUND-COLOR: white;")
txtstream.WriteLine("   FONT-FAMILY: font-family: Cambria, serif;")
txtstream.WriteLine("   FONT-SIZE: 10px;")
txtstream.WriteLine("   text-align: left;")
txtstream.WriteLine("   white-Space: nowrap;")
txtstream.WriteLine("   display:inline-block;")
txtstream.WriteLine("   width: 100%;")
txtstream.WriteLine("}")
txtstream.WriteLine("textarea")
txtstream.WriteLine("{")
txtstream.WriteLine("   COLOR: black;")
txtstream.WriteLine("   BACKGROUND-COLOR: white;")
txtstream.WriteLine("   FONT-FAMILY: font-family: Cambria, serif;")
txtstream.WriteLine("   FONT-SIZE: 10px;")
txtstream.WriteLine("   text-align: left;")
txtstream.WriteLine("   white-Space: nowrap;")
txtstream.WriteLine("   width: 100%;")
txtstream.WriteLine("}")
txtstream.WriteLine("select")
txtstream.WriteLine("{")
txtstream.WriteLine("   COLOR: black;")
txtstream.WriteLine("   BACKGROUND-COLOR: white;")
txtstream.WriteLine("   FONT-FAMILY: font-family: Cambria, serif;")
txtstream.WriteLine("   FONT-SIZE: 10px;")
txtstream.WriteLine("   text-align: left;")
txtstream.WriteLine("   white-Space: nowrap;")
txtstream.WriteLine("   width: 100%;")
txtstream.WriteLine("}")
txtstream.WriteLine("input")
txtstream.WriteLine("{")
txtstream.WriteLine("   COLOR: black;")
```

```
txtstream.WriteLine("    BACKGROUND-COLOR: white;")
txtstream.WriteLine("    FONT-FAMILY: font-family: Cambria, serif;")
txtstream.WriteLine("    FONT-SIZE: 12px;")
txtstream.WriteLine("    text-align: left;")
txtstream.WriteLine("    display:table-cell;")
txtstream.WriteLine("    white-Space: nowrap;")
txtstream.WriteLine("}")
txtstream.WriteLine("h1 {")
txtstream.WriteLine("color: antiquewhite;")
txtstream.WriteLine("text-shadow: 1px 1px 1px black;")
txtstream.WriteLine("padding: 3px;")
txtstream.WriteLine("text-align: center;")
txtstream.WriteLine("box-shadow: inset 2px 2px 5px rgba(0,0,0,0.5), inset -
2px -2px 5px rgba(255,255,255,0.5);")
txtstream.WriteLine("}")
txtstream.WriteLine("</style>")
```

3D


```
txtstream.WriteLine("<style type='text/css'>")
txtstream.WriteLine("body")
txtstream.WriteLine("{")
txtstream.WriteLine("    PADDING-RIGHT: 0px;")
txtstream.WriteLine("    PADDING-LEFT: 0px;")
txtstream.WriteLine("    PADDING-BOTTOM: 0px;")
txtstream.WriteLine("    MARGIN: 0px;")
txtstream.WriteLine("    COLOR: #333;")
txtstream.WriteLine("    PADDING-TOP: 0px;")
txtstream.WriteLine("    FONT-FAMILY: verdana, arial, helvetica, sans-serif;")
txtstream.WriteLine("}")
txtstream.WriteLine("table")
txtstream.WriteLine("{")
```

```
txtstream.WriteLine("    BORDER-RIGHT: #999999 3px solid;")
txtstream.WriteLine("    PADDING-RIGHT: 6px;")
txtstream.WriteLine("    PADDING-LEFT: 6px;")
txtstream.WriteLine("    FONT-WEIGHT: Bold;")
txtstream.WriteLine("    FONT-SIZE: 14px;")
txtstream.WriteLine("    PADDING-BOTTOM: 6px;")
txtstream.WriteLine("    COLOR: Peru;")
txtstream.WriteLine("    LINE-HEIGHT: 14px;")
txtstream.WriteLine("    PADDING-TOP: 6px;")
txtstream.WriteLine("    BORDER-BOTTOM: #999 1px solid;")
txtstream.WriteLine("    BACKGROUND-COLOR: #eeeeee;")
txtstream.WriteLine("    FONT-FAMILY: verdana, arial, helvetica, sans-serif;")
txtstream.WriteLine("    FONT-SIZE: 12px;")
txtstream.WriteLine("}")
txtstream.WriteLine("th")
txtstream.WriteLine("{")
txtstream.WriteLine("    BORDER-RIGHT: #999999 3px solid;")
txtstream.WriteLine("    PADDING-RIGHT: 6px;")
txtstream.WriteLine("    PADDING-LEFT: 6px;")
txtstream.WriteLine("    FONT-WEIGHT: Bold;")
txtstream.WriteLine("    FONT-SIZE: 14px;")
txtstream.WriteLine("    PADDING-BOTTOM: 6px;")
txtstream.WriteLine("    COLOR: darkred;")
txtstream.WriteLine("    LINE-HEIGHT: 14px;")
txtstream.WriteLine("    PADDING-TOP: 6px;")
txtstream.WriteLine("    BORDER-BOTTOM: #999 1px solid;")
txtstream.WriteLine("    BACKGROUND-COLOR: #eeeeee;")
txtstream.WriteLine("    FONT-FAMILY:font-family: Cambria, serif;")
txtstream.WriteLine("    FONT-SIZE: 12px;")
txtstream.WriteLine("    text-align: left;")
txtstream.WriteLine("    white-Space: nowrap;")
txtstream.WriteLine("}")
txtstream.WriteLine(".th")
```

```
txtstream.WriteLine("{")
txtstream.WriteLine("    BORDER-RIGHT: #999999 2px solid;")
txtstream.WriteLine("    PADDING-RIGHT: 6px;")
txtstream.WriteLine("    PADDING-LEFT: 6px;")
txtstream.WriteLine("    FONT-WEIGHT: Bold;")
txtstream.WriteLine("    PADDING-BOTTOM: 6px;")
txtstream.WriteLine("    COLOR: black;")
txtstream.WriteLine("    PADDING-TOP: 6px;")
txtstream.WriteLine("    BORDER-BOTTOM: #999 2px solid;")
txtstream.WriteLine("    BACKGROUND-COLOR: #eeeeee;")
txtstream.WriteLine("    FONT-FAMILY: font-family: Cambria, serif;")
txtstream.WriteLine("    FONT-SIZE: 10px;")
txtstream.WriteLine("    text-align: right;")
txtstream.WriteLine("    white-Space: nowrap;")
txtstream.WriteLine("}")
txtstream.WriteLine("td")
txtstream.WriteLine("{")
txtstream.WriteLine("    BORDER-RIGHT: #999999 3px solid;")
txtstream.WriteLine("    PADDING-RIGHT: 6px;")
txtstream.WriteLine("    PADDING-LEFT: 6px;")
txtstream.WriteLine("    FONT-WEIGHT: Normal;")
txtstream.WriteLine("    PADDING-BOTTOM: 6px;")
txtstream.WriteLine("    COLOR: navy;")
txtstream.WriteLine("    LINE-HEIGHT: 14px;")
txtstream.WriteLine("    PADDING-TOP: 6px;")
txtstream.WriteLine("    BORDER-BOTTOM: #999 1px solid;")
txtstream.WriteLine("    BACKGROUND-COLOR: #eeeeee;")
txtstream.WriteLine("    FONT-FAMILY: font-family: Cambria, serif;")
txtstream.WriteLine("    FONT-SIZE: 12px;")
txtstream.WriteLine("    text-align: left;")
txtstream.WriteLine("    white-Space: nowrap;")
txtstream.WriteLine("}")
txtstream.WriteLine("div")
```

```
txtstream.WriteLine("{")
txtstream.WriteLine("   BORDER-RIGHT: #999999 3px solid;")
txtstream.WriteLine("   PADDING-RIGHT: 6px;")
txtstream.WriteLine("   PADDING-LEFT: 6px;")
txtstream.WriteLine("   FONT-WEIGHT: Normal;")
txtstream.WriteLine("   PADDING-BOTTOM: 6px;")
txtstream.WriteLine("   COLOR: white;")
txtstream.WriteLine("   PADDING-TOP: 6px;")
txtstream.WriteLine("   BORDER-BOTTOM: #999 1px solid;")
txtstream.WriteLine("   BACKGROUND-COLOR: navy;")
txtstream.WriteLine("   FONT-FAMILY: font-family: Cambria, serif;")
txtstream.WriteLine("   FONT-SIZE: 10px;")
txtstream.WriteLine("   text-align: left;")
txtstream.WriteLine("   white-Space: nowrap;")
txtstream.WriteLine("}")
txtstream.WriteLine("span")
txtstream.WriteLine("{")
txtstream.WriteLine("   BORDER-RIGHT: #999999 3px solid;")
txtstream.WriteLine("   PADDING-RIGHT: 3px;")
txtstream.WriteLine("   PADDING-LEFT: 3px;")
txtstream.WriteLine("   FONT-WEIGHT: Normal;")
txtstream.WriteLine("   PADDING-BOTTOM: 3px;")
txtstream.WriteLine("   COLOR: white;")
txtstream.WriteLine("   PADDING-TOP: 3px;")
txtstream.WriteLine("   BORDER-BOTTOM: #999 1px solid;")
txtstream.WriteLine("   BACKGROUND-COLOR: navy;")
txtstream.WriteLine("   FONT-FAMILY: font-family: Cambria, serif;")
txtstream.WriteLine("   FONT-SIZE: 10px;")
txtstream.WriteLine("   text-align: left;")
txtstream.WriteLine("   white-Space: nowrap;")
txtstream.WriteLine("   display:inline-block;")
txtstream.WriteLine("   width: 100%;")
txtstream.WriteLine("}")
```

```
txtstream.WriteLine("textarea")
txtstream.WriteLine("{")
txtstream.WriteLine("    BORDER-RIGHT: #999999 3px solid;")
txtstream.WriteLine("    PADDING-RIGHT: 3px;")
txtstream.WriteLine("    PADDING-LEFT: 3px;")
txtstream.WriteLine("    FONT-WEIGHT: Normal;")
txtstream.WriteLine("    PADDING-BOTTOM: 3px;")
txtstream.WriteLine("    COLOR: white;")
txtstream.WriteLine("    PADDING-TOP: 3px;")
txtstream.WriteLine("    BORDER-BOTTOM: #999 1px solid;")
txtstream.WriteLine("    BACKGROUND-COLOR: navy;")
txtstream.WriteLine("    FONT-FAMILY: font-family: Cambria, serif;")
txtstream.WriteLine("    FONT-SIZE: 10px;")
txtstream.WriteLine("    text-align: left;")
txtstream.WriteLine("    white-Space: nowrap;")
txtstream.WriteLine("    width: 100%;")
txtstream.WriteLine("}")
txtstream.WriteLine("select")
txtstream.WriteLine("{")
txtstream.WriteLine("    BORDER-RIGHT: #999999 3px solid;")
txtstream.WriteLine("    PADDING-RIGHT: 6px;")
txtstream.WriteLine("    PADDING-LEFT: 6px;")
txtstream.WriteLine("    FONT-WEIGHT: Normal;")
txtstream.WriteLine("    PADDING-BOTTOM: 6px;")
txtstream.WriteLine("    COLOR: white;")
txtstream.WriteLine("    PADDING-TOP: 6px;")
txtstream.WriteLine("    BORDER-BOTTOM: #999 1px solid;")
txtstream.WriteLine("    BACKGROUND-COLOR: navy;")
txtstream.WriteLine("    FONT-FAMILY: font-family: Cambria, serif;")
txtstream.WriteLine("    FONT-SIZE: 10px;")
txtstream.WriteLine("    text-align: left;")
txtstream.WriteLine("    white-Space: nowrap;")
txtstream.WriteLine("    width: 100%;")
```

```
txtstream.WriteLine("}")
txtstream.WriteLine("input")
txtstream.WriteLine("{")
txtstream.WriteLine("    BORDER-RIGHT: #999999 3px solid;")
txtstream.WriteLine("    PADDING-RIGHT: 3px;")
txtstream.WriteLine("    PADDING-LEFT: 3px;")
txtstream.WriteLine("    FONT-WEIGHT: Bold;")
txtstream.WriteLine("    PADDING-BOTTOM: 3px;")
txtstream.WriteLine("    COLOR: white;")
txtstream.WriteLine("    PADDING-TOP: 3px;")
txtstream.WriteLine("    BORDER-BOTTOM: #999 1px solid;")
txtstream.WriteLine("    BACKGROUND-COLOR: navy;")
txtstream.WriteLine("    FONT-FAMILY: font-family: Cambria, serif;")
txtstream.WriteLine("    FONT-SIZE: 12px;")
txtstream.WriteLine("    text-align: left;")
txtstream.WriteLine("    display:table-cell;")
txtstream.WriteLine("    white-Space: nowrap;")
txtstream.WriteLine("    width: 100%;")
txtstream.WriteLine("}")
txtstream.WriteLine("h1 {")
txtstream.WriteLine("color: antiquewhite;")
txtstream.WriteLine("text-shadow: 1px 1px 1px black;")
txtstream.WriteLine("padding: 3px;")
txtstream.WriteLine("text-align: center;")
txtstream.WriteLine("box-shadow: inset 2px 2px 5px rgba(0,0,0,0.5), inset -2px -2px 5px rgba(255,255,255,0.5);")
txtstream.WriteLine("}")
txtstream.WriteLine("</style>")
```

SHADOW BOX

```
txtstream.WriteLine("<style type='text/css'>")
txtstream.WriteLine("body")
```

```
txtstream.WriteLine("{")
txtstream.WriteLine("    PADDING-RIGHT: 0px;")
txtstream.WriteLine("    PADDING-LEFT: 0px;")
txtstream.WriteLine("    PADDING-BOTTOM: 0px;")
txtstream.WriteLine("    MARGIN: 0px;")
txtstream.WriteLine("    COLOR: #333;")
txtstream.WriteLine("    PADDING-TOP: 0px;")
txtstream.WriteLine("    FONT-FAMILY: verdana, arial, helvetica, sans-serif;")
txtstream.WriteLine("}")
txtstream.WriteLine("table")
txtstream.WriteLine("{")
txtstream.WriteLine("    BORDER-RIGHT: #999999 1px solid;")
txtstream.WriteLine("    PADDING-RIGHT: 1px;")
txtstream.WriteLine("    PADDING-LEFT: 1px;")
txtstream.WriteLine("    PADDING-BOTTOM: 1px;")
txtstream.WriteLine("    LINE-HEIGHT: 8px;")
txtstream.WriteLine("    PADDING-TOP: 1px;")
txtstream.WriteLine("    BORDER-BOTTOM: #999 1px solid;")
txtstream.WriteLine("    BACKGROUND-COLOR: #eeeeee;")
txtstream.WriteLine("
filter:progid:DXImageTransform.Microsoft.Shadow(color='silver',      Direction=135,
Strength=16")
txtstream.WriteLine("}")
txtstream.WriteLine("th")
txtstream.WriteLine("{")
txtstream.WriteLine("    BORDER-RIGHT: #999999 3px solid;")
txtstream.WriteLine("    PADDING-RIGHT: 6px;")
txtstream.WriteLine("    PADDING-LEFT: 6px;")
txtstream.WriteLine("    FONT-WEIGHT: Bold;")
txtstream.WriteLine("    FONT-SIZE: 14px;")
txtstream.WriteLine("    PADDING-BOTTOM: 6px;")
txtstream.WriteLine("    COLOR: darkred;")
txtstream.WriteLine("    LINE-HEIGHT: 14px;")
```

```
txtstream.WriteLine("    PADDING-TOP: 6px;")
txtstream.WriteLine("    BORDER-BOTTOM: #999 1px solid;")
txtstream.WriteLine("    BACKGROUND-COLOR: #eeeeee;")
txtstream.WriteLine("    FONT-FAMILY: font-family: Cambria, serif;")
txtstream.WriteLine("    FONT-SIZE: 12px;")
txtstream.WriteLine("    text-align: left;")
txtstream.WriteLine("    white-Space: nowrap;")
txtstream.WriteLine("}")
txtstream.WriteLine(".th")
txtstream.WriteLine("{")
txtstream.WriteLine("    BORDER-RIGHT: #999999 2px solid;")
txtstream.WriteLine("    PADDING-RIGHT: 6px;")
txtstream.WriteLine("    PADDING-LEFT: 6px;")
txtstream.WriteLine("    FONT-WEIGHT: Bold;")
txtstream.WriteLine("    PADDING-BOTTOM: 6px;")
txtstream.WriteLine("    COLOR: black;")
txtstream.WriteLine("    PADDING-TOP: 6px;")
txtstream.WriteLine("    BORDER-BOTTOM: #999 2px solid;")
txtstream.WriteLine("    BACKGROUND-COLOR: #eeeeee;")
txtstream.WriteLine("    FONT-FAMILY: font-family: Cambria, serif;")
txtstream.WriteLine("    FONT-SIZE: 10px;")
txtstream.WriteLine("    text-align: right;")
txtstream.WriteLine("    white-Space: nowrap;")
txtstream.WriteLine("}")
txtstream.WriteLine("td")
txtstream.WriteLine("{")
txtstream.WriteLine("    BORDER-RIGHT: #999999 3px solid;")
txtstream.WriteLine("    PADDING-RIGHT: 6px;")
txtstream.WriteLine("    PADDING-LEFT: 6px;")
txtstream.WriteLine("    FONT-WEIGHT: Normal;")
txtstream.WriteLine("    PADDING-BOTTOM: 6px;")
txtstream.WriteLine("    COLOR: navy;")
txtstream.WriteLine("    LINE-HEIGHT: 14px;")
```

```
txtstream.WriteLine("    PADDING-TOP: 6px;")
txtstream.WriteLine("    BORDER-BOTTOM: #999 1px solid;")
txtstream.WriteLine("    BACKGROUND-COLOR: #eeeeee;")
txtstream.WriteLine("    FONT-FAMILY: font-family: Cambria, serif;")
txtstream.WriteLine("    FONT-SIZE: 12px;")
txtstream.WriteLine("    text-align: left;")
txtstream.WriteLine("    white-Space: nowrap;")
txtstream.WriteLine("}")
txtstream.WriteLine("div")
txtstream.WriteLine("{")
txtstream.WriteLine("    BORDER-RIGHT: #999999 3px solid;")
txtstream.WriteLine("    PADDING-RIGHT: 6px;")
txtstream.WriteLine("    PADDING-LEFT: 6px;")
txtstream.WriteLine("    FONT-WEIGHT: Normal;")
txtstream.WriteLine("    PADDING-BOTTOM: 6px;")
txtstream.WriteLine("    COLOR: white;")
txtstream.WriteLine("    PADDING-TOP: 6px;")
txtstream.WriteLine("    BORDER-BOTTOM: #999 1px solid;")
txtstream.WriteLine("    BACKGROUND-COLOR: navy;")
txtstream.WriteLine("    FONT-FAMILY: font-family: Cambria, serif;")
txtstream.WriteLine("    FONT-SIZE: 10px;")
txtstream.WriteLine("    text-align: left;")
txtstream.WriteLine("    white-Space: nowrap;")
txtstream.WriteLine("}")
txtstream.WriteLine("span")
txtstream.WriteLine("{")
txtstream.WriteLine("    BORDER-RIGHT: #999999 3px solid;")
txtstream.WriteLine("    PADDING-RIGHT: 3px;")
txtstream.WriteLine("    PADDING-LEFT: 3px;")
txtstream.WriteLine("    FONT-WEIGHT: Normal;")
txtstream.WriteLine("    PADDING-BOTTOM: 3px;")
txtstream.WriteLine("    COLOR: white;")
txtstream.WriteLine("    PADDING-TOP: 3px;")
```

```
txtstream.WriteLine("   BORDER-BOTTOM: #999 1px solid;")
txtstream.WriteLine("   BACKGROUND-COLOR: navy;")
txtstream.WriteLine("   FONT-FAMILY: font-family: Cambria, serif;")
txtstream.WriteLine("   FONT-SIZE: 10px;")
txtstream.WriteLine("   text-align: left;")
txtstream.WriteLine("   white-Space: nowrap;")
txtstream.WriteLine("   display: inline-block;")
txtstream.WriteLine("   width: 100%;")
txtstream.WriteLine("}")
txtstream.WriteLine("textarea")
txtstream.WriteLine("{")
txtstream.WriteLine("   BORDER-RIGHT: #999999 3px solid;")
txtstream.WriteLine("   PADDING-RIGHT: 3px;")
txtstream.WriteLine("   PADDING-LEFT: 3px;")
txtstream.WriteLine("   FONT-WEIGHT: Normal;")
txtstream.WriteLine("   PADDING-BOTTOM: 3px;")
txtstream.WriteLine("   COLOR: white;")
txtstream.WriteLine("   PADDING-TOP: 3px;")
txtstream.WriteLine("   BORDER-BOTTOM: #999 1px solid;")
txtstream.WriteLine("   BACKGROUND-COLOR: navy;")
txtstream.WriteLine("   FONT-FAMILY: font-family: Cambria, serif;")
txtstream.WriteLine("   FONT-SIZE: 10px;")
txtstream.WriteLine("   text-align: left;")
txtstream.WriteLine("   white-Space: nowrap;")
txtstream.WriteLine("   width: 100%;")
txtstream.WriteLine("}")
txtstream.WriteLine("select")
txtstream.WriteLine("{")
txtstream.WriteLine("   BORDER-RIGHT: #999999 3px solid;")
txtstream.WriteLine("   PADDING-RIGHT: 6px;")
txtstream.WriteLine("   PADDING-LEFT: 6px;")
txtstream.WriteLine("   FONT-WEIGHT: Normal;")
txtstream.WriteLine("   PADDING-BOTTOM: 6px;")
```

```
txtstream.WriteLine("    COLOR: white;")
txtstream.WriteLine("    PADDING-TOP: 6px;")
txtstream.WriteLine("    BORDER-BOTTOM: #999 1px solid;")
txtstream.WriteLine("    BACKGROUND-COLOR: navy;")
txtstream.WriteLine("    FONT-FAMILY: font-family: Cambria, serif;")
txtstream.WriteLine("    FONT-SIZE: 10px;")
txtstream.WriteLine("    text-align: left;")
txtstream.WriteLine("    white-Space: nowrap;")
txtstream.WriteLine("    width: 100%;")
txtstream.WriteLine("}")
txtstream.WriteLine("input")
txtstream.WriteLine("{")
txtstream.WriteLine("    BORDER-RIGHT: #999999 3px solid;")
txtstream.WriteLine("    PADDING-RIGHT: 3px;")
txtstream.WriteLine("    PADDING-LEFT: 3px;")
txtstream.WriteLine("    FONT-WEIGHT: Bold;")
txtstream.WriteLine("    PADDING-BOTTOM: 3px;")
txtstream.WriteLine("    COLOR: white;")
txtstream.WriteLine("    PADDING-TOP: 3px;")
txtstream.WriteLine("    BORDER-BOTTOM: #999 1px solid;")
txtstream.WriteLine("    BACKGROUND-COLOR: navy;")
txtstream.WriteLine("    FONT-FAMILY: font-family: Cambria, serif;")
txtstream.WriteLine("    FONT-SIZE: 12px;")
txtstream.WriteLine("    text-align: left;")
txtstream.WriteLine("    display: table-cell;")
txtstream.WriteLine("    white-Space: nowrap;")
txtstream.WriteLine("    width: 100%;")
txtstream.WriteLine("}")
txtstream.WriteLine("h1 {")
txtstream.WriteLine("color: antiquewhite;")
txtstream.WriteLine("text-shadow: 1px 1px 1px black;")
txtstream.WriteLine("padding: 3px;")
txtstream.WriteLine("text-align: center;")
```

```
txtstream.WriteLine("box-shadow: inset 2px 2px 5px rgba(0,0,0,0.5), inset -
2px -2px 5px rgba(255,255,255,0.5);")
    txtstream.WriteLine("}")
    txtstream.WriteLine("</style>")
```

www.ingramcontent.com/pod-product-compliance
Lightning Source LLC
Chambersburg PA
CBHW071102050326
40690CB00008B/1083